flawed light

Brett C. Millier

University of Illinois

Urbana and Chicago

flawed light

american
women poets
and alcohol

Library of Congress Cataloging-in-Publication Data
Millier, Brett Candlish.
Flawed light : American women poets and alcohol / Brett C. Millier.
p. cm.
Includes bibliographical references and index.
ISBN 978-0-252-03461-9 (cloth : alk. paper)
1. Women poets, American—Alcohol use. 2. Authorship—
Psychological aspects. 3. Women poets, American—Psychology.
4. Women poets, American—Biography. 5. American poetry—Women
authors—History and criticism. 6. American poetry—20th century—
History and criticism. 7. Alcoholism in literature.
I. Title.
PS151.M48   2009
811'.5099287—dc22 [B]   2008047509

Contents

Credits

Preface

This is a book about the role of alcohol in the lives of female American poets in the first half of the twentieth century, and about the way in which alcohol and/or alcoholism is reflected in their poems. In the poems of Dorothy Parker, Louise Bogan, Léonie Adams, Edna St. Vincent Millay, Elinor Wylie, Isabella Gardner, and Elizabeth Bishop, I look at figures for alcohol and inebriation that these writers used in their work in defiance of the masculine Modernist code of impersonality in art. As Alicia Ostriker summarized, "[T]he woman writer throughout most of our history has had to state her self-definitions in code, disguising passion as piety, rebellion as obedience. 'Tell all the truth but tell it slant' speaks for writers who in every century have been inhibited . . ." (6). The inhibiting factors have differed slightly from generation to generation, but have not disappeared.

I first began thinking about women poets and alcohol when working on a critical biography of Elizabeth Bishop, whose archive is full of evidence of the ways in which an addiction to alcohol bedeviled both her life and her work. While writing that book in the early '90s, I had somewhat reluctantly looked into what was known about alcoholism, but actively avoided attributing any aspect of her wonderful poems to that condition. It seemed, and still seems, an unanswerable question—would these poems have been different had Bishop not been an alcoholic? Would they have been written at all? But then after a well-known reviewer of my book claimed that I had exaggerated Bishop's alcoholism, that Bishop could not have been alcoholic because *he* knew alcoholic poets—Algernon Swinburne, Dylan Thomas, John Berryman—and Bishop "is not in that league at all," I grew militant.[1] To me, Bishop's alcoholism was a fact, and Anthony Hecht's refusal to acknowledge it was puzzling. He could name with ease those men who drank loudly and obviously and who wrote about drinking; but he could not recognize the same condition in Elizabeth Bishop. Did he (and others of her friends) not realize that Bishop struggled so desperately with alcohol? Or did he object to her being "exposed" as an alcoholic, in a way he did not with the male poets in her generation? It was clear that, either way, he was thinking about her drinking very differently than that of Berryman or Dylan Thomas. I suspect that the difference has a good deal to do with gender.

Since then, I have spent much time in the literature on alcohol use and alcoholism, and with studies of alcohol and creativity, which demonstrate both the effect of alcohol on the creative process, and the particular susceptibility of writers and artists to alcoholism and its negative life results. I have read most everything written on gender and alcohol, and the ways in which the experience of drinking and the consequences of alcoholism are different for women than for men. I have also been deep into biographies of these poets, where they exist, and in their letters, journals, and papers located in libraries across the country. All of this has been in preparation for reading their poems with this thesis in mind: that despite the shame and isolation these writers suffered as a result of their heavy drinking and, in some cases, their obvious alcoholism, and despite the oppressive restrictions on subject matter placed on women poets by the critical establishment in this era, these female poets nevertheless wrote about alcohol. Not very often explicitly about holding or drinking a bottle or a glass, but very often about the effects of alcohol on their bodies and minds and lives. What I first went looking for was what I called "characteristic imagery"—when the poet was writing covertly, if you will, about her struggle with alcohol, how did she figure that struggle, what imagery did she use? I imagined that each poet would have her own way of expressing the struggle—her own imagery—and to a certain extent, that turned out to be true. But the poets also share significant imagery, so that it has become possible for me to think in terms of typical tropes for alcohol across this gender and this genre and this era.

All of the writers I have studied in this context shared the difficult task of making themselves writers in an era when real writers were male, and when, as Ann Douglas has shown, values in poetry and prose were solidly masculine. Edna Millay commented frequently on the infuriating condescension with which her work was sometimes received, humorously, in verse (see Sonnet xxxi, "Oh, oh, you will be sorry for that word! / Give back my book and take my kiss instead. / Was it my enemy or my friend I heard, / 'What a big book for such a little head!'"[2]) and angrily in prose. Elizabeth Atkins's early study of Millay was the literal subject of a notorious review by John Crowe Ransom in 1937, in which he employed an astonishingly essentialized characterization of femininity to dismiss Millay and all other female lyricists (Marianne Moore is an exception) from the pantheon of "serious" poetry. The "lack of intellectual interest," Ransom noted serenely, "is that which the male reader misses in her poetry." The "intellectual power" of the male Modernists is finally too profound "to be commanded by the innocent woman-mind."[3] What the work ultimately suffers from is a "deficiency in masculinity," and when he finds poems to praise, it is because they are "excitingly womanlike" in that "the structures are transparently simple and the effects are immediate" and they concern themselves only with "a woman's sensibility in the midst of simple human and natural situations."[4] Reverberations from this review worked their way among the ambitious young female poets of the day, and the older generation as well, articulating (if not dictating) what seems to have been the central conflict in their psychic lives: the problem of Louise Bogan's signature lyric "The Alchemist": "I burned my life, that I might find / A passion wholly of the mind"[5]—how to have both "life," a life of the female body, with all its biological and emotional complexities and desires, and a distinctly masculine "life of the mind." Although this desire to eradicate the body in favor of the spirit is as old as Christian thought and was endemic among the nineteenth-century's "nightingale" poets, it has new resonance in the work of these poets, all of whom learned to drink, and started to write, during Prohibition.[6]

All of the women in this study were extraordinary lyric poets, though Bishop's work has proven to be perhaps the most enduring. All of them lived most of their lives in the era before "confessional" poetry, when the conventions of lyric supported a distance between the speaker of the poem and the poet herself, when Eliot's call for poetry that is an "escape from personality" still dominated. As women in a remarkable tradition of female lyric poets, their subjects and voices were circumscribed as well by their sex, as the work of Ostriker, William Drake, Cheryl Walker, and others has revealed. Nevertheless, their painful struggles with alcohol and its effects are recorded in their poems, and while the struggles and the imagery are individual to each poet, the preoccupations they share are instructive as well.

Acknowledgments

Because this project arose from my earlier work on Elizabeth Bishop, I am grateful first of all to those of Bishop's friends who were willing to talk with me about the secret shame of her life, her alcoholism. And I am grateful as well to Anthony Hecht, both for his poems and for the spur that his outrage at my suggestion that Bishop drank to excess gave me. My colleagues at Middlebury College were generous with their expertise about alcohol and addiction: Devon Jersild, Yonna McShane, and Carlos Velez-Balsini. My wise friend Jon Coffin both shared his wide knowledge and nurtured the project when it foundered.

Middlebury itself fully lived up to its commitment to the highest levels of scholarship among its faculty, with support for research travel, conference attendance, and publishing and permissions costs. Fellow tillers in the field of twentieth-century American poetry—Annie Finch, Al Gelpi, Tom Travisano, Cheryl Walker, and the late Diane Middlebrook—offered encouragement and suggestions in a variety of forms and venues.

Books like this don't happen without the blessed expertise of librarians and curators, and of libraries and their collections. The staffs of the Beinecke Library at Yale University, the Berg Collection of the New York Public Library, the Manuscripts Collection at the Library of Congress, Manuscripts and Special Collections at Washington University in St. Louis and at the University of Washington in Seattle, the Elizabeth Bishop Papers Vassar College Library, and the Louise Bogan Papers at the Amherst College Library all contributed time and guidance, as well as their marvelous holdings, to this project. *Contemporary Literature* first published my work on Bishop and alcohol in 1998, and graciously permits a revised version of that essay to appear in this volume.

Finally, I am most grateful to my family, Karl, Peter, and Annie Lindholm, who have both allowed me and encouraged me to be a partner and a mom as well as a teacher, scholar, and writer.

flawed light

Introduction

Women Poets and Alcohol

The relationship of alcohol and alcoholism to literary artists has received a good deal of attention in recent years. Tom Dardis's *The Thirsty Muse: Alcohol and the American Writer* (1989) is the best and best known of these studies, and Donald W. Goodwin's *Alcohol and the Writer* was published the previous year. Thomas Gilmore's more literary study, *Equivocal Spirits: Alcohol and Drinking in Twentieth-Century American Literature*, appeared in 1987. A spate of highly colored and anecdotal books about writers in the prohibition era followed in the next fifteen or so years—notably Marion Meade's *Bobbed Hair and Bathtub Gin: Writers Running Wild in the Twenties,* and Kelly Boler's *A Drinking Companion: Alcohol and the Lives of Writers.* Kathleen Drowne's scholarly *Spirits of Defiance: National Prohibi-*

tion and Jazz Age Literature appeared in 2005. A journal "of literature and addiction," *Dionysos,* was founded in 1989 and published numerous studies of individual writers and alcohol, and other essays by Barnaby Conrad, Scott Donaldson, Roger Forseth, Julie Irwin, Alfred Kazin, Robin Room, Sue Vice, and Ann Waldron have all appeared since 1980. Nearly all of these studies repeat the essentially biographical and anecdotal focus of the earlier books, and often repeat their subjects as well: much of the work rehearses the relatively well-known struggles of William Faulkner, Ernest Hemingway, F. Scott Fitzgerald, Eugene O'Neill, and, more recently, John Cheever.[1] The frequently cited statistic—that five of the first seven American Nobel Prize winners in literature were alcoholic—skews these discussions in the direction of both maleness and extreme celebrity. And very little of the work has extended the biographical to examine how the chronic consumption of alcohol affected the artistic practice even of these well-known writers, beyond noting that their later work is often inferior to their earlier work. No study of alcohol and artistic practice yet exists to compare with, for example, Alethea Hayter's *Opium and the Romantic Imagination* (1968), which identifies imagery and habits of composition attributable to opium use in the works of Coleridge, George Crabbe, Francis Thompson, and others.

A standard list of alcoholic and heavy-drinking American writers emerges from these studies, and its range is instructive. The commonly named writers are all dead, and the list goes something like this: James Agee, Conrad Aiken, W. H. Auden, Philip Barry, Robert Benchley, John Berryman, Maxwell Bodenheim, James M. Cain, Truman Capote, Raymond Carver, Raymond Chandler, John Cheever, James Gould Cozzens, Hart Crane, Stephen Crane, e. e. cummings, Bernard DeVoto, Theodore Dreiser, William Faulkner, Scott Fitzgerald, Dashiell Hammett, Ben Hecht, Ernest Hemingway, Stanley Edgar Hyman, Charles Jackson, James Jones, Jack Kerouac, Ring Lardner, Sinclair Lewis, A. J. Liebling, Jack London, Robert Lowell, J. J. Marquand, Don Marquis, Edna St. Vincent Millay, Donald Newlove, John O'Hara, Eugene O'Neill, Dorothy Parker, Edgar Allan Poe, William Sydney Porter (O. Henry), James Whitcomb Riley, E. A. Robinson, Theodore Roethke, Delmore Schwartz, Irwin Shaw, John Steinbeck, Wallace Stevens, Tennessee Williams, Thornton Wilder, Edmund Wilson, and Thomas Wolfe.

Robin Room has pointed out that a significant number of these writers were born between 1885 (Lardner, Lewis) and 1905 (O'Hara), and notes that this generation of artists spent its formative years in an atmosphere that was relatively "dry"—the years leading up to Prohibition—and thus found an easy form of social rebellion or dissent in the excessive public consumption of alcohol.[2] This helps to account for the remarkable "five of the first seven Nobel Prize winners" statistic. The middle cohort learned to drink when the sale and use of alcohol was literally prohibited by law, and Room sees these conditions as central to the writers' susceptibility to alcohol addiction. The later group, of course, had the model of the earlier writers on which to base their drinking habits.[3]

The drinking careers of many of these writers are well known even to the general public, and their celebrity has helped to build the popular stereotype of the drunken writer, amusing in the abstract, but seductive and dangerous to the young writer in search of a credible voice. The less well-known writers have had their drinking careers exhumed to illustrate the critics' assertions, and their names help to support the stereotype. The fact that most American writers did not and do not drink to excess lies implicit, but unstated, behind any such list.

The list also leans heavily in the direction of fiction writers; indeed, it has been remarked that famous American novelists would dominate even an international list of artists addicted to alcohol.[4] It includes the names of several important poets—Auden, Berryman, both Cranes, cummings, Lowell, Millay, Robinson, Stevens—but only Berryman has received any serious critical attention as an alcoholic writer.[5] This is in part attributable to the greater celebrity of the fiction writers. Yet a study of the effect of alcohol on the practice of twentieth-century poets is a next logical step in the study of literature and addiction.

Finally, the standard list includes the only two women whose literary careers and drinking careers approached that level of celebrity. Both Dorothy Parker and Edna St. Vincent Millay defied the powerful disapproval American society directed toward female drinkers in a big way—by drinking publicly to excess, in the company of their famous male writer friends. The fact that the list includes no names of women writers who were not celebrities (and does include the names of less-famous men) speaks to the points both that women's drinking, even among writers and artists, was largely hidden, and that the names of women drinkers are less likely than those of men to be bandied about for the amusement of readers. Female alcoholics, including artists, have both benefited and suffered from this collective aversion of public eyes.[6]

Sadly, there are other American women writers of the twentieth century who would fit almost anyone's definition of alcoholic. And like the list of male writers similarly afflicted, the women whose lives were most dominated by their need for alcohol tend to be among the very best writers this country has produced. Léonie Adams, Djuna Barnes, Elizabeth Bishop, Louise Bogan, Isabella Gardner, Lillian Hellman, Carson McCullers, Katherine Anne Porter, Marjorie Kinnan Rawlings, Anne Sexton, Jean Stafford, and Elinor Wylie might begin the alternative list.

This study gathers the unwoven threads of the work to date on writers and alcohol both to look at the role of alcohol in the lives of American women poets in the first half of the twentieth century and to show the way in which alcohol and/or alcoholism is reflected in both the form and content of their poems. In the work of Dorothy Parker, Louise Bogan, Edna St. Vincent Millay, Elinor Wylie, Léonie Adams, Isabella Gardner, and Elizabeth Bishop and, in counterpoint, Jean Garrigue, I look at figures for alcohol and alcoholism that must be present if one assumes, as I do, that almost all poets tell the story of their lives in their work. Female alcoholic poets of this era, because of the shame attached to their condition, could not write in explicit, personal ways about drinking or being drunk (and might not have been so inclined, by temperament). It stands to reason, then, that this major condition of their lives would be figured in imagery in their poems of self-analysis.

What I do not want to do is to reduce the work of gifted poets to the condition of symptoms of a disease, or to the accidental effusions of an artist who has lost control of her art, and her life. This is the risk faced by every critic who relates the circumstances of a writer's life to the form and content of his or her work (Tom Caramagno's work on Virginia Woolf's bipolar illness is a successful example), but for the critic writing about alcohol and alcoholism, the risk of such reductionism may be compounded by the temptation to impose moral judgment on the subject. For the poets I discuss here, negotiations with alcohol were a condition—like sex, physical health, or economic circumstances—under which they lived and worked. That condition is reflected in their poems. It was also, of course, not the only condition in their lives—and here my work depends on and reinterprets the many studies of the struggles of women poets of the era to find their public voices and their connections to one another.[7]

Why Alcohol?

Alcohol is a depressant drug, which slows the activity of the brain. The first parts of the brain to be affected by this depressant action are the so-called higher centers, the seats of self-judgment and self-control. The anesthetization of this part of the brain frees the mind temporarily from inhibition, anxiety, self-consciousness, and caution, according to how much is consumed. This disinhibition may be useful at first—to shy people it may ease social intercourse; to artists it may quiet the inner critic enough to permit inspiration—but continuing to drink impairs concentration, memory, and judgment so that the drinker becomes unable to make constructive use of that liberation.

The distinction between heavy drinking and alcoholism is notoriously hard to draw, and is nowadays measured for the most part in the number of "problems" a drinker has encountered because of his or her drinking.[8] The disease model of alcoholism is now widely accepted, but there is little agreement in the medical community as to what characterizes the disease. Most experts agree that alcoholism is not a unitary disease but a constellation of symptoms that affect different individuals differently, and that it has behavioral, social, and environmental, as well as medical and psychological, aspects. The tendency toward alcoholism may be genetically inherited.[9] George Vaillant finds his analogy in heart disease or hypertension—yes, the problem is medical and inheritable, but the progress of the disease can be affected by the patient's habits, behavior, and psychological state.[10] Only in the most severely ill alcoholics is the disease inevitably progressive.[11] Perhaps the most useful description of alcoholism, derived from the definition in the fourth edition of the *Diagnostic and Statistical Manual of Mental Disorders* (DSM-IV), states that an alcoholic is a person who cannot, on any given occasion, predict the amount that he or she will drink.[12] Locating the problem in terms of control removes from the attempt at definition the varied social contexts and constraints under which drinkers drink.

Research on the relationship between alcohol use and creativity is sparse and has been hampered by slippery definitions of "creativity," and research on true artistic or scientific genius and alcoholism has been bedeviled by the slipperiness of both terms. Several more-general examinations of genius and mental illness exist, however. Two such studies were conducted in Germany. Adele Juda noted among her 294 "highly gifted personalities" a "relative biologic inferiority of the artists [compared with scientists] exhibited by the higher number of psychic abnormalities among themselves and their families, the lower fertility and shorter life span, the higher number of single persons and illegitimate children, the increased infant mortality, and the higher divorce rate."[13] Nancy Andreason's study of thirty writers (twenty-seven men and three women) and their families found a high correlation between literary genius and affective disorders including alcoholism, and speculated that, pending further research, such disorders may be an advantage to the culture as a whole as an aid to producing works of literary merit.[14]

Most of the research on alcoholism and creativity is again anecdotal—surveys of artists' thoughts on their own drinking and the drinking of others, descriptions of the well-witnessed alcoholic careers of notable figures. Two studies examine the literal effect of alcohol consumption on creative performance. Lang and colleagues studied "40 male undergraduate social drinkers" in a "standard balanced placebo" experiment using vodka and tonic in which the subjects were led to expect either spiked or unspiked tonic and given one or the other, sometimes as expected and sometimes not. The results of the study showed that these manipulations produced very little effect on measured creativity (performance on the Torrance Tests of Creative Thinking). One interesting result was that those subjects who *thought* they had received alcohol (whether or not they did) evaluated their creative work more positively than did those who thought they had received plain tonic.[15] Although the idea of the "male undergraduate social drinker" patting himself on the back for his fine creative work while drunk is faintly amusing, it speaks to the role of one's mental state in determining one's response to alcohol, and to the breakdown in judgment about one's own work that artists often describe as occurring when they drink.[16]

A study by Hajcak in 1975, a dissertation project at Temple University, examined thirty-two undergraduate males of varying drinking habits, both while they were under the influence and when they were sober. Hajcak invited his subjects to his home and conducted the experiments in this informal setting. Subjects completed tests for originality and creative problem solving, and the results showed that originality was enhanced by alcohol consumption, but that problem solving was impaired, more so when alcohol was consumed in larger amounts. Hajcak speculated that his results might support the idea of alcohol as a help to creativity, despite the impairment of problem-solving ability, because "[a]n individual may learn to direct the increase in originality in the service of his particular talent as a result of repeated experience with creative tasks under the influence of alcohol."[17] However, the great majority of writers who have spoken on the subject state that they are unable to write under the influence of alcohol, and even the heaviest drinkers endeavor to keep their drinking and their writing separate.

Why writers drink is a different question from why they become alcoholic. It is likely, in fact, that no higher percentage of writers are alcoholic than of any other profession. But the circumstances under which many writers live and work may make them vulnerable to over-consumption. First, though, writers may drink because they like it, and they may drink to excess because the frenzy of drunkenness or the temporary connection to "divinity" is worth the inevitable pain. And alcohol may indeed be literally useful to them in their creative practice by providing a release of creative inhibitions. In the *Writer's Digest* "Booze and the Writer" survey, novelist Stephen King remarked that "[w]riters who drink constantly do not last long, but a writer who drinks carefully is probably a better writer" (30). Irish poet and critic Tom Paulin has identified potential creative ecstasy even in the hangover, bane of drinkers everywhere. There are three kinds of sufferers, he says: the dehydrated poet, for whom the world is eerily and painfully real; the paranoid poet, who is hunted and haunted; and the visionary poet, for whom "The world is changed to Pure Word, shimmering with absolute inspiration."[18] Gaston Bachelard, in the part of his study of the nature of poetic consciousness called *The Psychoanalysis of Fire,* insists on the value of "the water that flames"[19] to artistic inspiration, in particular to creating the fantastic and phantasmagoric in writing.

> One is mistaken if one imagines that alcohol simply stimulates our mental potentialities. In fact it creates these potentialities. It incorporates itself, so to speak, with that which is striving to express itself. It appears evident that alcohol is a creator of language. It enriches the vocabulary and frees the syntax. In point of fact, to return to the problem of fire, psychiatry has recognized the frequency of dreams about fire in cases of alcoholic delirium; it has shown that Lilliputian hallucinations are brought about by the excitation of alcohol. Now the reverie which leads to the miniature also leads to depth and stability: it is the reverie which in the final analysis best prepares us for engaging in rational thought. Bacchus is a beneficent god; by causing our reason to wander he prevents the anchylosis of logic and prepares the way for rational inventiveness.[20]

But most research and the anecdotal evidence also insist that the capacity to make use of alcohol-induced inspiration is nearly always impaired by drinking to the point of intoxication. The ecstasy continually sought after and described in the poetry of Baudelaire, for example, must come through the contemplation of beauty and not through artificial means, for the drug "promises equally rich manifestation in writing, but, in reality, it delivers fatigue, inertia, addiction, and, therefore, a loss of freedom and the capacity to write."[21] This double nature of alcohol—inspiration and ecstasy on the one hand, dissipation and death on the other—is as old as the two faces of Dionysius; Bacchus the beneficent god eventually withdraws his favor.

Working most often alone and unsupervised at odd hours in a business that involves moment-to-moment self-revelation and tremendous commitment and risk, writers experience tension and temptation together. Ernest Lehman made the case for the special needs of writers by saying, "Persons who live inside their heads as constantly as writers do are bound to awaken many sleeping dogs that lie there. In *non*-writers, many of those sleeping dogs merely slumber. Writers find it necessary to quiet the barking with alcohol."[22] Poet John Berryman, whose alcoholic poet-persona Henry enacted many of his creator's struggles with alcohol, describes this anxiety memorably in his Dream Song #67:

> I don't operate often. When I do,
> persons take note.
> Nurses look amazed. They pale.
> The patient is brought back to life, or so.
> The reason I don't do this more (I quote)
> is: I have a living to fail—
> [...]
> I am obliged to perform in complete darkness
> operations of great delicacy
> on my self.
> —Mr. Bones, you terrifies me. [...][23]

Alfred Kazin found the special pressure on American writers to be successful both in literary and monetary terms to lead to the alcoholic downfall of great talents in the Modernist generation.[24]

Both male and female writers in the twentieth century were attracted by the rebellion and romance of drinking during Prohibition; Kazin remarked that male writers in the first half of the century found alcohol a cheap and available ticket to apparent sophistication: "[T]hey drank to be different from the unsophisticated 'booboisie'; they drank to be the same as 'regular fellers'; they drank to acquire *class*."[25] Artists have always been inclined to embrace in themselves what makes them unique or at least unusual, even if it also makes them miserable. As the Symbolist vogue swept the literary world in the early twentieth century, both men and women took to heart the reputations of the poets of the French nineteenth century—Verlaine, Baudelaire, Rimbaud—who seemed to advise the poet to be in touch with the darkest parts of himself, to plunge to the depths of experience in order to describe it, through drunkenness, in fact.[26] Claire Lyu has since argued persuasively that, despite his subsequent reputation, Baudelaire in fact rejected artificial stimulants as counterproductive to poets:"He embodies the higher law of poetic inspiration, that a poet can write about experience, as of intoxication and addiction, without becoming intoxicated or addicted himself."[27] His "Le poème du hachisch" both explains the attraction of such stimulants to men of genius, and dismisses their effects as both false and enervating.[28] Nevertheless, the popular image of the French decadent poets battling ennui with drugs and alcohol had enormous influence on this generation of writers.

The connection between the writing gift and psychic orality has also been made: writers often smoke as well as drink, and those who don't drink alcohol when they write often drink something else: coffee, tea, soda. And the tool of the writer, language itself—both talk and writing—expresses orality as well. Anya Taylor has described her work on English writers and alcohol as a struggle to find the "interconnectedness" of writing and alcohol in "the conjunction of words and pleasure, of mirroring, repetition, storytelling and garrulity, of words and self-transcendence."[29] Edmund Wilson, the literal drinking companion of several of the poets in this study, devised a famous list of 107 synonyms for drunkenness, published under the title "The Lexicon of Prohibition" in 1927. The list is a double oral romp, beginning with *lit, squiffy, oiled, lubricated* and ending with *to have the screaming meemies, to have the whoops and jingles, to burn with a low blue flame.*[30]

Poets both male and female have drunk in order to free themselves of inhibitions imposed by a materialistic world; to shut down the painfully observant consciousness necessary to a writer (Ernest Hemingway is often quoted as having said that he drank in order "to stop writing"); to quiet a self-critical inner voice; to liberate shyness in social settings; to gain access to subconscious or unconscious material; to endow the mundane world with new beauty and strangeness.[31] Because certain of these writers were disposed in one way or another—genetically and/or psychologically—toward alcoholism, their experiments with alcohol would prove disastrous in their lives, if not in their work. Both the experiments and the disasters differ when the drinker is a woman.

Are writers more vulnerable to the disease of alcoholism (as opposed to mere drinking) than other people? Perhaps not. But it is interesting nonetheless that many of the psychological characteristics common to creative people are also common to alcoholics. Most alcoholics are not particularly creative, and most artists are not alcoholic; alcoholism is a psychopathology and, Freud notwithstanding, creativity is probably not. Nonetheless, both alcoholics and artists find themselves alienated and at odds with the world, are often inner-directed, and may be compelled to fantasize into being alternatives to untenable reality (both tend to lie, to put it more bluntly); both are notoriously insecure and dependent on validation from outside themselves. Both alcoholism and the urge to create result from "dissatisfaction" (in infancy, if you are a psychoanalyst), can be used to relieve anxiety, and are or resemble addictions, although one is a negative adaptation and one is positive.[32] And the intensity of artistic creation is figured in a list of metaphors worthy of Wilson himself: "fury," "fire," "ecstasy," "brainstorm," "flash," "rapture"; even "stew," "ferment," and "intoxication." Bachelard notes that "[s]ince alcohol is eminently combustible, it is easy to imagine that persons who indulge in spirituous liquors become, as it were, *impregnated* with inflammable substances."[33] He goes on to consider the persistent legends of people (often women) who were thought to have suffered spontaneous combustion, and the persistence of this metaphor in the collective imaginations of many cultures. "Nor, according to the alchemists," says Linda Schierse Leonard, "is there the transmutation of lead into gold without going through the fire. This is also the paradox of the alcoholic's 'Firewater.' In the very image of opposites is the paradox than can poison or redeem."[34]

Women and Alcohol

A discussion of the role alcohol has played in the lives of female writers, poets in particular, is necessary because the experience of alcohol and alcoholism is manifestly different for women than for men. Women's bodies process alcohol less efficiently than men's—women produce less of the enzyme that helps to digest alcohol, alcohol dehydrogenase. Women are more immediately and dramatically affected by alcohol as well. Their bodies contain less water and more fat, and because alcohol does not enter fatty tissue (which has little blood supply), alcohol is less diluted in their blood. Thus, a woman gets drunker faster and stays that way longer, on roughly a third less alcohol than her male companions need—all of which makes women much more vulnerable to the negative biological effects of steady drinking, as well as negative social judgments when she does drink.[35] A woman needs to drink less than half as much as a man, even a same-sized man, to develop cirrhosis of the liver, for example;[36] for women, the length of time between the onset of heavy drinking (for women, usually in response to a life crisis of some kind) and physical dependence on alcohol is much shorter.[37] Intoxication for women is affected by hormone levels; thus, alcohol may affect the female drinker differently at different times in her menstrual cycle, making it more difficult for her to judge her consumption. Women drinkers are more depressed, feel more guilt, are more ashamed, suffer from lower self-esteem, and commit suicide more often than their male counterparts as well.[38] And more women than men are what are known as "secondary alcoholics"— that is, they become alcoholic in response to a previous mental illness, most often depression.[39]

The experience of drinking, and of heavy drinking, is different for women as well. When Jack London described the seductive nature of John Barleycorn, he began with the virtues of the saloon and alcohol's connection to sociability, its capacity to break down barriers between men, to make them aware of their emotional ties with one another.[40] Women do a lot less drinking in bars, and most often drink with their husbands or boyfriends (and in fact mimic his drinking habits); when their drinking becomes problematic, they drink alone. Even homeless, so-called skid row women typically drink alone, taking the bottle around the corner or across the park to consume.[41] Perhaps this is so because of the harsher social judgment of women drinkers, which Jean Rhys described memorably in her most autobiographical novel, *Good Morning, Midnight* (1938): "Now the feeling of the room is different. They all know what I am. I'm a woman come in here to get drunk. That happens sometimes. They have a drink, these women, and then they have another and then they start crying silently. And then they go into the lavabo and then they come out—powdered, but with hollow eyes—and, head down, slink into the street."[42]

A drunken man may be amusing; a drunk woman is not. This negative, almost misogynistic judgment, in Rhys's case as in many others internalized, affects every aspect of a woman's relationship to alcohol and to the world of treatment and recovery.[43] If drinking in women is judged harshly, then the woman will drink alone. As her drinking problem deepens, her support system falls away (men leave their alcoholic wives far more often than women leave their alcoholic husbands) and she becomes more and more isolated. Her shame will encourage her to hide her condition longer than a man might. Thus, women's alcoholism (which develops faster than men's anyway) is likely to be more advanced when she presents herself for treatment. And because social pressure mitigates against heavy drinking for women, the woman who becomes an alcoholic is perceived as more deviant and perhaps pathological at the start. "First, a doctor who is faced with a female alcoholic, tries more to find out the reasons for such behavior than he does when he is faced with a man. Why on earth does she drink, he asks himself. The question almost implicitly draws a distinction between habitual, social, almost "normal" drinking that we find in male alcoholism, and female alcoholism which is pathological, abnormal, psycho-neurotic."[44] Not surprisingly, studies show that certain women lose rather than gain self-esteem when they enter Alcoholics Anonymous, and suffer depression and excessive self-criticism in most other coeducational treatment programs.[45]

Women who drink have, since the mid-nineteenth century, aroused tremendous anxiety in the culture for fear they would abandon their suitable roles as caretakers of children and become sexually aggressive.[46] Even mid-twentieth-century studies of alcoholic women are most often focused on sexual behavior and development. VanAmberg (1943) found that only twenty of his fifty female alcoholic patients had "satisfactory" psychosexual development,[47] and Curran (1937) also closely examined the erotic lives of his patients, finding most had been "tomboys" as young girls, and that their alcoholic hallucinations were nearly always critical and accusatory, most often of the patient's real or imagined sexual behavior.[48] This anxiety about gender roles, and the harshly critical inner voice expressed in sexual terms, is easily internalized from society at large. Wall (1937) also studied fifty institutionalized female alcoholics. He found thirty of them to be self-described tomboys as well, and found that they had begun drinking in response to "symptoms and emotional attitudes toward menstruation."[49] Thirty of his patients he identified as having engaged in "loose heterosexual activities."[50] Benjamin Karpman, whose substantial *The Alcoholic Woman: Case Studies in the Psychodynamics of Alcoholism* (1948) was based on his observations of women committed to St. Elizabeths Hospital in Washington, D.C., and was a standard text for years, stated unequivocally that alcoholism in women as well as men is "nothing more than a particular form of neurosis" caused by an unresolved "Oedipus situation" that could be cured through psychoanalysis.[51] He was at pains to say as well that *somewhere* "chaste" (that is, celibate if unmarried, or faithful to a spouse) alcoholic women must exist, but he had none for his study.[52] Although contemporary research has in part validated the connection between gender role anxiety and alcoholism[53] and has found in women alcoholics a frequent common denominator in a history of sexual abuse and incest, these have been discoveries of the feminist movement in nonalcoholic women as well. Thus, confusion about sex roles and psychic damage as a result of sexual abuse has become a part of the discovery of the more general inadequacy of a patriarchal society in meeting women's needs, and alcoholism itself is viewed as a response—even, at times, a valid response—to the tensions inherent in contemporary women's existence in that society. But only recently did the stereotypical female alcoholic go from being a prostitute to being a homemaker, hiding her bottles in the linen closet.

The negative social judgment of women's alcoholism has existed since the late 1920s, although Jersild and others argue that that judgment has less force today than it once had, accounting in part for the narrowing of the gap between the number of diagnosed male and female alcoholics, which stood for years at about two to one. But although a part of women's greater social freedom in the past quarter century has included the "right" to drink in public, the moral restriction on the amount and frequency with which she drinks has remained. As with many recent feminist gains, this double bind has yet to disappear and adds a level of confusion to young women's experience with alcohol. Even the unpathological desire to relax with alcohol is very often troubled by guilt and anxiety imposed from without, but impossible to ignore. Ironically, even the recent well-intentioned studies exposing the "hidden" problem of female alcoholism frequently seem to present all drinking by women as pathological.[54]

Women drinkers in the first half of the twentieth century faced an even less ambiguous message. To drink in public was frowned upon; to drink to excess was to declare oneself outside the bounds of acceptable female behavior. Such rebellion became more general during Prohibition, then narrowed again after its repeal.[55] The historical context in which these writers drank is different in important ways from our own time. For one thing, the culture of the first half of the twentieth century judged all alcoholism morally and negatively. E. M. Jellinek's *The Disease Concept of Alcoholism* wasn't published until 1960; the idea that drunkenness might be an illness rather than a vice was only beginning to recirculate in the 1930s.[56] And because it was still thought of in moral terms, a society protective of the reputation of its women issued a general denial as to the existence of female alcoholics. In 1892, T. D. Crothers could remark cheerfully that real American women (as opposed to immigrants) would never succumb to alcoholism, in part, he said, because they would sooner turn to more socially acceptable drugs such as opium or chloral. In addition, to his evident relief, families tended to keep their female alcoholic relatives safely hidden from public view so society need not confront the problem.[57] Although Prohibition brought to light women drinkers in the highest numbers since the notoriously wet early republic,[58] the post-repeal reaction focused particular scorn on the drinking of young women, particularly young women of the middle and upper classes. For a writer like Dorothy Parker to drink heavily in public had its political uses. But even for her, to join the ranks of drinking writers involved a sacrifice of traditional femininity related to the many gender conflicts raised by trying to be a writer at all.

In discussing alcoholism in writers of the first half of twentieth century, it is vitally important to remember, as Rosemarie Johnstone has warned, that the famous meeting between Edwin T. and Bill W. that led to the founding of Alcoholics Anonymous did not happen until 1934 and the organization took several years to achieve widespread acceptance. Prior to that time, the paradoxical understanding that alcoholism is an incurable (but arrestable) "disease," the solution to which is essentially moral and spiritual, was not widely shared.[59] Problem drinkers had no access to this self-understanding, and were not regarded by others with this model in mind. Thus, our reading of the lives and works of earlier drinkers must reflect the fact that they struggled with alcohol without the benefit of a clear and established path to recovery. Their recourses to medical intervention and psychoanalysis were for the most part ineffective, and their attempts to achieve abstinence or controlled drinking alone, by force of will, usually failed as well. It does no good to criticize writers born near the turn of the century for failing to embrace a concept and an ideology that was not widely abroad in the culture until the mid-1950s. And even more contemporary artists have been slow to adopt the AA ideology, unwilling to accept the quasi-religious basis of the program, and unable to perform the surrender of "self-will" that is the first of the Twelve Steps. When John Berryman committed suicide in 1972, his fellow poets were shocked and grieved, but Elizabeth Bishop wrote to her friend Robert Lowell with wonder and apparent disapproval, "John had been on the wagon (AA of all things)."[60]

The Alchemists

All of the poets in this study belong to the generation of female Modernists who, in Cheryl Walker's compelling formulation, translated the nineteenth-century woman poet's commitment to "renunciation," that "piercing virtue," into "masks, outrageous and austere." The masks they fashioned were designed to deflect the scrutiny of a male critical establishment unable or unwilling to value female experience as material for poetry, and that regarded unconventional female behavior as profoundly disturbing. Although the mechanisms of celebrity and the tremendous cultural upheavals of the 1920s made several of them—Parker, Millay, Wiley—famous and infamous avatars for a national anxiety about gender roles, and others—Adams, Bogan, Bishop—fiercely guard their privacy, none who wished to be taken seriously as a poet dared let down her mask on the page.

Despite the shame attached to being an alcoholic woman, and despite the injunction against making use of the "merely personal" in poetry, all of these poets wrote in one way or another about alcohol, and about the complex negotiations each conducted with the ambiguous "sanctuary" the drug provided. Imagery both common to all the poets and characteristic of each speaks eloquently of the attraction in that temporary oblivion, and its cost. Most of these poets lived into the era of "confessional" poetry, when other poets of the so-called middle generation opened their work both formally and in terms of content to material and "facts" that they had avoided or disguised in the past. By contrast, most of these poets stopped writing rather than reveal themselves explicitly or directly in their poems. Wylie and Millay died before the confessional era; Bogan published almost nothing after 1948, and Adams published literally nothing after her marriage in 1933. Parker wrote no poetry after 1931. Gardner wrote a few very self-revealing poems in the 1960s, and Elizabeth Bishop ("You just wish they'd keep some of these things to themselves") could muster only nine original poems for her final volume, *Geography III* (1976), many of which had been with her in draft form for fifteen years or more. She would finish three new poems before her death in 1979. One comparison is hard to avoid: the late work of both John Berryman and Robert Lowell, the most prominent male alcoholic poets of this era, is often criticized for its prolixity and lack of restraint— the ever-expanding *Dream Songs*; Lowell's proliferating sonnet sequences in *Notebook* (1969), *The Dolphin* (1973), *For Lizzie and Harriet* (1973), *History*

(1973), and *Day by Day* (1977). By contrast, most of the female poets fell silent or resurrected earlier, unfinished poems instead.

One artifact of my work on this study has been the development in my mind of a kind of typical trajectory for the lives of these women poets.[61] Generally speaking, they grew up with problematic or absent parents, particularly mothers; they were ambitious from early in their lives to write and to make art, and that ambition was often thwarted by family and social expectations; they achieved success relatively early and suffered serious depression soon after; chronic illness and unhappiness followed; marriages and relationships failed; childbearing became a problem of one kind or another; health deteriorated; as she aged, it became more and more difficult to produce satisfactory work; and the poet ended her life in painful isolation or in a lopsided relationship with a selfless caretaker. Alcohol is one among several possible explanations for this downward trajectory, although it is only one. What follows is an examination of the art these poets made, both under and about these conditions.

Chapter 1

"Just a Little One"

Dorothy Parker as Archetype

Dorothy Parker (1893–1967) was the most famous female drinker of her day, famous first because her celebrated sense of humor so perfectly reflected the values of her time, but also famous because she drank alongside and drink for drink with the best-known male writer/drinkers of the day. With her near-contemporary Edna St. Vincent Millay, Parker was a female icon of the twenties in America; an icon, however, of the era's darker side. Millay's apparent gaiety and perpetual flirtatious girlhood became in Parker's life and work a stagnant despair, barely disguised beneath the writer's razor wit. For Parker, the free and ir-responsible consumption of alcohol was first her ticket to equality with the male writers of the so-called second American Renaissance, and then the undoing of both her life and her work.

An innovator and important interpreter of the short story genre, Parker was nowhere near the poet that the other figures studied here were. But her light verse was hugely popular—along with Millay she was perhaps the best-known poet of the 1920s. The darkly humorous poems were flawlessly constructed and almost unfailingly clever (it was she, after all, who penned the still-famous "News Item": "Men seldom make passes / At girls who wear glasses"[1]), but Parker herself acknowledged the limitations of both her ambition and her achievement in poetry. However, the trajectory of Dorothy Parker's life resembles those of the lives of the other poets in this study in ways that suggest and support the idea that to be a *female* drinking writer—even a journalist and writer of light verse—in the first half of the twentieth century was indeed different from being a male one. Although Parker was atypical among these poets in that she drank heavily in public and in the company of men (a shocking number of the founding members of the famous Algonquin Round Table eventually succumbed to alcoholism), the circumstances of her life and career predict the circumstances of her younger followers. Neither should Parker's role as a direct influence on other female writers be underestimated; she was friendly with Elinor Wylie and continuously aware of Millay; and she and Bogan were both involved in the early *New Yorker*. Nearly all of the subjects of this study dabbled for a time in Parkeresque light verse, cynicism, and satire, and (particularly Bogan and Millay) in her pioneering short story genre, the direct-discourse character sketch—and all of them knew of her reputation as both exemplar and voice of the twenties' desperate commitment to the pursuit of "fun." Parker's close connection with the two most famous male American writers of her day (and the two most famous drinkers)—she was friendly with Scott Fitzgerald and in adoring (on her side) competition with Ernest Hemingway—was an inspiration to them as well. And Parker in her heyday was also an icon of New York City itself—literary mecca, arts capital, scoffer at Prohibition, "the New York bottle," as Hemingway called it, "the city on a still."[2] The city figures centrally in all of these poets' lives, most often as a nemesis closely associated with destructive drinking.

Like Elinor Wylie, Louise Bogan, Isabella Gardner, and Elizabeth Bishop—and a great many other women who suffer from alcoholism—Dorothy Rothschild was a gifted, perceptive, and intelligent child who lacked adequate mothering.[3] Like nearly all of the poets in this study—Bishop, Bogan, Gardner,

Millay, and even Jean Garrigue—she grew to be a rebellious and iconoclastic young woman with literary ambitions that flew in the face of the more conventional expectations of her family and her social class. Like Bogan, Wylie, and Adams, she began to drink in response to her husband's drinking and to unhappiness in her first marriage. Like all of these poets, she learned to drink destructively during Prohibition, when the drinking habits of a great many Americans shifted from casual to desperate.[4]

Parker also shares with these writers the experience of what we would now call clinical depression, the extreme self-doubt and self-deprecation, even self-hatred, that has besieged a great many women who embarked on unconventional career and life paths, and that is a trademark of most accounts of the so-called alcoholic personality.[5] And she shares with them the experience of feeling failure even in the face of the most obvious and documented success; all of these women spent the years immediately following their first positive public recognition in nearly complete despair, and in all of them alcoholism took hold during that time. All were what is known as "secondary alcoholics"—they used alcohol to self-medicate that depression and despair. The pattern of chronic unhappiness in their lives, an unhappiness independent of literal circumstances, is unmistakable. Like both Millay and Wylie, Parker was famous, a celebrity in the emerging twentieth-century American style, and like them she was forced to live in the gap between her reputation as a fast woman of loose sexual morals, perpetually in pursuit of another man and a good time, and the struggle of her real life: to grow up and beyond that superficial image, to live well, and to make lasting art.

Also like all of these poets, with the possible exception of Elinor Wylie, Parker's drinking affected her work, not so much in quality (this may be an interesting difference between the most famous male alcoholic writers of this generation and their female counterparts) but in quantity. The slim Modern Library volume that gathered all of the poems and short stories that Parker wanted to preserve resembles the slim volumes of the collected works of Bishop, Bogan, Gardner, and Adams as well.[6] All five were perfectionistic about writing, and unable to write during periods when their drinking fell out of control; and all took some care to conceal their deepest personal conflicts in their work. Although all wrote poems and short stories that were essentially autobiographical, each distanced herself from the material through conscious artistic strategy. While Parker's glittering satire and humor often directly concerned the drinking habits of her circle and her own failed love affairs, she affected a generalized tone and was almost too literally honest to be taken seriously in her suffering. Millay's girlish flippancy is closely related to Parker's dry cynicism and Gardner's reflexive wit. Wylie's obsessive preference for a fantasy world became Adams's and Bogan's intentional obscurity, which became in early Bishop a studied preference for impersonality and "objectivity," even in the treatment of her most personal material. This self-defensive authorial posture has been widely noted in the women poets of this period ("Another armored animal," as Marianne Moore dryly put it) and is generally attributed to pressure toward impersonality in art asserted by Eliot and the other male Modernists. It is also a result of each poet's profound doubts about the legitimacy of using her own emotional life as material for poetry, lest such revelation limit both her audience and her reputation as woman and artist.

Like all of these women except Bishop, who was lesbian, Parker married—and like all of them including Bishop, her most satisfactory serious relationship was with a person—her second husband, Alan Campbell—willing to surrender his own needs and claims to be her full-time caretaker. At least one parallel relationship exists in the lives of each of the other poets as well, although Louise Bogan lived the second half of her life a good deal more independently than did the others. Dorothy Parker was also childless, as were most of these women (Bogan and Wylie each had single children very early, whom they abandoned to the care of others at least for a time; Gardner had two very troubled children); as with Millay, this was in part a choice—both she and Parker purposefully delayed marriage and the possibility of children, and had abortions at the end of unhappy love affairs. And like Wylie and Adams, she suffered acute pain and regret later in life over her inability to carry a child to term; each had multiple miscarriages quite possibly related to alcohol consumption. And like all of these poets except Bishop, who remained in the care of lovers and friends to the end of her life, Parker died essentially alone—like Millay she had lost her caretaking husband to a shocking and unexpected death. She lived her last few years alone in the Volney Hotel in Manhattan, alcoholic to the end.

Also like Elinor Wylie, Parker's posthumous reputation has suffered at the hands of unsympathetic (and quite redundant) male biographers.[7] Although there is no doubt that Parker was a difficult person, at times self-pitying, shockingly selfish, and unwise in managing her personal life, all three full-length biographies seem determined to make Parker the chief agent and author of her own unhappiness. The tone taken by all three writers seems to cast the most negative possible interpretation on each turn of Parker's personal life, and all three seem to blame Parker deeply for her failure to conform to stereotypically feminine values—her lack of love for her family; her lack of interest in housekeeping and cooking; her childlessness, including her abortion and her belated grief over her miscarriages; her numerous sexual affairs, some with married men; and, indeed, her masculine drinking habits.[8] Although it is not possible to exonerate Parker entirely from her habit of exaggerating her suffering, it may be possible to view that suffering in light of the suffering in the lives of others in this study in order to illuminate the conditions under which female writers in the first half of the twentieth century lived and wrote.

Born in 1893, two months prematurely and nine years after her nearest sibling to a mother ailing in health and spirit, Dorothy Rothschild lost that mother altogether with the death of Eliza Marston Rothschild when Dorothy was five. Her father, J. Henry Rothschild, a Jewish clothing wholesaler of no relation to the famous banking Rothschilds, remarried shortly thereafter, to a stern and humorless Protestant woman who saw her mission as saving young Dorothy's soul from the taint of her father's Jewish blood. When this stepmother also died three years later (Dorothy was nine), one biographer writes, "Now Dorothy had two murders on her conscience. The sudden deaths of Eliza and Eleanor became the twin traumas of her early life, her ticket to self-pity, a passe-partout to self-hatred and an unalterable conviction that she deserved punishment . . ."[9] Although Dorothy idolized her older sister Helen and admired her social ascent toward a conventionally advantageous (and Christian) marriage, she found no model for her own life there, either. Tiny, awkward, and underdeveloped physically, Dorothy took refuge from her own confusion and shame in her reading and writing—and in her sharp tongue and precocious humor. Well-educated at Miss Dana's School in Morristown, New Jersey, she was prevented from going to college by the death of her father in December 1913 and the collapse of her financial resources. Instead she launched herself into the lively literary world of New York City, sending light verse to Franklin P. Adams's miscellany column in the *New York Herald*, "The Conning Tower," and selling her first poem, "Any Porch," to *Vanity Fair* in late 1914. Hired as a ten-dollar-a-week copywriter for *Vogue* magazine in 1913, she honed her craft by writing incisive captions for the magazine's many fashion photographs. "Brevity is the soul of lingerie" is perhaps her most memorable, accompanying a montage of images of ladies' underwear.

On her own in the city, Dorothy Rothschild first lived in a boarding-house on West 103rd Street with no money but in the lively company of her fellow boarders. There she became adept at playing the "good sport" woman in a group of men, a role she carried off with great success—but less and less satisfaction—over the next fifteen years. In 1916, she met and fell in love with Edwin Pond Parker II, scion of a pedigreed Connecticut family and already an alcoholic. She married in order to change her name, she said, just as Eddie went off to World War I as an ambulance driver. While it seems clear that she was genuinely in love with Parker—she wrote him daily and entertained him with humorous poems while he was overseas—in his absence, she claimed the career that would make her famous.

Hired in 1918 by Frank Crowninshield as the drama critic for the oh-so-chic *Vanity Fair*—the only female drama critic on the lively New York arts scene—Dorothy Parker became famous at the age of twenty-four as the mistress of a wicked wit, and was an adept practitioner of what her friend Robert Benchley called the "Elevated Eyebrow School of Journalism."[10] When Benchley was hired as managing editor at the magazine, and Robert Sherwood joined the staff as well, Parker became the female member of this trio of extraordinarily gifted comrades—Mrs. Parker, Mr. Benchley, and Mr. Sherwood, they called one another. At the start, only Sherwood among them was a drinker. Parker was herself a teetotaler, and Benchley an ardent Prohibitionist, the son of an alcoholic father. Parker first drank in response to her husband's drinking and with his encouragement, and in response to a crisis in her marriage, as is typical of female alcoholics generally. Eddie's experience at the front did not cure him of his habit of binge drinking (he was so often beside himself with alcohol that his friends called him "Spook") and left him a morphine addict. His return in August 1919 marked the beginning of the end of the marriage, and the beginning of Dorothy Parker's experience with alcohol.

Late in Eddie Parker's absence, in June 1919, Dorothy Parker was invited to a lunch at the Algonquin Hotel, hosted by the press agents of several New York theaters, welcoming Alexander Woollcott, the *New York Times* drama critic, home from the war. Also present at the table were Franklin P. Adams, the city's most recognizable literary voice, and the young Harold Ross, who had been a colleague with Woollcott and Adams on the staff of the *Stars and*

Stripes, the house organ of the American Expeditionary Forces.[11] From this beginning grew the fact and the legend of the Algonquin Round Table (it was a few months later that hotel manager Frank Case actually provided the group with its trademark round table). Its charter members included Woollcott, Adams, and Ross, as well as Parker, Benchley, and Sherwood, along with Heywood Broun, John Peter Toohey, George Kaufman, and Marc Connelly. Later they were joined (off and on) by Edna Ferber, Frank Sullivan, Charles MacArthur, Herman Mankiewicz, Harpo Marx, Donald Ogden Stewart, Murdock Pemberton, Deems Taylor, Arthur Samuels, Alice Duer Miller, Laurence Stallings, and John V. A. Weaver.[12] Ring Lardner was also associated with the group, though he rarely attended. A few women other than Parker, Ferber, and Miller joined in from time to time: Margalo Gillmore, Tallulah Bankhead, Peggy Wood (all actresses); Ruth Hale, Jane Grant (the wives of Broun and Ross, respectively); and Margaret Leech, a novelist.[13] Nearly half of these gifted writers, actors, editors, and musicians were or would eventually become alcoholic.

The group met and became famous for its witty repartee, the highlights of which were faithfully recorded in Adams's column. In this way, Dorothy Parker became the spokeswoman for the postwar generation's determination to leave worry and responsibility and traditional values behind in the relentless pursuit of a good time (Hemingway's discarding of the ideal words "sacred, glorious, and sacrifice" in *A Farewell to Arms* comes to mind). Later Dorothy Parker would remember the group's darker side—its relentlessly cynical pose, its incessant competitiveness, its use of insults as the currency of exchange; but at the start, it was all good fun, witty rejoinders, and word games. They made "I-Can-Give-You-a-Sentence" famous: Parker's most-quoted contribution is her "You can lead a horticulture but you can't make her think." (Far away in a private girls' school outside Boston, young Elizabeth Bishop tried the game out on her friends: "feeding their pilot biscuits to the gulls: *menstrurations* all over the beach."[14])

Parker ultimately found little personal sustenance in the relationships she formed at the Round Table—only Robert Benchley remained her close friend—and when in January 1920 she was fired by *Vanity Fair* (and Benchley resigned in protest), she was cast out on the competitive literary seas of New York City to survive on her wits. A week after the firing, Prohibition went into effect, and during the next eighteen months Parker both found her way as a freelance critic, poet, and short story writer and learned to drink in the way that would be her downfall. By 1922, both Parker and Benchley were drinking in order to relieve the anxiety and uncertainty of their improvisational lives. Disliking the taste of most liquor, Parker drank straight Scotch, a "quick, safe, and reliable" alternative among Prohibition's home-brewed choices[15] and more and more she drank away from her husband, in the easy masculine camaraderie of New York speakeasy culture. "Scotch helped her to function better," according to Marion Meade. "It seemed almost miraculous how little sips, spaced regularly throughout the day, could act as an effective tranquilizer."[16] "Never did Dorothy appear drunk," her friends reported. "But she was seldom completely sober either."[17] Like most of her writer-friends at the time, Parker could write only when she was not drinking—and when she was not writing, she drank.[18]

In 1921, Parker embarked on a love affair with a married newspaperman, Charles MacArthur, also a heavy drinker and member of her speakeasy crowd. When the affair ended unhappily, Parker underwent a hospital abortion (having convinced a doctor, with money, that the procedure was medically necessary) and plunged into a prolonged depression. In mid-January 1922 she attempted suicide—having ensured in advance that the man delivering her takeout dinner would find her before it was too late. This unhappy episode became fodder for the Round Table's humor (which culminated in a toast offered by a jealous Ernest Hemingway halfway around the world in France: "'Here's to Dorothy Parker. Life will never become her so much as her almost leaving it.'"[19]), and marked a permanent shift in Parker's life and work. This is the point at which her reputation as a devil-may-care wit separated from her real life as a depressed, suffering, and alcoholic woman. Her work recorded the shift, but it was perhaps too subtle for her general audience to catch. Writes Meade,

> The content of her verse began to change. . . . Satin gowns turned into shrouds, decomposing corpses clinically observe the activity of worms, the living dead ghoulishly deck themselves with graveyard flowers. There were alarming glimpses, no more than a series of snapshots, of the tragedies that would be recognized by twentieth century women as peculiarly their own: the gut-searing loneliness of the women who have "careers," the women who don't marry, the women who are condemned to seek love forever in the barren soil of husbands and children and even animals; women howling primitively for nourishment, flanked on one side by rejecting mothers and on the other by rejecting lovers. Her verse began to acknowledge the timeless subject of female rage.[20]

To Meade's list, one could add the frustration of being a female writer in a time that celebrated the stereotypically masculine in nearly every aspect of life.[21] Parker's "Song of Perfect Propriety" summarizes her frustration:

I'd like to straddle gory decks,
And dig in laden sands,
And know the feel of throbbing necks
Between my knotted hands.
Oh, I should like to strut and curse
Among my blackguard crew . . .
But I am writing little verse,
As little ladies do. (PDP 103)

By 1925, Parker had become physically dependent on alcohol, needing larger and larger amounts to relieve the anxiety and depression she continued to feel. She was cautioned by doctors to stop drinking and began to take the tranquilizer Vernol as an antidote to alcohol-induced anxiety. Early in 1926, she again attempted suicide by taking an overdose of the drug. At this her friend Robert Benchley is said to have remarked, "'Dottie, if you don't stop this sort of thing, you'll make yourself sick.'"[22] Deprived of the drug as she recovered in the hospital, she had her friends smuggle alcohol in. Parker underwent several weeks of psychiatric treatment following this episode, but eventually abandoned the search for answers to her condition.[23]

Just as Parker left for Europe for the first time in February 1926, self-consciously joining the growing community of expatriate American writers gathering in France, where the wine still flowed freely, her first book of poems appeared. At Parker's suggestion, the cover illustration of *Enough Rope* featured a knotted noose and the suggestion of suicide—of giving up, opting out, embracing death and oblivion. It is a volume of "light verse" with a dark subtext that appealed enormously to Americans in the mid-1920s. By early 1927, the book was in its third edition, selling faster than any volume of American poetry ever. It was eventually reprinted thirteen times.[24] Parker was characteristically uncomfortable with the critical praise the book received, and while its sales made her life a little easier, she was not buoyed in spirit by its success.

The second poem in the volume establishes the tone. "The Small Hours" says explicitly what the other poets in this study imply with their recurring images of unconsciousness and passivity:

No more my little song comes back;
And now of nights I lay
My head on down, to watch the black
And wait the unfailing gray.
Oh, sad are winter nights, and slow;
And sad's a song that's dumb;
And sad it is to lie and know
Another dawn will come. (PDP 75)

In other poems, such as "The Trifler," the volume's two obsessive concerns—death and the failure of heterosexual love—are joined. "Death's the lover that I'd be taking," she offers, in a Dickinsonian turn. "Gone's my heart with a trifling rover. / Fine he was in the game he played—/ Kissed, and promised, and threw me over, / And rode away with a prettier maid" (PDP 76). In "Epitaph," the speaker succeeds in dying, celebrating that fact in a way that calls to mind the *Ariel* poems of Sylvia Plath. The poem ends, "And I lie here warm, and I lie here dry, / And watch the worms slip by, slip by" (PDP 80). The book's contemplation of death culminates with the thoroughly memorable "Résumé":

Razors pain you;
Rivers are damp;
Acids stain you;
And drugs cause cramp.
Guns aren't lawful;
Nooses give;
Gas smells awful;
You might as well live. (PDP 99)

The book is shockingly honest in its assessment of the situation of women in the negotiations of love, and in its self-criticism and awareness of the ways in which women contribute to their own unhappiness and enslavement. "Ballade at Thirty-Five" develops around the sad refrain, "I loved them until they loved me," for example; and many of the poems record the petty dishonesty of both men and women in their relations with one another. Most memorable, of course, is this "Unfortunate Coincidence":

By the time you swear you're his,
Shivering and sighing,

And he vows his passion is
Infinite, undying—
Lady, make a note of this:
One of you is lying. (PDP 96)

Parker soon published two more volumes of this "light verse," *Sunset Gun* in 1928 and *Death and Taxes and Other Poems* in 1931, but wrote no more poetry after that. The "Coda" to *Sunset Gun* aptly summarizes her worldview at this time:

There's little in taking or giving,
There's little in water or wine;
This living, this living, this living
Was never a project of mine.
Oh, hard is the struggle, and sparse is
The gain of the one at the top,
For art is a form of catharsis,
And love is a permanent flop,
And work is the province of cattle,
And rest's for a clam in a shell,
So I'm thinking of throwing the battle—
Would you kindly direct me to hell? (PDP 240)

The poems make little mention of alcohol or drinking itself. Instead they relentlessly record a desperate and depressed state of mind in which anesthesia—by death or by drug, or, occasionally, by falling in love—is the only hope for relief.

Parker returned from Europe in the fall of 1926 to take up her duties as the chief fiction reviewer for the fledgling *New Yorker*, which had published its first issue in February 1925. Under the sobriquet "Constant Reader," Parker offered evaluations of everything the magazine sent her way, from the autobiography of an English countess ("'The affair between Margot Asquith and Margot Asquith will live as one of the prettiest love stories in all of literature'"), to A. A. Milne's *Winnie the Pooh*: "'Tonstant weader fwowed up.'"[25] She also began taking herself more seriously as a writer of short stories, although she became more rather than less dependent on alcohol at the same time. After her divorce from Edwin Parker was finalized in 1928, she evidently felt more free to write about her marriage, and more confident in her ability to tell the story, even of her own weakness within it.

"Big Blonde" is everywhere acknowledged to be Parker's masterpiece in the short story mode. In it, she tells the story of Hazel Morse and the decline of her marriage to "Herbie," a heavy drinker and one of her barroom admirers. Although she gave her heroine precisely opposite physical characteristics from her own (Hazel is "a large, fair woman" who shone in the heyday of "the big woman"; Parker was tiny with dark hair and dramatic dark eyes), much about Hazel's experience parallels Parker's own. Hazel starts out as "a good sport. Men liked a good sport" (PDP 187). Affable and uncomplaining, she never lacks for male companionship, but yearns, after "a couple thousand evenings of being a good sport among her male acquaintances," for a settled domestic life. Provided with one by Herbie's earning power, she is unable to keep him interested in the small concerns and sadnesses of her domestic day. They grow apart; he complains that she has become "a lousy sport."

> She could not recall the definite day that she started drinking, herself. There was nothing separate about her days. Like drops upon a windowpane, they ran together and trickled away. She had been married six months; then a year; then three years.
>
> She had never needed to drink, formerly. She could sit for most of a night at a table where the others were imbibing earnestly and never droop in looks or spirits, nor be bored by the doings of those about her. If she took a cocktail, it was so unusual as to cause twenty minutes or so of jocular comment. But now anguish was in her. Frequently, after a quarrel, Herbie would stay out for the night, and she could not learn from him where the time had been spent. Her heart felt tight and sore in her breast, and her mind turned like an electric fan.
>
> She hated the taste of liquor. Gin, plain or in mixtures, made her promptly sick. After experiment, she found that Scotch whisky was the best for her. She took it without water, because that was the quickest way to its effect.
>
> Herbie pressed it on her. He was glad to see her drink. (PDP 191–92)

Herbie and Hazel quarrel when they are drunk, and eventually Herbie leaves. Hazel's decline following his departure features deep depression, more and more alcohol (with less and less apparent effect), and affairs with kind but uncommitted men. The story culminates in Hazel's attempted suicide with Vernol and alcohol, an account that closely parallel's Parker's own 1926 experience. When she wakes to find herself still alive, she wearily shares a

drink with her household maid, earnestly praying that her days of unconsciousness have restored alcohol's effectiveness: "[M]aybe whisky would be
her friend again" (PDP 210).

Parker's significant extramarital experience in the speakeasy culture of
New York in the 1920s also produced her brilliant taxonomy of feminine
drunkenness, "Just a Little One." A first-person monologue told from the
point of view of a woman visiting a speakeasy in the company of a male
friend, the story records the falling away of inhibition and the rising garrulity in the cadence and diction of the woman's speech. "I like this place,
Fred," the story begins, in full sarcasm from the start. "And they let you
right in, without asking you a single question. I bet you could get into the
subway without using anybody's name. Couldn't you, Fred?" (PDP 241). In
its description of the speakeasy itself and the literally underground culture
of alcohol consumption that Prohibition brewed, the story is very much
of its moment. But more important, amid its satire and frustration (that the
protagonist must be in the company of a man, even a loser like Fred, in
order to drink at the bar, for example), is a record of the rationalizations
and evasions, the self-deceptions and social liabilities, of a woman drinking
to excess in a public place. "'Why, I don't know, Fred—what are you going
to have? Then I guess I'll have a highball, too; please, just a little one. Is it
really real Scotch? Well, that will be a new experience for me. You ought to
see the Scotch I've got home in my cupboard; at least it was in the cupboard
this morning . . . '" (PDP 241). The speaker consumes at least six drinks in
the course of her four-and-a-half page narration, each one with a disclaimer
that serves as the story's refrain: "Are you going to have another one? Well,
I shouldn't like to see you drinking all by yourself, Fred" (PDP 241); "Oh,
darling, do you really think I ought to? Well, you tell him just a little bit of
a one. Tell him, sweet" (PDP 242); "What's the sense of feeling good, when
life's so terrible? Oh, all right, then. But please tell him just a little one" (PDP
244); "Yes, I think we ought to, honey. I think we ought to have a little drink,
on account of our being friends. Just a little one, because it's real Scotch, and
we're real friends" (PDP 244); "Look, I'll tell you what let's do, after we've had
just a little highball . . ." (PDP 245). The speaker's decline expresses itself in
typically feminine forms (in addition to the more universal slurred speech,
failing logic, and general loquaciousness): "All right, what do you care if
I'm crying, I can cry if I want to, can't I? I guess you'd cry, too, if you didn't
have a friend in the world. . . . Just give me back my hand a second, till I get
this damned mascara out of my eye" (PDP 243–44). It ends with the speaker

29

begging Fred to help her collect stray animals from the city streets ("Three highballs, and I think I'm St. Francis of Assisi," as she'd said earlier [242]). But not right away: "Let's have a drink and then let's you and I go out and get a horsie, Freddie—just a little one, darling, just a little one" (PDP 245).

Like most alcoholics, Parker drank destructively because she was an alcoholic, but she began drinking in the first place for reasons of her own. Relief from anxiety, self-medication for depression, help with being the social "good sport" she wanted to be, and even help with the problems inherent in being a writer at all, lay behind her decision to take up alcohol after having been a virtual abstainer until the age of twenty-nine. Parker's friend Diana Sheean commented that Parker "'gave off an aura of troubledness. I think she drank because of her perception. She wanted to dull her perceptions. Her vision of life was almost more than she could bear.'"[26] This echoes the experience of many other writers who sought to dull temporarily the observing critical voice utterly necessary to the practice of their art. Perhaps in Parker's case that search for respite became an absolute avoidance of the necessary tension, anxiety, and self-criticism. Her friend Beatrice Ames Stewart offered this glimpse into Parker's complex thinking: "Her talent was the most precious thing in the world to her. She respected her talent even more than her attraction for beautiful men. She had an absolute, solid gratitude for her talent. She said to me, 'I'm betraying it, I'm drinking, I'm not working. I have the most horrendous guilt.'"[27]

A story circulates among the various biographies of Parker that in 1931, the point at which her friends shifted from admiring her capacity for drink ("For such a small woman, she does well") to worrying about how much she was putting away, Robert Benchley suggested that she visit with Alcoholics Anonymous. Parker did so, the story goes, "and brought back word to the drinkers at Tony's that she thought the organization was perfectly wonderful." Benchley asked her if that meant that she would join, and Parker is said to have replied, "Certainly not. They want me to stop *now*."[28] The story is anachronistic, if not apocryphal—Alcoholics Anonymous was not founded until 1935 and not well established for several years after that. And part of the story of Parker's alcoholism, and that of the other writers in this study, is their lack of access to and later lack of interest in the formal program of that organization. For Parker to have adopted absolute abstinence as a means to cure her alcoholism in 1931 would have been flying in the face of what her whole culture—particularly that of literary New York—was telling her she ought to value in life. Despite the misery her drinking was causing her, she identified it closely with her vocation as a writer.

"Big Blonde" won the 1929 O. Henry Prize for the best American short story of the year, and on the strength of that success, Parker was invited to Hollywood to write for a major studio. The fragmentary and unsatisfying (but well-paid) work contributed to her sense of purposelessness, and she returned to New York a few months later very much at a loss. She left for Europe in late 1929 in hopes of restoring her spirits, but suffered during her travels from acute but unidentified liver illness. Following (at their request) Gerald and Sara Murphy, the wealthy friends and hosts of Fitzgerald and others, to Switzerland to await the death of their son Patrick from tuberculosis, Parker earnestly tried to cut back on her drinking but could not sustain a long period of even relative sobriety. Although she was apparently a genuine comfort to the Murphys in their grief, she grew more depressed herself in the atmosphere of death and decline. Back in New York in February 1932, she again attempted suicide, this time with barbiturates.

Like Edna St. Vincent Millay, Parker had had her political convictions aroused over the execution of Sacco and Vanzetti in 1927. She and Millay were perhaps the two most famous writers at the Boston demonstration on the night of their deaths. As the stock market crashed and the twenties came to an abrupt end, the obvious inequalities of life in Depression-era New York kept Parker both engaged and saddened by what she saw around her, and for the rest of her life she gave her name, her time, and her money to political causes that eventually—in the McCarthy years—cost her her Hollywood livelihood. A fierce defender of Spain during its civil war, an early and committed member of the Anti-Nazi League, and much of the time beside herself at the world's apparent indifference to the Third Reich's treatment of Jews, Parker never lost her interest in political and social justice. When she died, she left her entire estate to Dr. Martin Luther King Jr.

In 1933, Parker met the man who would be her second husband, Alan Campbell, a handsome and possibly homosexual former actor eleven years her junior. In response to her tremendous needs—Parker was indeed no housekeeper, no money manager, and abjectly dependent on alcohol at this time—Campbell essentially abandoned his own ambitions to take up his role as full-time caretaker to Parker. While it seems clear that they fed each other's worst habits of drinking and taking prescription sedatives, they also attempted to give one another the semblance of a settled domestic life. They signed on together as a screenwriting team, and sold their services to the highest bidder among the Hollywood studios; they bought an ancient farm in Bucks County, Pennsylvania, that they lovingly (and somewhat eccentrically) restored. Although they fought often (and in fact divorced in 1947 only to remarry in 1950), Parker and Campbell were absolutely necessary to one another throughout their difficult time together. This was the period of their screenwriting (and Hollywood's) heyday; the period of Dorothy's miscarriages and her fervent desire to bear a child; of the premature deaths of her Algonquin friends—Fitzgerald in 1940, Woollcott in 1943, and Benchley in 1945, among others; the period of her blacklisting because of her political convictions and her appearance before the House Un-American Activities Committee (where she did, indeed, refuse to name names); and the period of her physical decline as a result of alcoholism. But it was Alan Campbell who died first, the victim of an apparently accidental overdose of alcohol and barbiturates, on June 15, 1963. Parker herself drifted for the next four years, writing little and drinking a great deal, until she herself died of a heart attack, alone in her suite at the Hotel Volney in New York, at the age of seventy.

Parker's stories and plays are searching analyses of women in her own situation. "Big Blonde" is the best and most critically acclaimed of these stories, but Parker herself was most proud of *The Ladies of the Corridor*, a play she cowrote with Arnaud d'Usseau, about the lives of divorced, widowed, and abandoned women living alone in a New York residence hotel very much like the Volney. The play's tone and mood resembles that of "Big Blonde" as the lost and insignificant women mark off their meaningless days, drowning their boredom and sorrow in alcohol, drugs, and sordid affairs. Mildred Tynan is the witty philosopher in the group, the drinker who defends her habit to her housekeeper. "A couple of drinks, and I've got some nerve. Otherwise I'm frightened all the time."[29] When Mildred commits suicide at the play's end, we see that she had not conquered her fear after all, any more than her corridor-mates who go on (ostensibly) living. *The Ladies of the Corridor* (its title is taken from Eliot's "Sweeney Erect") was not a success on the stage and Parker was bitter about the critics' and the public's unwillingness to hear her message about the "appalling human waste"[30] represented in the lives of those forgotten women and, by implication, of single women generally. Parker would also work on the screenplays for *A Star Is Born* and *Smash-Up: The Story of a Woman*, both of which tell the story of women ultimately undone by their dependence on alcohol and drugs.

Dorothy Parker's experience differs from that of the other women in this study chiefly on account of her extreme celebrity and her willingness—indeed, her *need*—to drink to excess in public places and in the company of men. Only Elizabeth Bishop suffered as much from alcohol dependency, and Parker's every instinct for publicity and sociability became in Bishop such acute shame and instinct for privacy that she conscripted (and harmed) people she loved in a desperate "conspiracy of silence" about her drinking. Louise Bogan translated that instinct for privacy into a doctrine of self-concealment so powerful it eventually silenced her lyric voice.

Chapter 2

The Alchemist

Louise Bogan

At the same time that Louise Bogan (1897–1970) is remembered and studied as one of the finest lyric poets America has produced, the fact that she was a woman and that she defended formal lyric poetry in an age of expansive experimentation has made evaluation of her work somewhat reductive. Lumped with far less gifted and less psychologically sophisticated "poetesses" in the American tradition, Bogan has only recently come to be seen as a worthy descendent of Emily Dickinson, and a Modernist innovator in her own right. Her achievement in poetry has also been overshadowed by her extensive critical writings; for thirty-eight years she was the poetry critic for the *New Yorker* magazine, the

Photograph by Lotte Jacobi

arbiter of taste in such matters for a literate and influential audience, and for two generations of female poets.

But Louise Bogan's work in poetry, and her life as well, suffered from what her biographer, Elizabeth Frank, called "a principle of arrest": "[S]omething stopped Louise Bogan dead in her tracks, not once but many times."[1] Gloria Bowles has argued persuasively that this principle of arrest might be termed an "aesthetic of limitation"—a set of rules for poetry by women, both self-imposed and internalized from without, rules so strict that they "would almost inevitably lead to silence."[2] Indeed, Bogan published only 132 poems in her adult lifetime (and edited those to 105 for *The Blue Estuaries,* her "collected poems"). She wrote very little poetry after 1937, and none at all between 1941 and 1948. Bogan also struggled all her life against paralyzing depression, and was hospitalized for its treatment three times. She drank heavily from her mid-twenties on, and although, as Frank concludes, "she had never, during a lifetime's hard drinking, become an alcoholic (that is, never ceased to function because of alcohol, or needed alcohol to function)," there were periods in Bogan's life in which alcohol threatened to become a cause rather than merely a symptom of her general unhappiness.[3]

Bogan herself referred to the period 1930 to 1933 as a time of "despair, neuroses and alcoholism" and she twice hospitalized herself with what she called "breakdowns" during these years (wwl 145).[4] Like others of her generation Bogan learned to drink during Prohibition, bootleg gin and whiskey, as a part of a self-consciously rebellious and bohemian lifestyle. Her friends were heavy drinkers; she was close to Edmund Wilson, perhaps the heaviest-drinking productive American writer ever, and to Theodore Roethke, who made something of a religion of physical debasement. She herself began to "drink steadily," she said, after meeting her second husband, Raymond Holden, in 1923 ("although I had been known to crook my arm, on two continents, before that") (wwl 190), and her reputation as a heavy drinker was secure enough in 1944 that even so discreet a commentator as Marianne Moore could comfort a friend against Bogan's harsh review by saying "I hear she drinks a great deal."[5] But unlike Scott Fitzgerald or William Faulkner or even Elizabeth Bishop, Bogan's abuse of alcohol was never separable from her other psychological difficulties. She drank badly when she was suffering from depression; she drank less when she was happy. If she was ever alcoholic, she was a so-called secondary alcoholic; that is, abusing alcohol in response to a primary psychological illness—a condition much more common in women than in men.[6]

Nevertheless, reflections of Bogan's lifelong negotiation with alcohol, and with depression, occur with great frequency throughout her poetry, particularly in the poems of *Dark Summer* (1929) and *The Sleeping Fury* (1937). She wrote several poems explicitly about alcohol, and the central preoccupations of her work overall—the split between mind and body, intellect and passion; the operations of the unconscious and the subconscious on the conscious mind of the artist; the temptation toward oblivion or an unfeeling death-in-life, often figured in devastated or abandoned landscapes—can all be fruitfully seen in terms of those negotiations as well.

Louise Bogan was born of the unhappy marriage of Daniel and Mary "May" (Shields) Bogan in Livermore Falls, Maine, a bustling mill town on the Androscoggin River. In 1897, the year of Louise's birth, Daniel Bogan was superintendent in a pulp mill in the town, the first of many such relatively white-collar mill jobs he would hold during her childhood. Louise was their third child; a son, Charles, had been born in 1884 and a second son, Edward, had died in infancy.

A product of deepest New England and its hard-drinking Irish communities, Louise moved often with her family, to a variety of hotels and boardinghouses and other temporary dwellings: to Milton, New Hampshire, in 1901; to Ballardvale, Massachusetts, in 1904; to Roxbury (near Boston) in 1909. These moves were prompted both by economics and by the family's unhappiness. May Shields Bogan was a beautiful and unstable woman prone to flaunting her many extramarital affairs (on at least one occasion witnessed by her daughter) and to mysterious and lengthy disappearances. Louise Bogan remembered her childhood as a time of violence and terror, but revealed few specific incidents in her poems or autobiographical prose: "But can I tell the whole truth? I never have, even to Dr. Wall" (JAMR 176). Her inability to face squarely the demons of her early life is one possible explanation for both her chronic depression and the retreat of her ability to write poems. She did remember that once, something she had seen shocked her to such an extent that she went blind for two days. "What had I seen?" she wrote in her journal. "I shall never know" (JAMR 26).

Bogan associated her mother both with the violence, shame, instability, and unhappiness of her childhood homes and with her own gifts as an artist and a lover of beauty. Her efforts to make sense of the relationship were fragmentary: she was eventually able to admit that she had "never truly feared" her mother: "Her tenderness was the other side of her terror" (JAMR 27). And she came to recognize the human in the monster of memory: "A terrible, unhappy, lost, spoiled, bad-tempered child. A tender contrite woman, with, somewhere in her blood, the rake's recklessness, the baffled artist's despair" (JAMR 35). She was stern with herself, and with others, about the temptation to self-pity: "We must not bring back and describe 'the bad mother'—'the Dragon mother'—to justify ourselves. Only to understand.—To hold the portrait of this evil figure unresolved, into age, is madness" (JAMR 167). And about disciplining one's urge to mean-spirited confession: "But I still cannot describe some of the nightmares lived through, with love. So I shan't try to describe them at all" (JAMR 172).

Although there is no direct evidence that May Shields Bogan was herself alcoholic, it is very likely that Louise's older brother Charles was. His mother's favorite, Charles was unable to make a life for himself and lived unhappily with his parents until, as Louise put it, "death providentially took him" in the First World War. She remembered that near the end of his life, "he used to knock down doors and smash windows with chairs, and be brought home, beaten to a pulp" (WWL 99). Bogan's poem for Charles, "To My Brother Killed: Haumont Wood: October, 1918," remembers the apparent futility of his life first in terms of alcohol: "O you so long dead, / You masked and obscure, / I can tell you, all things endure: / The wine and the bread" (BE 77). It has long been one of the commonplaces of alcohol studies that an overindulgent mother may predispose a young man to alcoholism, and that for women, the mother's absence or unreliability may be an antecedent.[7] Louise and Charles conform to this model, although the mother involved is the same.

Despite these difficulties, Louise was quite well educated, in a New Hampshire convent from 1906 to 1908, and at Boston's excellent Girls' Latin School from 1910 to 1915, where she received a classical education in Latin, Greek, French, mathematics, history, science, and the arts, and distinguished herself as class poet.

Sent by her parents to Boston University in 1916, Bogan did extremely well, publishing poems in the university's literary magazine. She earned a scholarship to Radcliffe for her sophomore year, to the immense pride of her mother. But going to Radcliffe would have meant continuing to live at home, and Louise elected instead to escape. She chose the only respectable means available to her: she got married. Curt Alexander was a German immigrant and U.S. Army officer not at all liked by Bogan's parents, and her break with them was swift and, for a time, complete. Louise moved with her husband to New York City, where she made brief acquaintance with the vibrant Greenwich Village literary community, and then, when war was declared in April 1917, to Panama. There in the heat and humidity, awaiting the birth of her daughter, Louise was forced to recognize her folly in marrying a man with whom she had nothing in common but physical attraction and began to plan her escape. She wrote poems about her condition, including "Betrothed" and "The Young Wife." Mathilde (Maidie) Alexander was born in October, and in May 1918, Louise took her daughter and moved home with her parents in Massachusetts. At the war's end she was briefly reconciled with her husband, but in the summer of 1919, she left Alexander for good. With chilling single-mindedness, she consigned her daughter to the care of the parents she had been desperate to escape two years before and found herself an apartment in New York City from which to launch her career as a woman of letters. Curt Alexander died in 1920, and his army widow's pension made it possible for her to stay in the city.

From a temporary job at Brentano's bookstore in New York, Bogan quickly became acquainted with the city's lively literary community. The young, radical, energetic, and hard-drinking crowd included, early on, Lola Ridge, Malcolm Cowley, William Carlos Williams, Mina Loy, Maxwell Bodenheim, John Reed, Louise Bryant, Conrad Aiken, and, most important to Bogan, Edmund Wilson. She embarked on a program of intense self-education in New York, reading widely and taking careful notes, disciplining and honing her writing skills with great dedication and seriousness. Painfully conscious of her lack of higher education (she carried a lifelong resentment of people with advanced degrees), Bogan determined to read more widely and deeply than any of her contemporaries. With Wilson as her first tutor, she learned both to read critically and to drink with pleasure and then abandon.

Bogan's education as a poet had begun with her teenage enthusiasm for Swinburne and her absorption of Arthur Symons's famous book on the French Symbolists. Here Bogan learned not only to embrace the romanticism of her own nature and to invest the autobiography and emotion in her poems deeply in symbols, but also to know the nineteenth century's apparent enthusiasm for opium and alcohol as a means for the poet to loosen the claims of society upon his mind. Baudelaire's recommendation at the end of "Le Voyage"—"Plonger au fond du gouffre, Enfer ou Ciel, qu'importe? / Au fond de l'Inconnu pour trouver du *nouveau*!" ("To plunge to the depths of the abyss, Hell or Heaven, what does it matter? / To the depths of the

Unknown in order to find the *new!*")—was taken by numerous writers of Bogan's generation to recommend intoxication quite literally, and helped further to erode the social pressures that might under other circumstances have discouraged Bogan, as a woman, from drinking. Bogan's most important contemporary American literary influences—Elinor Wylie, Edna St. Vincent Millay, and E. A. Robinson—were all heavy drinkers as well.

Perhaps more important for Bogan, though, was the Symbolists' implicit support of her instinctive belief that poetry must arise from deep in the poet's unconscious mind, and will likely arise only as a result of mental conflict, struggle, or suffering. "The certain method of stilling poetic talent," she wrote, "is to substitute an outer battle for an inner one. A poet emerges from a spiritual crisis strengthened and refreshed only if he has been strong enough to fight it through at all levels, and at the deepest first" (JAMR 116). Bogan added thorough reading of Freud and his disciples to her Symbolist education, and the result was a poetic method that began in personal psychic pain and conflict, transformed that pain and its causes into symbols arising from the subconscious, and dropped reference to actual outside experience altogether: "The poet represses the outright narrative of his life. He absorbs it, along with life itself. The repressed becomes the poem. Actually, I have written down my experience in the closest detail. But the rough and vulgar facts are not there" (JAMR 72). Bogan's determination to leave "vulgar facts" out of her poems left them open to charges of idiosyncrasy and obscurity, with some justice. And her "passion for reticence" in poems and in public life "bordered on obsession," according to her biographer.[8] This fear was her own version of the Modernist call for "impersonality" in poems, certainly, but it may also have been the middle-class (or aspiring middle-class) woman's residual discomfort with her own unconventional background and life choices, heavy alcohol use among them. In any case, it is a stance common to female poets of this generation.

Bogan articulated most of her "aesthetic of limitation" very early on, and it was fully expressed in her first book of poems, *Body of This Death* (1923). In addition to the "rules" against explicit self-revelation and confession, Bogan bound herself by a host of restrictions she felt necessary to save women poets from "appearing ridiculous" in the masculine literary world. As with most of the rules in Bogan's life, these restrictions were not without conflict for her. Bogan believed—and articulated this belief more and more strongly in the 1940s and '50s, when she saw the "poetic logicians" taking over—that women had a special service to perform for poetry, to ensure that emotion was not lost to it. But emotion is the woman poet's greatest danger, as well, and was frowned upon by the male Modernists. "Small emotion" and the treacle of "'feelings unemployed'" in bored housewives could not be fit subjects for poetry; authenticity for Bogan was a matter of scale. Large emotion was necessary for significant poetry.[9]

In the fall of 1962, Bogan gave a talk at Bennington College in which she mused about the role of women in society and about the strengths and limitations of feminism, and gave her fullest articulation of both her belief in the special contribution women could make to poetry and the limits of that contribution. Although the great subjects of literature were for Bogan as available to women as to men ("Who am I? From whence did I come? Is there a design in the universe of which I am a part? Do you love me? Shall I die forever?" [JAMR 157]), women's attitudes toward those subjects— she even says "women's deportment"—must be carefully controlled. "[T]he brutal, rough, swaggering, masculinized gesture never, somehow, works. . . . [T]he gentle, tender, nurturing feminine nature perhaps precludes ultimate coarseness or harshness, either in tone or in choice of material." Surrealism, for example, is a man's province, as is "the hallucinatory, the shocking, and the terrifying effect; . . . the calculated irrational and the direct or indirect erotic" (JAMR 155). Women poets cannot and should not swear in a masculine way. She then draws up a list: "First, in literature (or in any other art) women must not lie. Second, they must not whine. Third, they must not attitudinize (in the role of the *femme fatale* least of all). And they must neither theatricalize nor coarsen their truths. They must not be vain, and they must not flight or kite in any witch-like way. Nor, on the other hand, go in for little girlishness and false naïveté. Nor 'stamp a tiny foot at the universe'" (JAMR 156); and women should avoid sonnet sequences because they are particularly tempting to women's special liabilities—the tendency to "go on and on," and to effect an attitude of subservience or an artful death wish (JAMR 157).

To be sure, one might deplore vanity or self-pity and praise technical excellence in anyone's work—Bogan's poetic values are solidly classical. But the articulation of these restrictions, which Bogan had developed over a lifetime, has the effect of closing down the rhetorical space upon which a woman poet might stand to say her piece, and creating in the woman poet—Bogan herself, and those other female poets who looked to her for guidance—such censorious self-consciousness that saying anything at all grew more and more difficult. Maturity for Bogan meant moving away from the merely personal in poems; the less traceable the personal revelation in her poems was, the more satisfactory she found them. Bogan excised many poems in *Body of This Death* from later collections because she later found them too personal and—her sharpest criticism—"mawkish."

Bogan was probably right about the necessity of these restrictions for a woman poet if she was to be taken seriously by the male critical establishment. Alicia Ostriker explained the strategy in *Stealing the Language:*

> The woman poet who adopts an impenetrable tone is less in danger of being dismissed as sentimental or overemotional by critics. . . . To approach the strategy of this style from another angle, we need look no further than Laing's observation that an ontologically uneasy person may adopt, to the point of caricature, the personality of his oppressor. Control, impersonality, and dispassionateness are supposedly normative masculine virtues in any case, and are favored by the contemporary literary climate. The cooler the voice, the warmer the reception is a good rule of thumb. An intelligent woman poet may have every reason in the world to construct, as her fortress, a perversely exaggerated version of an acceptable style. The intelligent reader, on the other hand, need not be fooled.[10]

Bogan did ultimately ally herself with the relatively "minor" tradition of lyric poetry and, with lots of ambivalence, of lyric poetry by women such as Lizette Reese, Imogen Guiney, Elinor Wylie, and Edna St. Vincent Millay. She felt less sympathy for the Modernist work of Marianne Moore, Gertrude Stein, and H. D., but she reevaluated this identification almost continuously throughout her life.

By the time *Body of This Death* was published, Bogan had spent five months alone in Vienna, a "sabbatical" designed to give her time to think and write. And she had met and fallen in love with her second husband, Raymond Holden, a sometime poet and novelist who had been a friend of Robert Frost. When she and Holden moved in together in 1924, Bogan retrieved her daughter from her parents and began the first stretch of domestic happiness she had ever known. The two were married in July 1925.

The life Bogan and Holden made for themselves in New York and Boston (and for a time in Santa Fe, New Mexico, where they retired briefly for Holden's health) was rather frantically social. As insiders at the new *New Yorker* magazine (Holden was for a time its managing editor), they were near the center of a young, smart, witty, and hard-drinking circle, including close friends Rolfe Humphries and his wife, Dr. Helen Spencer; Léonie Adams;

Witter Bynner; and others. Bogan's correspondence during this period contains many comfortable anecdotes about who got drunk at what party and who vomited on the carpet, who was brewing what at home (Holden's own bathtub gin was especially prized by his friends), how long the hangover lasted, bawdy jokes about drinking, and this or that friend's prodigious capacity. It was all very easy and sociable, with scarcely a trace of moral conflict or anxiety. Genevieve Taggard and Robert Wolf quarreled with Bogan and Holden in 1924, and, as Bogan reported, "they called both Raymond and myself habitual drunkards and reminded me that I would probably fill a dipso's grave because it was in the blood" (WWL 13–14). In retrospect, this might be taken as an early indication of the eventual damage that alcohol would do to the marriage and to Bogan and Holden themselves, but at the time, Bogan was able to take it lightly—or as lightly as she could ever take a slur on her Irish heritage.

Bogan and Holden eventually grew weary of this social whirl (and Holden was fired by the *New Yorker*), and they retreated happily to an old farmhouse in Hillsdale, New York, in the summer of 1928. During the next nine months they lovingly restored the house, moving in in May 1929. This was the most peaceful season of their marriage, and Bogan was able to report in December 1928 that "Raymond and I have taken up chess and given up liquor—almost, that is" (WWL 43). Bogan lived well and wrote well during this time, including her first attempt at a long poem, the Yeatsian dialogue "Summer Wish." She gardened and canned and contemplated the turns of the seasons. But this happiness was short-lived. In December 1929 the beloved house burned to the ground, taking with it all of Bogan's journals, notebooks, and works in progress as well as nearly all of the family's personal belongings. Bogan and Holden collected their insurance money and moved resolutely back to New York City, but the marriage would not recover from the shock, and neither would Bogan—or not for a long time.

Bogan's second book, *Dark Summer,* appeared in the middle of the happy time, in September 1929. Generally more difficult and less accessible than *Body of This Death,* the book contained poems written between 1922 and 1929—and contains the only two long poems Bogan ever completed, "The Flume" (1924) (which she excised from her collected poems) and "Summer Wish" (1929). Despite her happiness at the time of its publication, the book is overwhelmingly dark, as its title suggests—as if to foretell the struggle to follow.

It is only in retrospect that Bogan labeled the period 1930 to 1933 as a time "of alcoholism and despair." As she is drinking the most addictively and destructively (and the least socially) of any time in her life, all mention of alcohol drops from her correspondence. Her journals of the period are filled with her anguish over her marriage—she was convinced that Holden continually betrayed her with other women—and her suffering with acute and paralyzing depression, but she does not discuss and hardly mentions her drinking. If there is a story to be told of Bogan's drinking in this period, it is a story written in the silences and gaps of her journals and letters, and in the poems she did not write or could not finish, so determined was she not to fall back on the merely personal. A part of the story of her recovery from depression and her return to controlled drinking is her gradual willingness to credit her own experience with significance, to resist the temptation to think of her life only in literary terms, and to move away from utter dependence on symbols in her poems.

Bogan hospitalized herself in April 1931, having suffered from paralyzing depression for more than a year. She had also begun to drink heavily, by herself, during the day. At the Neurological Institute in New York, she followed a routine of occupational therapy, hydrotherapy, and individual counseling sessions. "I refused to fall apart," she told her editor, John Hall Wheelock, "so I was taken apart, like a watch" (WWL 57). After a few weeks, she moved to Cromwell Hall, a private sanitarium in Connecticut, and there she continued her mild program of knitting and weaving and needle-showers, the comfort and rest cure typical of treatment for women's depression since the late nineteenth century. Her notes about her therapy contain no mention of alcohol or drinking. She returned to New York and the wider world in June, feeling better but not well.[11]

Bogan had a difficult time writing poems during this period, but she began to write and publish criticism more regularly. Her first *New Yorker* poetry review appeared in 1931, and twice a year for the next thirty-eight years she would offer the magazine's readers her survey of the season's new poetry books. She also turned with some enthusiasm and success to writing short stories, most of which she published in the *New Yorker*. Three of these, "Saturday Night Minimum" (1935), "Sunday at Five" (1931), and "Conversation Piece" (1933) are serious attempts to capture the alcohol-sodden social world of the Prohibition era, in a manner reminiscent of the sketches of Dorothy Parker. In "Sunday at Five" the narrator rages at the banality and pretense of cocktail party conversation, her irritation growing as she waits and waits for another drink. "Conversation Piece" is a more sophisticated attempt to record the rise in anger and resentment toward the other guests and her husband in the course of the protagonist's consumption of five drinks.

In "Saturday Night Minimum," Bogan spends some time dissecting specific social effects of alcohol—here the husband drinks brandy and the speaker/wife drinks rye, and both are made more eloquent by alcohol. The patrons pour down their drinks "without hardly a swallow." The story is again about the false nature of these self-conscious interactions, but here Bogan attempts to record the effect of alcohol on the speaker's thinking about the dancer who entertains the crowd in the bar, and her own relationship with her husband:

> You can't be blamed for what another person winds around you, and builds you into. Another person, busily engaged in spinning round you their attention, their ideas of what would please them, their wishes, their efforts toward love, may finish the process, and begin to hate you, but that isn't your fault. You have been yourself all the time. You haven't noticed that any reeling and winding has been going on, and that you're halfway in and halfway out of a whole web emanating from another.
>
> So that when the reverse process starts, you are safe from it, as well. You are just where you always were, attacking, it may be, a wider field of reference on different levels, surrounded by entire constellations of neatly related ideas.
>
> With the third rye, the reverse process gained such momentum, that it was all over when she looked again at the spot-lighted girl.

"On Saturday nights there was a minimum charge attached to the drinks," is the story's last line.[12]

In other short stories of this period, Bogan began to write for the first time of her own childhood difficulties, of the grimy mill towns where her family suffered and she grew up. These began with the remarkable "Journey Around My Room," based on Xavier de Maistre's nineteenth-century *Voyage autour de ma chambre,* in which Bogan takes her *New Yorker* readers on a tour of her bedroom with the intention of answering the question of how she came to this place and point in her life.[13] Two other memoirs, the beginnings of an autobiographical novel that Bogan hoped to call *Laura Da[i]ley's Story,* were also written during this period. "Dove and Serpent" and

"Letdown" are both accounts of defining moments in Bogan's adolescence. Both were published in the *New Yorker*, at which point Bogan abandoned autobiographical prose altogether.

The short stories reflect both the new self-awareness Bogan had acquired in therapy and the tension that remained in her marriage to Raymond Holden. Although the two continued to work on the relationship, Bogan grew less and less happy in it and her depression returned. The crisis in both the marriage and her psyche was postponed temporarily when Bogan applied for and was granted a Guggenheim Fellowship for study in Italy in 1933. She left in April, and although the trip was important to her continuing development as an artist and a critic, it was personally difficult from start to finish. Her negotiations with Holden continued through the mail, her depression did not lift, she was lonely, and she drank too much. When her trip was cut short by a drop in the value of the dollar, she returned to New York in September to face the end of her marriage and with certain knowledge that she would have to complete the overhaul of her life and mind she'd begun at the Neurological Institute in 1931.

She took up the task in November 1933, when she once again checked herself into the hospital with what she admitted this time was "a bad nervous crack-up." What role alcohol may have played in this illness we do not know, although once she left the hospital, her drinking was apparently under control. However, her doctor at New York Hospital's Westchester Division, on Bloomingdale Road in White Plains, New York ("Bloomingdale's," familiarly), was James H. Wall, a young psychoanalyst who had something of a subspecialty in the treatment of female alcoholics. His 1937 article, "A Study of Alcoholism in Women" contained his observations on fifty patients he treated at the Bloomingdale facility between 1920 and 1933. If Bogan had been included in his study, it would have been at its very end and she is not among the three detailed case studies he reports.[14] Nevertheless, Wall would have approached her treatment with an awareness of the particular needs and difficulties of female abusers of alcohol. His essay is the most sympathetic of the mid-century studies of female alcoholism, and many of his observations have been upheld by more systematic research over the past sixty years; for example, that women's alcoholism tends to begin in response to a partner's drinking and/or to a major life crisis such as miscarriage or divorce (rather than in heavy social drinking, as it often does for men); that premenstrual tension prompts excessive drinking; and that depression and other mental or emotional illness tended to precede women's problem drinking. Although none of Bogan's notes or correspondence suggests that alcohol was a major focus of her therapy, she did report many years later that "Dr. Wall said I could be as eccentric as I pleased, so long as I didn't take to drink" (WWL 250).

Bogan spent seven months at the Bloomingdale facility, working hard to find a way past her depression. Her therapy was difficult and painful, as she forced herself to acknowledge the violence and losses of her childhood. Although she was not suicidal, she had lost her desire to push forward in life, and the tasks of her therapy were "to recover joy and outsmart the death-wish"—and to find a way to write again.[15] Dr. Wall counseled rest from writing and from all struggle in order to promote recovery, and a purposeful and forgiving "letting go" of her life's antagonists in order to maintain it. "One by one," her biographer reported, "she gave up the remnants of her early hurting self: the provincial girl; the noble, reckless romantic; the jealous wife, with a touch of paranoia."[16] Wall counseled her toward a truce with the passage of time, and thus with the limitations of all human endeavor.

To be sure, Bogan did not stop drinking after this hospital stay, but she was not much troubled by her alcohol consumption again until the last few years of her life. She left the hospital in better psychological shape than she had ever been, and a part of that health was evidently an acceptance of herself as the heavy drinker she was. While she periodically vowed to cut down or to drink only beer or only hard liquor, and sometimes apologized for her need of a drink to sleep or to relax, in general she was at ease with the role of alcohol in her life. She and Edmund Wilson remained intellectual and drinking companions, and to certain correspondents she was entirely frank. "[L]ast night I sort of knocked myself out with claret," she wrote to her close friend Morton Zabel, "and you can imagine how much claret it took to knock *me* out: me who should go down in history as the heartiest female drinker among the female poets (closely edged up on, it is true, by E. Millay, L.[éonie] Adams—who used to astonish [Ford Madox] Ford by downing pony after pony of brandy, and staying cold sober—and E.[linor] Wylie, God rest her soul)" (WWL 144).

In May 1934, Bogan left her husband for good and moved on to other relationships, despite her conviction that "[t]here can be no new love at 37, for a woman."[17] She was passionate and romantic, and enjoyed the love of men, despite her unwillingness to talk and write openly about her affairs. The life she sought after her hospitalization was shaped and disciplined by her work as a writer, but leavened and energized by her relationships. In the spring of 1935, she began a brief but happy liaison—and a long friendship—

with the young poet Theodore Roethke. She wrote cheerfully to Wilson, "I, myself, have been made to bloom like a Persian rose-bush, by the enormous love-making of a cross between a Brandenburger and a Pomeranian, one Theodore Roethke by name. He is very, very large (6 ft. 2 and weighing 218 lbs.) and he writes very very small lyrics. 26 years old and a frightful tank. We have poured rivers of liquor down our throats, these last three days, and, in between, have indulged in such bearish and St. Bernardish antics as I have never before experienced★★★Well! Such goings on! A woman of my age! He is amusing, when not too far gone in liquor" (WWL 84). The affair lasted only two months; soon after Bogan took on the role of mentor to the younger poet. She gave him firm and specific criticism of his poems in progress, and counseled him about the impact of alcohol in an artist's life. "I don't know what to say about the drinking," she wrote to Roethke in the fall of 1935. "If you didn't have such a good, happy, and sensitive mind, I'd say, go on and drink, if you want to. Lots of excellent people have drunk and drunk and produced. But drinking seems to have you down, at the moment, and to hell with anything that gets a person of your potentialities down. . . . You are thoughtless and unhappy and spoiled" (WWL 99). Roethke was rarely in control of his drinking and in fact embraced his alcoholism and manic episodes as necessary complements to his gifts as an artist; or, as one of his many psychiatrists said, as "'the running expenses he paid for being his kind of poet."[18] During those manic episodes, Roethke sometimes subjected his body to extremes of exercise and alcohol, in search of a mystical state of exhaustion and oblivion. Like Wilson, Bogan's other great drinking companion, Roethke had the freedom and confidence of his sex in both his literary endeavors and his spectacular breakdowns. Bogan was resolutely practical and sane, despite her severe depressions—another of the ways she prevented herself from "appearing ridiculous" in the eyes of the male literary establishment.

Bogan prepared the manuscript of her third book, *The Sleeping Fury*, to reflect her progress from misery to acceptance. "It rises and falls," she told Morton Zabel, "from despair, to exaltation, and back again: Bogan in cothurnus and Bogan in flat heels." She wanted to represent "the 1930–33 period" of "despair, neuroses and alcoholism," but also to show her recovery: "All ends on a note of calm: me and the landscape clasped in each other's arms" (WWL 145). Poems had been slow to come to Bogan in the thirties—she feared that her therapy had vanquished the intensity she required to summon the epigrammatic lyrics she most valued. And she urged herself away from the temptation to write about her personal struggles. She prayed earnestly for more poems for *The Sleeping Fury:* "Ten others, and they must be objective as possible."[19] The poems eventually came to her, and *The Sleeping Fury* was generally acknowledged as her strongest volume to date.

The Sleeping Fury would be the last of Bogan's books to contain substantial new work, as she became less a practicing poet and more a critic and teacher. But 1937 was in many ways the fresh beginning of the rest of Bogan's life. In May, her divorce from Raymond Holden became final; she would not marry again. In April, she was able to complete the unexpired term of her 1933 Guggenheim Fellowship by traveling in Ireland. She suffered—and drank heavily—on the trip, coming face to face with her Irish heritage and thus, once again, with her childhood demons. Panicked and distraught, she rushed home in mid-June, badly in need of rescue. She found it, first, in the person of "a tall thin man" who came to her aid on the Southampton boat train and "took care of me like a baby" on the crossing. She saw Dr. Wall on her return, who prescribed complete rest. When she recovered her equanimity, she took up an affair with the "tall thin man"—whose name is not known, and whom she never introduced to her friends. He was an Irish electrician from near the Bronx, and the relationship lasted eight happy years, years of "perfect freedom, perfect detachment, *no jealousy* at all—an emphasis on *joy*"[20] (JAMR xxx). The success of the relationship was permitted, in part, by the fact that the two were of a similar social class, formal educational background, and ethnic origin—Bogan was, for the first time, free to be herself. "O, why didn't I know about the trades, years ago?" she wrote to Roethke. "I wasted a lot of time on the professions."[21] These circumstances may also account, in part, for Bogan's determination to keep the relationship secret from her literary friends. The two parted ways in 1945, and this was the last recorded love affair of Bogan's life.

Also in 1937 Bogan solved her ongoing problem of where to live. Moving to an apartment at 709 West 169th Street (later to a second apartment in the same building), Bogan had a home of her own for the first time ("I feel like a newly-wed"[22]). With views of the Hudson River and the Psychiatric Institute on 168th Street, sister institution of the Neurological Institute, where she had been hospitalized in 1931, she felt oriented and appropriately grounded.

But she wrote no poems between the publication of *Poems and New Poems* in 1941 and 1948. The violence and moral horror of the Second World War discouraged her about the power of poetry against such hatred, and she was troubled by what she saw as the obscurity of her own position. She went

48

in search of a new publisher (without success until 1954), and the loss of the steady encouragement of her longtime editor, John Hall Wheelock, also troubled her efforts to write poems. She had once remarked to Wheelock that "[a] woman writes poetry with her ovaries," and she began to feel that her time had passed.[23]

Bogan found a publisher in the new Noonday Press in the early 1950s, and set about preparing her *Collected Poems 1923–1953*. She had only three new poems to add; two of which rank among her finest. "After the Persian" and "Song for the Last Act" are unmistakably valedictory, and both are written from a position beyond pain and conflict. A year later, in 1955, Bogan published a volume of *Selected Criticism, Poetry and Prose*. Both volumes were respectfully reviewed, and she shared the 1955 Bollingen Prize with her friend Léonie Adams.

Ruth Limmer speculated that Bogan's near silence in poetry after 1940 arose from her deeply ingrained fear of revealing herself. At the same time, Limmer wrote, it is difficult to see what she would want to keep private.[24] For a private nature, however, privacy itself is the end. Although Bogan may have grown ashamed of her gradual return to uncontrolled drinking, and although her psychological difficulties had always included an element of paranoia, reticence and privacy were central to her way of confronting the world when she was healthy as well as when she was ill.

And yet, heavy drinking is very likely to separate a poet with Bogan's values and preoccupations from those values and strengths. To consume alcohol is to deaden feeling—and Bogan was, as she said, a poet of feeling. Bogan's art was a delicate balance between acceptance of emotion and of images from the subconscious—and the firm control of those emotions and images in formal structures of meter and rhyme, and in technical craftsmanship. Alcohol may facilitate the poet's initial access to subconscious material, but both authenticity of feeling and artistic control are compromised by continuing to drink. Bogan's high standards for poetry, which grew higher as she grew older, prevented her from publishing such compromised work. Among her papers are fragments of numerous unfinished poems, a great many of which approach her personal suffering more directly than any of her published verse. And surely for a poet to medicate her suffering with alcohol is to "substitute an outer battle for an inner one," which is fatal to good poetry, according to Bogan (JAMR 116).

Bogan's last years were a combination of honors and continued hard work and dark depression and worsening alcoholism. She went annually between 1957 and 1964 to the MacDowell Colony in Peterborough, New Hampshire, where she found the time and peace to write poems as well as her strong critical prose. She traveled in Europe, and continued to teach. She prepared the manuscript for *The Blue Estuaries: Poems 1923–1968,* for Farrar, Straus, and Giroux, which had acquired Noonday Press. The volume included a dozen new poems, most of which had been started much earlier. Most of these last poems are in free verse, as Bogan grew more willing to accept poems in the forms in which they came to her. *The Blue Estuaries* appeared in 1968 and received strong reviews from William Meredith, who called her "one of the best woman poets alive" and wondered at how her "reputation has lagged behind a career of stubborn individual excellence,"[25] and from Hayden Carruth, who praised the poems despite their small number. Whatever "stopped Bogan in her tracks" nevertheless left intact her marvelous control over her art.

Bogan's depression had returned with painful force in the early 1960s, and in June 1965 she once again checked herself into the Neurological Institute. For the first time, antidepressant drugs[26] became a part of her therapy, and she was also prescribed other tranquilizers—such overmedication, prescribed in the absence of frank discussion about alcohol use, was and is all too typical of the treatment of psychiatric illness in women. The combination of her medications—she suffered from diabetes as well—and her drinking left her prone to dozing off and falling episodes and to regular and painful bouts of weeping. Although Bogan had never been suicidal, it was the consensus among her friends that she had all but given up by the fall of 1969.[27] In September, she resigned her position as poetry reviewer for the *New Yorker,* ending her thirty-eight years of association with the magazine; she was simply unable to write the reviews she wanted to write. "No more struggling *not* to be a square," she told Ruth Limmer (WWL 381).

Louise Bogan died at her apartment sometime in the early hours of February 4, 1970, of a coronary occlusion. A memorial service, arranged by her friend William Jay Smith, was held at the Academy of Arts and Letters on March 11, attended by 120 of her friends and admirers. At the service, W. H. Auden noted Bogan's personal strength. "Aside from their technical excellence," he said of her poems, "what is most impressive is the unflinching courage with which she faced her problems, her determination never to surrender to self-pity, but to wrest beauty and joy out of dark places."[28] For Bogan, beauty was a product of intellect and joy an expression of the body; to reconcile the two was her life's—and her art's—work.

L ouise Bogan's first published book, *Body of This Death*, contains several of the poet's most memorable poems, and in general reveals her life-long preoccupations. Betrayal is a constant theme, particularly sexual betrayal, and she arrived early at her great theme of passion versus intellect, heart versus mind, body versus soul. The specter of the disappointment and sorrow of her marriage to Curt Alexander broods over the book, without being explicitly expressed. Like Emily Dickinson's "gift of screws," Bogan's poems are made of meticulously distilled experience, distanced from the source by objective language. Often presented (in title) as songs or chants or arias, they call attention to themselves as rhetorical acts in a common language. The commitment to public discourse did not protect Bogan from occasional obscurity—her distillations and symbolizing sometimes made indecipherable the emotion at the center of a poem. But Bogan saw herself in the tradition of sixteenth- and seventeenth-century English poetry, filtered through nineteenth-century American poetry by women, through the French Symbolists and through Freud. She disciplined her emotion and its conscious expression to the formal meter and rhyme she instinctively preferred. Such formality also served to discipline emotion for Bogan, and to give shape to the chaotic gifts of her unconscious and subconscious. This is what Bogan meant when she demanded that poets work through psychic difficulties on all their levels.

Consistent with these values, Louise Bogan wrote about her struggle with alcohol—if she wrote about it at all—in "veiled forms."[29] She did not write when she was drunk, although she was occasionally able to make use of language or images that came to her under the influence of alcohol. "[S]ipping [hard liquor] is excellent for releasing the subconscious at the time," she once explained, "it is rather bad for the next morning's clarity of mind" (WWL 80). And her drinking was so linked to her depression (alcohol is, of course, a depressant), that when she achieved the "clarity of mind" with which to write poems about her suffering, the two are inseparably linked.

Body of This Death includes Bogan's signature poem, the nearly perfect lyric, "The Alchemist":

> I burned my life, that I might find
> A passion wholly of the mind,
> Thought divorced from eye and bone,
> Ecstasy come to breath alone.
> I broke my life, to seek relief
> From the flawed light of love and grief.

With mounting beat the utter fire
Charred existence and desire.
It died low, ceased its sudden thresh.
I had found unmysterious flesh—
Not the mind's avid substance—still
Passionate beyond the will. (BE 15)

The conflict described in this poem is restated in perhaps a dozen other Bogan lyrics—the fervent but hopeless wish for escape from physical life and passion into a life wholly mental or intellectual. Diane Middlebrook argued persuasively that these two modes of existence are inevitably gendered, and that the poem describes the woman poet's struggle to reconcile the rules of masculine discourse (dispassionate intellect), while finding her own passionate, sensate voice and way of being.[30] But the three elements at odds in the poem—flesh, mind, will—are central to any discussion of human nature and existence, and may also go some way toward explaining the near universal presence of alcohol in human society. This is not to say that the poem is "about" alcohol in any direct way; only that for a nature preoccupied with the conflict between body, mind, and will, alcohol is likely to offer surprisingly specific, if temporary, relief.

The suggestion of alcohol in the poem's title—distillation is the alchemist's method (the words "alchemy" and "alcohol" are both Arabic in origin, but otherwise etymologically unrelated)—tempts one to speculate. The "spirits" of alcohol act temporarily to resolve conflict between body and mind by suspending the will. Alcohol acts on the body to affect the mind's function ("It'll sort of ease the pain a bit, and it levels out my thinkin'" sings the Irish band *The Fury*), and the effect of continued drinking is to separate the mind and body entirely (as in a blackout), and then to still them both (as when one passes out). Bogan's early poems, like those of Elinor Wylie, continually imagine a place out of the glare of the "flawed light of love and grief," of feeling and passion; in, for example, the marble statue of the girl, whose "inquietudes of the sap and of the blood are spent," in "Statue and Birds"; or the speaker of "Medusa," forever suspended ("I shall stand here like a shadow"); or the passive protagonist of "Knowledge," who, having learned "how passion warms little," vows to "lie here and learn" about the slow movements of trees; or the more general contemplation of the aftermath of passion in "Stanza" ("Wearily sleeps the hardy, lean / Hunger that could not be appeased.") This exhausted, passive position is also figured as a burned-over or abandoned landscape.[31] The spent fire in "The Alchemist" suggests the "hidden deserts" and "torn fire" of "A Tale"—the poem that opened four of Bogan's six poetry volumes; the "ravaged country" from which the speaker invokes the virtue of chastity in "Ad Castitatem"; the bitter "winter-burning" fields of "The Crows." Sometimes this landscape has been ravaged by fire, but as often it takes the form of a vacant lot or uncultivated waste. Bogan's preference for the arrangements of art over the chaos of nature is a defining aspect of her consciousness, and the absence of human attention or love represented in a weedy field is closely linked to the troubles of her childhood, including, perhaps, the emotional absences of an alcoholic family. "*Terre Vague,*" she wrote in an attempt at memoir, "uncultivated land, filled with 'chance vegetation.' The unbuilt lots of my childhood, filled with tansy and chicory; sometimes with some scrub of trees. . . . The edge of things; the beaten dead end of nature" (JAMR 20). Later she tried again to articulate the fascination: "The incredibly ugly mill-towns of my childhood, barely dissociated from the empty, haphazardly cultivated, half wild, half deserted countryside around them" (JAMR, 23). Even in Bogan's most "objective" poems this figure appears and carries this burden of association. "Memory" counsels that memories themselves should not be hoarded or closely kept, but regarded "Rather, like shards and straw upon coarse ground, / Of little worth when found, / Rubble in gardens, it and stones alike, / That any spade may strike" (BE 18). The language and imagery of abandonment and waste belongs to the discourse of alcoholism as well as of Bogan's landscapes and memories.

Bogan's second book, *Dark Summer* (1929), is an extended contemplation of darkness, as Elizabeth Frank has argued: "Throughout the volume both *dark* and *darkness* recur with obsessive frequency. . . . While each [poem] . . . gives a particular force to its use of *dark* or *darkness,* in all of them it comes to stand for latency, concealment, and imminence, for whatever lies at a remove from will and control."[32] Bogan's intense and educated interest in the subconscious and the unconscious suggests a first meaning for "whatever lies at a remove from will and control," but her continual experimentation with extinguishing will and losing control through drinking may also inform the poems, written during the first years of her marriage to Raymond Holden. The book continues to envision the retreat from pain into insensate oblivion, as *Body of This Death* had, but here the sense of an inevitable aftermath, a resumption of forward movement, is palpable. The title poem simply describes the ominous suspension:

> Under the thunder-dark, the cicadas resound.
> The storm in the sky mounts, but is not yet heard.
> The shaft and the flash wait, but are not yet found.
>
> The apples that hang and swell for the late comer,
> The simple spell, the rite not for our word,
> The kisses not for our mouths,—light the dark summer. (BE 41)

In the lovely sonnet "Simple Autumnal," written about the same time as "Dark Summer," refusing to grieve or to feel sorrow suspends the speaker in the "year's delay"; time is stopped at the moment of autumn when the trees are aflame with foliage, "Full season's come, yet filled trees keep the sky / And never scent the ground where they must lie" (BE 40). To admit sorrow and allow grief would "break the seal stamped over time / And set the baskets where the bough is bent," but as the poem ends the speaker is not yet ready to move forward. (This imagery recalls Léonie Adams's many equinoctial poems.) In "Tears in Sleep," the speaker recalls weeping aloud from within a dream, and resisting her companion's urge to awaken, "I would not wake at your word, I had tears to say" (BE 44). The unwillingness to relinquish unhappiness even in response to love (the speaker lies in a "happy bed" and claims her grief is "false") is another version of shutting down in order to avoid pain. It is a commonplace of alcohol counseling that problem drinkers drink in order to avoid painful feelings and that health cannot return until the feelings are acknowledged and experienced. Bogan does not specify a means of suspending grief and sorrow, in these poems or anywhere else, but we know that alcohol was one of her methods.

Dark Summer is also preoccupied with the passage of time, and with mutability generally. Elizabeth Bishop said that among her own reasons for drinking was a desire to avoid the sensation of passing time; indeed, anyone who has ever drunk too much knows that one always recovers to find at least one thing missing—a chunk of time, long or short. Bogan made no such connection, but in these poems, written during the time when she first began to "drink steadily," she said, a terrible ambivalence about time's operations is everywhere inscribed. "Come, Break with Time" (which Bishop identified as her favorite Bogan poem) offers a derisive invitation to escape

54

time into a state of suspension or passivity—while acknowledging that the heartbreak will inevitably come, eventually:

Break, since you must.
Time has its fill,
Sated with dust.
Long the clock's hand
Burned like a brand.

Take the rocks' speed
And earth's heavy measure.
Let buried seed
Drain out time's pleasure,
Take time's decrees.
Come, cruel ease. (BE 51)

The "cruel ease" the poem solicits, which destroys time's dominion for good or for ill, has several possible forms. Alcoholic oblivion may be one.

There are also burned-over and abandoned landscapes in the poems of *Dark Summer*, notably in "Feuer-Nacht" ("The leaf-shaped flame / Shears the bark piled for winter, / The grass in the stall. / Sworn to lick at a little, / It has burned all." [BE 36]). But if Bogan's experience with alcohol is reflected in the poems at all, it is most compellingly reflected in the despair and irresolution, the dis-ease of even the volume's most hopeful lyrics.

By the time of *The Sleeping Fury* (1937), after her therapy with Dr. Wall, Bogan had shed many of her earlier preoccupations—with sexual betrayal and emotional devastation—and the tension and darkness of *Dark Summer* have eased. This is a knowing book, in which the poet looks her demons directly in the face. And the book contains the only poems Bogan would ever write about alcohol itself. "At a Party" is a kind of encapsulation of her short stories about social drinking. The speaker demands that her spirit "Be still" "and let the flesh speak out," for here, "art and usury combine." The last stanza acknowledges the vitality of the gossip and competition so typical of literary gatherings: "And each bright symbol of their power / Speaks of my triumph, and your fall. / Step forth, then, malice, wisdom's guide, / And enmity, that may save us all" (BE 70).

The same kind of irony informs "To Wine," which follows "At a Party" in the volume. The poem looks squarely at the emotional numbing alcohol provides, and the false resolution of pain it represents.

Cup, ignorant and cruel,
Take from the mandate, love,
Its urgency to prove
Unfaith, renewal.

Take from the mind its loss:
The lipless dead that lie
Face upward in the earth,
Strong hand and slender thigh;
Return to the vein
All that is worth
Grief. Give that beat again. (BE 71)

Here Bogan acknowledges that alcohol offers a "leveling out" of emotion—if you drink, the urgency and anxiety of love, the mandate of life, is quieted. This might seem a salutary effect at first, but the list of what the cup can take away grows longer and darker; it takes memory in addition to grief and anxiety, and replaces it with unfocused longing, longing for "all that is worth / Grief"—and the cycle of pain and loss begins again. The cup is "ignorant and cruel"—that is, not an agent itself, but the destructive instrument of one's own mind, which serves to trap the speaker in a pattern of troubled love and loss. Bogan here seems to acknowledge the role her drinking may have played in the unhealthy choices, as she saw them now, she'd made in love and marriage.

Bogan's other persistent emotional difficulties are laid to rest in *The Sleeping Fury* as well. "Putting to Sea" launches the speaker on a psychological and emotional journey to an unknown land. The journey is perilous and the dangers uncertain, but after healing from the bruises of hate, the poet can venture forth with enthusiasm: "And learn, with joy, the gulf, the vast, the deep" (BE 84). The title poem, "The Sleeping Fury," looks at the torment of the poet's recent past with new perspective. The poet's demon, the "fury," is expressed in terms familiar from Bogan's memories of her own mother, but is now quiet:

Your hair fallen on your cheek, no longer in the semblance of serpents,
Lifted in the gale; your mouth, that shrieked so, silent.
You, my scourge, my sister, lie asleep, like a child,
Who, after rage, for an hour quiet, sleeps out its tears. . . .

And now I may look upon you,
Having once met your eyes. You lie in sleep and forget me.
Alone and strong in my peace, I look upon you in yours. (BE 78–79)

The resolution represented in the poems of *The Sleeping Fury* was hard-fought and lasting for Bogan, although it also represented the end of her life as a productive poet.

The very small group of new poems in *Poems and New Poems* (1941) opens with "Several Voices Out of a Cloud," a somewhat violent attack on the ideological hacks Bogan saw dominating the world of poetry, and also a reiteration of Bogan's claim that poetry arises from the poet's deepest internal conflicts and not from "outer" struggle. The poem is uncharacteristically contemporary, in a manner both reminiscent of Auden and anticipating Isabella Gardner: "Come, drunks and drug-takers," it invites, and then lists those who should be disqualified: "Parochial punks, trimmers, nice people, joiners true-blue, / Get the hell out of the way of the laurel. It is deathless / And it isn't for you" (BE 93). This association of drinking with the artist's very vocation is a lesson Bogan imbibed with her French Symbolist education, as well as her American writer's education during Prohibition.

"Evening in the Sanitarium" (which was originally published with the subtitle "Imitated from Auden") is Bogan's recollection of her hospitalizations, suffused with Audenesque irony. The poem expresses some regret at the loss of her fellow patients' eccentricities. They are cured, or mostly cured, "Some alleviation has been possible": "O fortunate bride, who will never again become elated after childbirth!" "Everything will be splendid: the grandmother will not drink habitually"; "Childhoods will be put away, the obscene nightmare abated." What they will have instead, however, hardly promises fulfillment: "To the suburban railway you will return, return, / To meet forever Jim home on the 5:35" (BE 111). The poem's speaker does not tell the story of her own recovery directly, although Bogan's own journey is suggested in the "childhoods . . . put away, the obscene nightmare abated."

Among Bogan's very last poems, included in *The Blue Estuaries,* three revisit the sea voyage metaphor of "Putting to Sea" as a means of expressing "the gulf, the vast, the deep" of the subconscious or semiconscious mind. Unpublished poems, as well, show Bogan working toward an identification of the ocean's depths with her own, and yet all of these poems also use marine imagery to reassert her early preoccupation with psychic retreat or stasis, imagery she may have used to represent her use of alcohol. Almost all of her seascapes express the ocean in terms of uneasy suspense (again, one thinks of Elizabeth Bishop's icy water "suspended / above the stones and then the world" in "At the Fishhouses"), and a return of the inability to feel— suggesting that this may be Bogan's means of figuring her return to heavy drinking. The fluid, shifting, harsh, and somehow suspended ocean is a fit metaphor for the fluid, shifting, harsh, and arresting influence of alcohol.

One undated fragment works toward her late poem, "Night," and invites the ocean to "come again, distilled through the blood" . . . "Symbolized / by that shining curve of / advancing & healing water," for "Something still waits, not in the salt / tear, but in the salt blood" (ACL 16:54). Other fragments specifically identify the ocean setting as Swampscott, Massachusetts, which Bogan had first visited in the summer of 1934, just after her separation from Raymond Holden, and revisited many times. One begins "It is Swampscott; it is March; it is I. / Clouds, over the sea, motionless lie" (ACL 16:36). The sense of arrested motion found its way into Bogan's later, published ocean poems as well. "Zone," which contemplates the painful ambiguity of early spring in the north, does so in marine terms:

> We have struck the regions wherein we are keel or reef.
> The wind breaks over us,
> And against high sharp angles almost splits into words,
> And these are of fear or grief.

And the sense of passive endurance returns as well:

> Now we hear
> What we heard last year,
> And bear the wind's rude touch
> And its ugly sound
> Equally with so much
> We have learned how to bear. (BE 109)

"Psychiatrist's Song" records the speaker's dream of a journey over the ocean "in a boat without oars." The dreamer reaches the unknown shore—which, as Sandra Cookson points out, resembles the destination of "Putting to Sea" as well—and walks "fearlessly" up the beach.[33] The sea vanishes, and dry land appears, "with, closely waiting, / A hill all sifted over with shade / Wherein the silence waits." The dreamer embraces the safety of the shore, and even the uncertainty of "waiting": "Farewell, phantoms of flesh and of ocean! / Vision of earth / Heal and receive me" (BE 134–35). And finally, the final version of "Night," the poem that gave *The Blue Estuaries* its title, offers a curious personification of the ocean's movement:

> The cold remote islands
> And the blue estuaries
> Where what breathes, breathes
> The restless wind of the inlets,
> And what drinks, drinks
> The incoming tide;
>
> Where shell and weed
> Wait upon the salt wash of the sea, (BE 130)[34]

Movement and feeling are once again apparently suspended; the absence of humans in the scene leaves the breathing and drinking to be done by the landscape itself. But here Bogan uses the large movements of time and nature—movements so large that they seem not to be moving at all—to call forth a characteristically ambiguous affirmation: even as life slows and closes, even as consciousness shuts down, desire does not fade:

> —O remember
> In your narrowing dark hours
> That more things move
> Than blood in the heart.

Louise Bogan's struggle with alcohol and depression ultimately confirmed what she knew as a young woman, at the time of "The Alchemist"— that "unmysterious flesh," including "the heart," will make its claims regardless of the mind's "will" to transcend them. "The flawed light of love and grief" is all the illumination available in the lives of these poets.

Chapter 3

"I must not die of pity"

Edna St. Vincent Millay's Addictions

In *The Cup of Fury*, his 1956 "outing" of alcoholism in his fellow writers, Upton Sinclair convicts Edna St. Vincent Millay (1892–1950) on dubious evidence:

> . . . Edna St. Vincent Millay came to Pasadena in 1940 on a lecture tour. I greeted her in a dressing room of the Pasadena Community Theatre, and we sat down to chat. With her was her husband, Eugen Boissevain, a Dutch importer. I had met him years before in Greenwich Village; he was a charming, kind fellow who had previously been married to Inez Millholland, the suffrage worker. When it came time for Edna to go on stage and speak, Eugen drew a flask from his back pocket and handed it

to his wife. She took a heavy swig. Nothing was said; evidently, this was routine.

I went out and listened while she read a dozen or more of her poems to an audience of ladies; then when it was over, I went behind the scenes again; and there Eugen produced the flask again, and I watched Edna empty it.[1]

Millay's earliest biographers defended her against this charge with as much passion and with evidence just as flimsy;[2] in 2001, Nancy Milford vindicated Sinclair, at least in part. It is significant that Sinclair offers his anecdote specifically as an example of "enabling" behavior on the part of the spouses of alcoholic artists (Millay is not one of his principal subjects). He goes on in the next paragraph to lament the mutual destruction of Scott and Zelda Fitzgerald. Millay and Fitzgerald, along with Isadora Duncan, are the only female artists Sinclair discusses at all in his heavily AA-influenced tract, which includes thematic biographies of some twenty-five other male drinking writers, actors, and painters, all of them dead by 1956.

But Edna St. Vincent Millay was, along with Dorothy Parker, the most famous female drinker of her day. Parker would eventually displace her, as Millay retreated in 1925 from the New York and Greenwich Village scene to a supportive marriage and life in the Berkshire foothills. In her own time, Millay was closely identified with the rebellious youth culture of the 1920s and the post–World War I reevaluation of moral and behavioral standards, as much an icon of the Jazz Age as were the Fitzgeralds. Sinclair claims that "she set the tempo of the time; she served as a minstrel for the madness."[3] She was the "It-girl" of her era, a legend whose real life came to resemble the life of her reputation less and less. Ironically, she drank less in her days as a famous bohemian defying Prohibition than she did in the sad last years of her life, when, wracked by illness, injury, and loss, she succumbed first to a morphine addiction (from which she recovered) and then to alcoholism. Today she is acknowledged as a master of the sonnet form, and avatar of the "other Modernism"—the vital group of largely female poets whose work captured the popular—if not the critical or academic—imagination in the 1920s and '30s.

Millay was born in 1892, and grew up in an impoverished but lively and wholly supportive all-female household in Camden, Maine. Her father, Henry Millay, had been dismissed from the family by her mother, Cora Buzzell Millay, when "Vincent" was eight. Why remains something of a mystery, although alcohol and gambling seem to have been precipitating causes. The family—Cora, Vincent, Norma, and Kathleen—were close, artistic, and ambitious, and Vincent showed her own literary gift early. Her family envisioned greatness for her, and she was rescued from the limitations of life in rural Maine by a wealthy patroness. After a stellar (in literature and theater) and somewhat notorious career at Vassar College, Millay arrived in New York in 1917 and soon earned a spot in the company of the Provincetown Players, the low-budget but highly modern playwright's theater, headed by George Cram "Jig" Cook, which produced some of the most important plays of its day. The Players were her introduction to the life of Greenwich Village bohemia, and despite her poverty, Millay (and her mother and sisters, who joined her in the city at various times) lived an exciting and fulfilling life of literature and art and men and parties until the passage of the Volstead Act in 1919 changed the frank and open culture of the Village forever.[4]

It was not that New Yorkers stopped drinking with the arrival of Prohibition. Ann Douglas, in *Terrible Honesty: Mongrel Manhattan in the 1920s*, summarizes the City's response:

> New York was nowhere less amenable to reform than in its drinking habits. Prohibition, passed into law in 1919 and not repealed until 1933, was a joke in most of urban America, but in New York it was an all-out full-scale farce. Seven thousand arrests for alcohol possession or drinking in New York City between 1921 and 1923 (when enforcement was more or less openly abandoned) resulted in only seventeen convictions; observers estimated the number of illegal speakeasies, dives, and drugstores as somewhere between a monstrous 32,000 and an unbelievable 100,000. "YANKEES TRAINING ON SCOTCH" ran the shameless headline of a 1922 story about Babe Ruth's team. Bishop John Cannon, tireless leader of the Anti-Saloon League, referred to New York as "Satan's Seat." Some people during Prohibition, playing on John Winthrop's famous words about the "city on a hill," called New York the "City on a Still."[5]

But if Greenwich Village had been something of a youthful and avant-garde utopia, what was added to the mix with the arrival of Prohibition was an element of secrecy and desperation and alienation, the absence of which had been one of the Village's cultural values in the teens. "Our own nation had passed the Prohibition Amendment as if to publish a bill of separation between itself and ourselves; it wasn't our country any longer," Malcolm

Cowley wrote.[6] Millay herself is said to have hated the speakeasy culture that replaced the open and free consumption of alcohol—and sex, and ideas—of her earliest days in New York. While a good many of the well-known writers with whom Millay came in contact in the Village were or became alcoholic, whether they would have done so without the added incentive of defying the law and proving one's independence from middle-class values is at least a matter of debate.[7]

The Greenwich Village bohemians were united in their rejection of Prohibition. In their written condemnations of the law, something of the moral and philosophical significance of alcohol to their chosen lifestyle becomes clear.[8] Millay's own relatively lighthearted tract was written for *Vanity Fair* and published under her prose-writing pseudonym, Nancy Boyd. Entitled "Our All-American Almanac and Prophetic Messenger," the 1924 essay (written while Millay was living in France) condemns the lingering puritanism of American culture, and offers a logical extension of Prohibition's attempt to regulate the private happiness of individuals, beginning with "NEW YEAR'S DAY, 1925. Cabarets closed, New York City; dancing abolished. Many private houses raided. Sale of crêpe paper and colored balloons prohibited. Two men surprised in Central Park with pockets full of confetti; and given sixty days each. Slogan HAPPY NEW YEAR changed by Act of Congress to VIRTUOUS NEW YEAR. . . . Cigarettes banned, 1926." Linking the free use of alcohol with the free artistic imagination, a common theme in the Village's anti-Prohibition writings, Millay goes on to predict the eventual "excommunication" of Santa Claus by the "Society for Suppression of Imagination in Children" and the banning of all children's fantasy literature. Music is banned, theaters are closed, literature and the production and reading of books is prohibited. Elsewhere in her almanac, Anthony Comstock, the well-known opponent of birth control, is "canonized" and laws are passed (prohibiting haircuts and requiring side-saddles for women, for example) in support of "the holy cause of Female Modesty"; the equality and freedom of women is also related, in Millay's view, to the freedom to drink. After providing for the abolition of summer and of baseball, Millay predicts the "Total eclipse of the Western Hemisphere" as the final result of the government's attempt to deny its citizens the pleasures of alcohol.[9]

Upton Sinclair ironically quotes Susan Glaspell, novelist and wife of Jig Cook, the alcoholic director of the Provincetown Players in Millay's time, on the subject of the positive use her husband was able to make of alcohol, before Prohibition and after. Millay and her crowd would have agreed with

Glaspell: "'All his life this man had a habit of occasionally getting drunk and seeing truth from a new plane. He saw then, saw what was pretending, in himself, and others. It would begin in good times with friends—self and timidity going down in the warmth of sympathetic drinking. There was a sublimated playfulness, ideas became a great game, and in play with them something that had not been before come into being.'" Glaspell goes on to quote her husband as having once said that some people "'drink only with their bellies. But true drinking is an affair of the head and heart. There must be a second, finer ferment in the mind—a brewing and refining of raw wit and wisdom.'" "'Long afterwards,'" Glaspell continues, "'he had what I venture to call a somewhat God-like relation of wine and vision. Drinking was one of the things in which Jig succeeded, in which he realized himself as a human being and artist. Yet he saw the black thing it may become.'"[10]

Sinclair quotes Glaspell at length, including a long passage in which she sentimentally recalls idyllic "hangover days" in which she and her husband shared "'a rarefied sense of being something nearer pure spirit'" following "'a violent encounter with life.'" "'I cannot recall ever having read a greater piece of nonsense from the pen of a modern emancipated woman,'" Sinclair comments, dismissing utterly what Cook, Glaspell, Millay, Cowley, and others insisted had been an article of faith among the Greenwich Village artists.[11]

The Greenwich Village bohemia that Millay had so enjoyed changed with the coming of Prohibition and the disillusion and despair following the end of the First World War. The beautiful and somewhat ethereal Millay was besieged by male admirers and had to extricate herself from an intense and difficult affair with Floyd Dell, and to come to terms with her own passion for Arthur Davison Ficke, who, except for one memorable weekend, shared her ambivalence about surrendering one's self to love and physical passion rather than to art alone. This conflict between the needs of the body and the creative spirit would trouble Millay's life and dominate her poems, and links her with all of the other poets in this study. Edmund Wilson, Adolphe Roberts, Scudder Middleton, John Reed, and Witter Bynner are among the other literary figures with whom Millay was, at one time or another in the early 1920s, romantically associated. But her friend Max Eastman found "[h]er determination to be a poet, and not some man's woman or even some child's mother," to be "absolute,"[12] and she was to suffer for her self-enforced lack of attachments.[13]

By 1920, Millay was famous, the most talked about and quoted poet of her day. On April 7, she wrote giddily to her friend Jessie Rittenhouse, still smarting over the passage of the Eighteenth Amendment, "I find myself suddenly famous, Jessie dear, and in this unlooked-for excitement I find a stimulant that almost takes the place of booze."[14] Indeed, her second book, *A Few Figs from Thistles*, appeared that year, and despite the fact that Millay had written and would write far more serious and better poems, this collection of light verse became her trademark publication; like Dorothy Parker, she would struggle to live it down. This is the collection from which the famous "First Fig" is taken, which became the manifesto of a generation:

> My candle burns at both ends;
> It will not last the night;
> But ah, my foes, and oh, my friends—
> It gives a lovely light! (CPM 127)

There seems little doubt that the candle burns, at least in part, alcohol. Other poems similarly establish Millay as the "minstrel to the madness" of the iconoclastic twenties, even as she herself was growing weary of the endless round of activity New York represented. In "Recuerdo" she recalls some of her initial conquest of the city:

> We were very tired, we were very merry,
> We had gone back and forth all night on the ferry.
> We hailed, "Good morrow, mother!" to a shawl-covered head,
> And bought a morning paper, which neither of us read;
> And she wept, "God bless you!" for the apples and pears,
> And we gave her all our money but our subway fares. (CPM 128)

"Thursday" captures some of the studied indifference with which Millay approached her relationships with men:[15]

> And if I loved you Wednesday,
> Well, what is that to you?
> I do not love you Thursday—
> So much is true.
>
> And why you come complaining
> Is more than I can see.
> I loved you Wednesday,—yes—but what
> Is that to me? (CPM 129)

In "The Singing-Woman from the Wood's Edge," she takes on the tyranny of even Greenwich Village's tendency to essentialize female sexuality: "After all's said and after all's done, / What should I be but a harlot and a nun?"—an early expression of the body/mind conflict her later poems would also enact (CPM 133). "Grown-up" foresaw the end of youthful passion and freedom, perhaps in marriage: "Was it for this I uttered prayers, / And sobbed and cursed and kicked the stairs, / That now, domestic as a plate, / I should retire at half-past eight?" (CPM 138). Such a retreat to domesticity had always held some attraction for Millay, though she would continue to run away from the possibility of a settled life—or even of steady companionship—for several more years.

A few months after the sensational reception of *A Few Figs from Thistles,* Millay published what she considered the true sequel to the youthful *Renascence: Second April,* a book of relatively dark and contemplative poems in a very different spirit from *Figs.* Her popular and critically acclaimed play, *Aria de Capo,* an antiwar satire featuring Pierrot as a drunken and disillusioned denizen of the Jazz Age, and Columbine as his flapper-mistress, also appeared in 1920, and by the fall of that year she was exhausted with overwork and weary of her New York life. Frank Crowninshield, editor of *Vanity Fair* and also Parker's mentor, stepped in to her rescue with the assignment to become the magazine's European correspondent. Like all of the best known members of the so-called Lost Generation, Millay abandoned the chaos and contradictions of the Prohibition-era United States for Paris and the rest of the continent early in 1921. "Salvation by exile," Cowley called it.[16]

Millay's stay in Europe was as tumultuous as her life in New York had been, but it is less well documented. She fulfilled her duties to *Vanity Fair,* writing the pseudonymous prose sketches she collected in 1924 under the title *Distressing Dialogues* by Nancy Boyd, but relatively little poetry. She wrote plays and hoped to write a novel. She partook of the life of parties and drinking so well documented by other expatriate American writers, to the limits, anyway, of her meager financial resources, which she supplemented through liaisons with better-heeled men. She had several love affairs, including an important one that ended with Millay pregnant. She is said not to have told her lover, and to have gone to England where her mother provided her with an herbal abortion.[17] Weary of the Paris scene, she traveled throughout Europe in the company of her mother, who had joined her by virtue of a $500 advance Millay had received from Horace Liveright for the novel she was unable to write. They returned to New York in February 1923.

Back in New York, Millay's spirits continued to founder even as her reputation grew. In March 1923, she became the first woman ever to win the Pulitzer Prize for poetry and began the intensive work in the sonnet form on which much of her posthumous reputation rests. Her physical and emotional decline continued, however, until, late in the spring, she was invited to a weekend party in Croton, New York, where she met and fell in love with Eugen Boissevain, the man who would become her husband and caretaker—and the chief enabler of her alcoholism, if Sinclair is to be believed.[18]

Eugen Boissevain was a kind and enthusiastic man whose considerable fortune had been made in the import business. His first wife had been the well-known lawyer and suffragist Inez Millholland, and he was himself a committed feminist and happy in the company of strong and creative women. It is apparent that he took Millay under his emotional and financial wing, seeing to it that she received adequate support, rest, and medical care. Her friends acknowledged that Boissevain probably saved her life.[19]

In the months following her marriage, Millay prepared her third volume of serious verse, *The Harp-Weaver and Other Poems*, for publication and embarked on her first extensive reading tour. She is said to have disliked the enterprise of public readings, but having grown used to earning her own living, she recognized that her position as a well-known public figure was the key to her financial independence. Her defenders attribute those swigs from the flask to that ambivalence. In April 1924, Boissevain and Millay sailed around the world, beginning with a tour of China. On their return, they purchased a 700-acre farm near Austerlitz, New York, which they christened "Steepletop" and which would be their permanent home.

Eugen Boissevain resolved Millay's fears of losing her creative gift to a stifling marriage by devoting his considerable personal and financial resources to securing his wife's comfort, privacy, and freedom from worry.[20] Millay drank a good deal during her marriage, and the acquisition of alcohol during Prohibition was certainly a subject in her letters to friends and family.[21] But what is apparent is that Millay flourished in both health and work for at least ten years, publishing three more volumes of poetry (*The Buck in the Snow* [1928], *Wine from These Grapes* [1934], and *Huntsman, What Quarry?* [1939]) as well as the remarkable sonnet sequence *Fatal Interview* (1931), which records the emotional and physical rise and fall of a love affair, reputedly Millay's own serious and prolonged affair with twenty-two-year-old (Millay was thirty-seven at the time) George Dillon. The sonnets' publication caused something of a scandal, and increased Millay's reputation as a convention-flouting bohemian.[22] She produced a major play, *The Princess Marries the Page* (1932) and collaborated with Dillon on a translation of Baudelaire's *Flowers of Evil* (1936), an enterprise that engaged her entirely and led her to do extensive biographical research on the French poet and to contemplate his linking of physical degradation and intoxication to poetic genius. She received numerous honors and awards during these years, including honorary degrees from several colleges and universities and election to the National Institute of Arts and Letters in 1929. She lent her reputation and presence to the 1927 march protesting the executions of Sacco and Vanzetti. She continued to travel and to do public readings, including a successful radio series. Her continued productivity during these years is all the more remarkable, given the ascendancy achieved by Modernist principles and values in poetry—values of impersonality and obscurity, as Millay saw it, that she would continue to reject even as the dominant fashion eventually rejected her and her work.

In 1936, Millay's fortunes took several turns for the worse. In May, the manuscript for her ambitious philosophical mix of prose and poetry, *Conversation at Midnight,* was destroyed in a hotel fire. Her rewritten version never pleased her as the original had. In the summer she suffered a serious back injury in a car accident, one that involved her in great pain and in fairly constant medical treatments for nearly five years. It was during this period that Millay's friends began to talk of her addiction to morphine and her later cold-turkey recovery from that addiction, at the same time that rumors of excessive drinking by both Millay and Boissevain circulated.[23] Max Eastman reported that, bored in their rural isolation, "What Eugen and Edna did was to stimulate their hearts and dull their cerebral cortices with alcohol," taking "an inner short cut to a condition not remote from poetic exaltation, a heightened consciousness without the drive toward action," and that, alas, "chemical stimulation blunted the edge of Edna's otherwise so carefully cherished genius" during this period.[24] But he was at a loss to explain entirely her strange behavior:

> She seemed to be mysteriously sick a great deal of the time, and notwithstanding her moralism she had nothing of the soldier in her. She cultivated for all it was worth the privilege of being sick. She lived largely upstairs in her bedroom, and would fly up there from the slightest annoyance—a noisy guest, an untimely call from a neighbor or a passing friend. . . . She babied herself and Eugen babied her; the most was made of every reason

why she should not spend her energy. . . . one felt on entering Steepletop that some very fragile piece of china, inestimable in value, was in unstable equilibrium upstairs, and that even the air-waves, if too much agitated, might unbalance it.[25]

Eastman felt that this "life-pattern" of unhealthy dependency, drug use, and excessive drinking "went from bad to worse" in the 1930s and '40s and precipitated the end of their friendship.[26]

That blunting of creative sensibility and judgment, reported so often by drinking artists, also lead Millay into the greatest conflict of her creative life. Her increasing despair over the Spanish civil war, over Germany's actions in Europe and Japan's in Asia, and her country's failure to come to the defense of the oppressed and overrun sent her into emotional despair from which she would scarcely recover. It also prompted her to give all of her creative powers to the cause of world political justice. It sickened her to write what she judged to be bad poetry in the service of propaganda, but she felt that the world's crisis demanded it of her. In May 1940 she began writing verse urging her fellow citizens to prepare for war; *Make Bright the Arrows* appeared in the fall of 1940, and she donated the proceeds to buy ambulances for the Red Cross. Millay was excoriated by critics for prostituting her talent, and the poems are indeed so bad that she included only two of them in her *Collected Poems*. In 1942, she produced the ballad *The Murder of Lidice*, about the German takeover of a Czechoslovakian village, for radio broadcast. Soon after, she suffered a serious nervous breakdown, from the strain, she said, of feeling obliged to write bad poetry against deadlines, and perhaps also from the unhealthiness of her lifestyle during the previous years. She was quite ill and unable to write anything at all for more than two years. Milford has documented the major role that alcohol and other drugs, particularly morphine, played in this crisis.[27]

Millay eventually returned to work on serious poetry; her last poems were collected in *Mine the Harvest* (1954). The last years of her life were sad ones, as she suffered the deaths of her sister Kathleen and other close friends, and her own uncertain health and stability. Edmund Wilson reported visiting the poet at Steepletop in 1948 and finding her much changed in physical appearance, deeply anxious, and dependent on her husband.[28] In August 1949, Eugen Boissevain died of a stroke following surgery for lung cancer. He was nearly seventy years old, and his death flung Millay into a drinking binge that required hospitalization. When she was released, she returned alone to Steepletop, where she managed to pass a productive, if solitary, year. On October 19, 1950, she died. Alone in her house, she fell to her death down its long staircase, her glass of wine left sitting on one step. She was fifty-eight years old. Nancy Milford quotes the characteristic lines she had written and then circled in the notebook found near her body: "I will control myself, or go inside. / I will not flaw perfection with my grief. / Handsome, this day: no matter who has died."[29]

Millay, along with many other female writers of this era, enacted in her life and poems profound ambivalence about the place of their stereotypically feminine aspects—attachment to the physical world, passion, sensuality, emotion, even regard for the body itself—in lives they self-consciously dedicated to intellectual work: the conflict articulated in Bogan's "The Alchemist." In Millay this conflict is expressed in her flip rejection of the role of woman living for the love of man ("I find this frenzy [of physical passion] insufficient reason / For conversation when we meet again" [CPM 601]), as well as in the sometimes self-defeating isolation she enforced in her life. Elizabeth Atkins wrote in 1936 that the unity of Millay's sonnets in particular lay in the fact that "they all deal with the bewilderment of a girl strangled with a passion for intellectual beauty and for physical vitality, which refuse to sit at opposite ends of a bench, like Titian's 'Sacred and Profane Love' (if that is really his subject) coolly appraising each other's separate identity."[30] One of the salutary effects of alcohol for Millay, as well as for Elinor Wylie, Léonie Adams, Elizabeth Bishop, and Louise Bogan, was to spiritualize the physical self, to render the body and its contingencies invisible to the mind, to erase the difficulty of governing the body's responses and behaviors. This bodilessness is painfully temporary, of course; one of the awful revelations a hangover brings is the gross fact of the poisoned and suffering body, asserting its primacy over the mind once again.

The poems of Millay comment in interesting ways on the characteristic imagery of female poets writing about alcohol, particularly imagery evoking states of oblivion or unconsciousness, often associated with the sea. Much of Millay's poetic project consists of exhortations *against* withdrawal and despair, against the easy retreat from conflict and pain (as in those lines she composed on the night of her death)—she argues, in fact, for keeping the body and the mind in equilibrium as much as possible. Elinor Wylie, by contrast, obsessively sought such withdrawal; her "highest form of existence

[was] sensationless."[31] For both poets, writing itself is a defense against the threat of emotional breakdown; a "momentary stay against confusion," in Robert Frost's words; or, as Millay famously put it: "I will put Chaos into fourteen lines / And keep him there" (CPM 728). Their versions of what Cheryl Walker has called the "sanctuary poem" reflect both the tradition of such poems by women writers, and the modern availability of a simulacrum of that oblivion, alcoholic numbness.[32]

Millay's work overall is much less high-spirited than her most famous poems suggest. Certainly there are poems that portray festive drinking, as the "very tired and very merry" ferry riders of "Recuerdo" suggest. Or in her poem for Stephen Vincent Benét, brother of Elinor's Bill, "To S.V.B.—June 15, 1940," which recalls their earlier days in Paris: "All of us knew our guarded truth: / We called, 'L'addition!' not, 'The cheque!' / I always ordered French vermouth, / So I could say, 'Un export sec!'" (CPM 413). But the dominant mood of Millay's Collected Poems is a good deal more contemplative, and indeed more troubled, than one might expect from her reputation.

She was also a dedicated and attentive nature poet; what might serve as imagery in the work of the other poets in my study appears in Millay as setting and subject, familiar and specific plants, animals and landscapes. Millay does have sea imagery in common with the other poets, perhaps in part because the shoreline she recalls and describes is the same one—the coasts of New England and maritime Canada—that most of the others also experienced. And the sea represents for her the same sort of semidesirable oblivion. It is the seascape of her childhood, and of her life after 1933, when she and her husband purchased Ragged Island, in lower Casco Bay, Maine, to live on a part of every year. Most of her sea poems speak directly of her memory and longing for the sea and its shore. As "Exiled" expresses, "Searching my heart for its true sorrow, / This is the thing I find to be: / That I am weary of words and people, / Sick of the city, wanting the sea" (CPM 105). Even her metaphoric use of the sea is, like Elizabeth Bishop's, grounded firmly in precise and detailed description of that place. "Low-Tide" is a good example, its rhythm mimicking the movement of the sea, even as it develops the image of withdrawal to unconsciousness and death:

These wet rocks where the tide has been,
Barnacled white and weeded brown
And slimed beneath to a beautiful green,
These wet rocks where the tide went down

Will show again when the tide is high
Faint and perilous, far from shore,
No place to dream, but a place to die:
The bottom of the sea once more. (CPM 79)

"Inland" blends the nostalgic memory of the sea with the wish for oblivion, expressed in the characteristic romantic overstatement of Millay's earliest poems. Who longs for anything as the poet longs,

Starting up in my inland bed,

Beating the narrow walls, and finding
Neither a window nor a door,
Screaming to God for death by drowning,—
One salt taste of the sea once more? (CPM 90)

But "Above These Cares" envisions the speaker in uneasy harmony with the sea's changing moods, again expressed in realistic and tangible detail. Below the sea's surface lies entanglement and anxiety, curiously associated with the urge to "drink it dry":

Above these cares my spirit in calm abiding
Floats like a swimmer at sunrise, facing the pale sky;
Peaceful, heaved by the light infrequent lurch of the
heavy wave serenely sliding
Under his weightless body, aware of the wide morning,
aware of the gull on the red buoy bedaubed with
guano, aware of his sharp cry;
Idly athirst for the sea, as who should say:
In a moment I will roll upon my mouth and drink it dry.

Painfully, under the pressure that obtains
At the sea's bottom, crushing my lungs and my brains
(For the body makes shift to breathe and after a fashion flourish
Ten fathoms deep in care,
Ten fathoms down in an element denser than air
Wherein the soul must perish)
I trap and harvest, stilling my stomach's needs;
I crawl forever, hoping never to see

Above my head the limbs of my spirit no longer free
Kicking in frenzy, a swimmer enmeshed in weeds. (CPM 307)

This willfully divided self—the freed spirit floating like a swimmer on the surface; the trapped body crushed by the weight of watery "care"—comments on the mind/body split we see in all these poets. Here, the body is essentially and eternally entangled, doomed to forage like a lobster on the bottom. Her spirit must resist the urge to turn toward the sea and "drink it dry." In doing so—and the gesture may be an attempt to lift the weight of care from the body—the spirit risks becoming entangled in the weeds and drowning. That the spirit is tempted to drink in order to relieve the body of care makes this an apt metaphor for Millay's ambivalence about withdrawal, characteristically expressed in terms of drinking and the sea.

Very often drinking alcohol-like liquids is a metaphor for Millay—as she believed that the consumption of alcohol was an inalienable right and related activity for those seeking ecstasy in beauty and art, so her poems sometimes feature drinkers of beauty seeking to lose themselves in its pleasures. This drinking in of beauty is dangerous and not for everyone, but thrillingly attractive. This is the sestet of her earliest published sonnet, "Thou art not lovelier than lilacs,—no":

> Like him who day by day unto his draught
> Of delicate poison adds him one drop more
> Till he may drink unharmed the death of ten,
> Even so, inured to beauty, who have quaffed
> Each hour more deeply than the hour before,
> I drink—and live—what has destroyed some men. (CPM 561)

Even drinking of the river "Lethe," classically associated with death and forgetfulness in poetry, is for Millay rededicated to the cause of embracing pure beauty, beyond struggle and pain:

> Ah, drink again
> This river that is the taker-away of pain,
> And the giver-back of beauty!
>
> In these cool waves
> What can be lost?—

Only the sorry cost
Of the lovely thing, ah, never the thing itself!

The level flood that laves
The hot brow
And the stiff shoulder
Is at our temples now.

Gone is the fever,
But not into the river;
Melted the frozen pride,
But the tranquil tide
Runs never the warmer for this,
Never the colder.

Immerse the dream.
Drench the kiss.
Dip the song in the stream. (CPM 253–54)

This imagery suggests preservative qualities in the river Lethe, which lets go "the sorry cost / Of the lovely thing," but keeps pure the lovely thing (the kiss, the song) itself—embalms it, perhaps, as with alcohol. One thinks of Louise Bogan's "To Wine," which invites the "Cup, ignorant and cruel" to "Take from the mind its loss," but knows that such relief is both temporary and illusory.

Millay's poems express anguish over her "cares," personal losses in her life: the death of her mother in 1931, of several dear friends, of her husband; over the inevitable decline of passion in a love affair, over the injustice and misery she saw in the world around her; over the situation of women in the social and political world. Far more often than not, however, these same poems demand that the poet resist the urge to escape pain through death or symbolic oblivion or willful unconsciousness.[33] Sonnet cxxvi, from *Huntsman, What Quarry?*, faces down death's persistent invitation: "Thou famished grave, I will not fill thee yet," and promises to expend so much of herself in living that when she comes to die, "I'll be but bones and jewels on that day, / And leave thee hungry even in the end" (CPM 686). Sonnet cxxxix, from the same volume, also takes the metaphor of eating food to assert hope against a death from despair. Food for the body feeds the mind and spirit:

I must not die of pity; I must live;
Grow strong, not sicken; eat, digest my food,
That it may build me, and in doing good
To blood and bone, broaden the sensitive
Fastidious pale perception: we contrive
Lean comfort for the starving, who intrude
Upon them with our pots of pity; brewed
From stronger meat must be the broth we give.
Blue, bright September day, with here and there
On the green hills a maple turning red,
And white clouds racing in the windy air!—
If I would help the weak, I must be fed
In wit and purpose, pour away despair
And rinse the cup, eat happiness like bread. (CPM 699)

This kind of pep talk for the languishing soul, calling it from self-pity to self-preservation and even action, distinguishes Millay from most of the other poets in this study. Although she by all accounts succumbed to the losses in her life, as we all must, she wrote of her determination not to.

"Moriturus," a "sanctuary" poem from *The Buck in the Snow*, distinguishes between the wish for withdrawal and solitude and the wish for death itself by asking for the grave, but with consciousness intact:

If I could have
Two things in one:
The peace of the grave,
And the light of the sun;
My hands across
My thin breast-bone,
But aware of the moss
Invading the stone, . . .

Knowing that this is impossible, however, the long poem ends with the poet bitterly and characteristically resisting the death that inevitably comes for her. Her seduction and rape metaphor is reminiscent of Emily Dickinson:

Withstanding Death
Till Life be gone,

I shall treasure my breath,
I shall linger on.

I shall bolt my door
With a bolt and a cable;
I shall block my door
With a bureau and a table; . . .

With his hand on my mouth
He shall drag me forth,
Shrieking to the south
And clutching to the north. (CPM 199–207)

Other poems offer a more specific exhortation against, if not literal suicide, then against the symbolic suicide of psychological and emotional withdrawal, literally through drinking. Millay's founding utterance, "Renascence," spoke at length on the subject of not succumbing to despair, of seeking transcendence in nature. In the much later "*Fontaine, Je Ne Bourai Pas De Ton Eau!*" Millay actively refuses the oblivion offered by the fountain she contemplates ("I will not drink thy water!"), acknowledging that the excesses in her life have brought her trouble, but also experience transcending mere pain:

I know I might have lived in such a way
As to have suffered only pain:
Loving not man nor dog;
Not money, even; feeling
Toothache perhaps, but never more than an hour away
From skill and novocaine;
Making no contacts, dealing with life through agents, drinking one
    cocktail,
betting two dollars, wearing raincoats in the rain;
Betrayed at length by no one but the fog
Whispering to the wing of the plane.

"Fountain," I have cried to that unbubbling well, "I will not drink thy
    water!"
Yet I thirst
For a mouthful of—not to swallow, only to rinse my mouth in—peace.
And while the eyes of the past condemn,

The eyes of the present narrow into assignation. And . . . worst . . .
The young are so old, they are born with their fingers crossed;
I shall get no help from them. (CPM 349)

The "thirst / For a mouthful of . . . peace" the speaker might have had, had she lived a more cautious life; here she successfully resists achieving it by artificial means. It evokes the imagery of alcohol and the wish for oblivion, which troubled Millay increasingly as she grew older. Such negotiations with oneself and with the problematic substance are common to the experience of addiction, which Millay struggled with throughout her adult life. By contrast, the poems of Elinor Wylie, who was slightly older than Millay but much later to a writing career and very much aware of Millay's example as she began writing, show little of that ambivalence: they continually contemplate, wish for, and enact withdrawals to unconsciousness and symbolic death by drowning.

Chapter 4

"Hold to Oblivion"

Elinor Wylie's Intolerable Life

One of the events that depressed Edna St. Vincent Millay in the late 1920s was the early death of her friend and fellow lyric poet Elinor Wylie (1885–1928). Wylie, who had suffered from severe hypertension for most of her adult life, died in December 1928 of a stroke, in part because, her friends reported, she refused to give up drinking alcohol as her doctor had prescribed.[1] Millay wrote a sequence of six elegies for Wylie, published in *Huntsman, What Quarry?* in 1939, and continued to grieve over her death for many years.

Elinor Wylie was as notorious as Millay had been famous. The eldest of five children of an alliance between the wealthy and politically prominent Hoyt family (her father was an assistant attorney general in the McKinley administration and solicitor general under Teddy Roosevelt) and the socially prominent McMichael family of Philadelphia, Elinor Hoyt was an eager and excellent student who had wanted to go to college, but instead was forced to follow the path of a debutante into an early and unhappy marriage. Her first husband, Philip Hichborn II, was abusive and apparently mentally ill, and their child proved, through no fault of his own, little incentive for his mother to stay and preserve the forms and conventions of her elevated social class. Perhaps emboldened by the death of her father in December 1910, Elinor Hichborn eloped with her longtime lover Horace Wylie, a prominent Washington attorney, also married and the father of young children at the time. The elopement produced an enormous scandal that was chronicled in newspapers up and down the East Coast; "Philadelphia and Washington never forgave her," one biographer wrote, and the lovers were forced to leave the country and settle for five years in the English countryside under assumed names. In 1915, they returned to Boston and were married. The scandal of her marriages followed Elinor Wylie throughout her life, as did the restlessness and romantic searching that had prompted her fall from social grace in the first place. In 1927, a year before Wylie's death, Millay herself declined an honor from the League of American Penwomen on the grounds that the organization had rejected Wylie based on her infamous personal life.[2] Wylie's third husband and tireless ally, William Rose Benét, recalled the impact of that fateful "choice," to prefer the dictates of personal happiness over those of social convention, on Wylie's life: "It made her life harassed, it made her wary of human contact, it developed the satirical spirit in her, though never the cynical. It even played its part in undermining her physical constitution, and only the greatest powers of recuperation, mental and spiritual as well as physical, could have brought her through the perplexity of the years to the short period during which her superb talents as a writer fully manifested themselves."[3]

Elinor Hichborn found in the older Horace Wylie her substitute for the college education she craved. Judith Farr has hypothesized that she was deeply uncomfortable with sexual intimacy, and made her drastic choices—to defy social expectation and essentially to abandon her young son—in search of "congenial security"; more specifically, companionship and stimulation for her remarkable mind.[4] Wylie was a capable guide to Elinor's already ambitious reading habits, being himself a bibliophile with wide-ranging scholarly interests and warmly encouraging of her literary ambitions.

Elinor Wylie's personal and poetic reputation has been the victim of biographers and critics scarcely more sympathetic than the hostile society she faced in her lifetime. Like Dorothy Parker, she is a woman critics love to hate. Among the major studies, only Farr, in her 1983 *The Life and Art of Elinor Wylie*, has found it possible to look beyond her scandalous reputation and her somewhat grasping and self-dramatizing ways to see her life and work in the context of the struggle of women writers to find a voice in the rapidly constructed hegemony of poetic Modernism. The full-scale biography, Stanley Olson's *Elinor Wylie: A Life Apart*, is a mean-spirited production and thus only marginally useful in a search for the causes and conflicts in Wylie's admittedly difficult existence. Thomas Gray's entry in the Twayne U.S. Authors series begins by proclaiming its author's mystification at Wylie's persistent poetic reputation, and illustrates beyond a doubt the inadequacy of New Critical approaches in coming to terms with the work of the female lyric poets of the early twentieth century. Taken together, these sources provide an uneasy and incomplete portrait of Elinor Wylie's external existence, and say very little about her inner life. Unlike Millay's and Parker's, Elinor Wylie's short though spectacular existence prompted no outpouring of memoirists and would-be biographers, rushing forward to say "I knew her, and this is what she was really like."[5] And she left no bounty of critical writing, like Bogan, or letters, like Bishop, by which we might come to know her mind. What she did leave was four novels and four volumes of poetry whose dominant mode is autobiographical allegory.

The mother and the youngest brother and sister of Elinor Hoyt were apparently alcoholic. Anne McMichael Hoyt was, according to Olson, a self-dramatizing hypochondriac of the nineteenth-century sort, who spent most of her time invalided in her room, demanding that "restoratives and cordials" be brought to her at regular intervals.[6] Morton Hoyt, the charming, impulsive, and irresponsible black sheep of his family, and his sister's favorite sibling, "had an inordinate love of drink"[7] and at one point attempted suicide in a drunken leap from a ship.[8] (Two other siblings were successful suicides, as was Wylie's first husband, Philip Hichborn.) Olson concedes that Elinor Wylie's "pleasures were more subdued and certainly a great deal more refined than her brother Morton's," but noted also that she was "not abstemious: she loved wine and brandy."[9] In her remarkably self-revealing poem "Portrait in Black Paint, With a Very Sparing Use of Whitewash," Wylie described her subject as capable of "liv[ing] on aspirin and Scotch" some of the time, and as "vain," "lazy," "crazy," and "slightly alcoholic."[10] Almost of necessity in an adversarial relationship to the social world around her, Wylie sought solace in art and ideas, and also in alcohol, with very great detriment to her already delicate health.

In 1919, Elinor and Horace Wylie returned to live in Washington, D.C. in an uneasy return from social exile, and Elinor began to write poems in earnest. In 1912, she had had privately printed in London (at her mother's expense) her first volume of poems, but now, back home, she began to make literary acquaintances and connections—earliest among them Sinclair Lewis, a notorious alcoholic, and William Rose Benét, also a heavy drinker and eventually her third husband. On a summer 1919 visit to Mt. Desert Island, Maine, she felt she found her voice and idiom.[11] In 1921, she sold her first formal volume of poems to Harcourt, Brace and Howe, and launched her short but meteoric literary career.

By 1922, Wylie had effectively left her second husband and was living in New York City with Benét—a move she made with the conscious purpose of pursuing her literary and intellectual interests in the ideal location and in the company of a wealthy and supportive man of letters. The publication of *Nets to Catch the Wind* had revealed Wylie's astonishing lyric gift, and she was to follow that, in the remaining seven years of her life, with three more books of poems—*Black Armour* (1923), *Trivial Breath* (1928), and *Angels and Earthly Creatures* (1929)—and four intellectually ambitious and meticulously researched novels—*Jennifer Lorn* (1923), *The Venetian Glass Nephew* (1925), *The Orphan Angel* (1926), and *Mr. Hodge and Mr. Hazard* (1928). She also served for a time as poetry editor of *Vanity Fair* magazine, and as an editor of the Literary Guild book club. It is as productive a seven-year span as any well-known writer has ever enjoyed.

Wylie's poems were highly valued in her own time. Her intelligence and restraint were praised by contemporary critics, sometimes at the expense of other female lyric poets. Horace Gregory and Marya Zaturenska admired her "poetic intelligence and wit," which distinguished her from "many women writers" who "'write from impulse and as rapidly as they think,'" and are immune from "'the slow process of reasoning through which men have to pass.'" They eschew the necessary use of the "'pruning knife and the pumice stone.'"[12] Wylie's was a "self-conscious art," an "expression of a larger movement toward conscious art in poetry, a movement which at its best includes such diverse figures as Conrad Aiken and T. S. Eliot and the later William Butler Yeats."[13] While critics acknowledge her limitations—as she herself did—many are compelled by the crafted verbal music of her poems and by the gorgeousness of the imagery she employed. Morton Dauwen

Zabel expressed some impatience with that imagery ("her pages spill with meteors, moonstones, goblins, knights, fairy goldsmiths, mandrakes, blacka-moors, and saints; with filigree, mistletoe, snowflakes, wasp-nests, stalactites, bronze, goldfish, silver, moonbeams, *marbre, onyx* and *émail* upon which a labor no longer rebellious was required for fashioning and shaping. Tray after tray of choice images is heaped before the enchanted banquet. . . ."), but acknowledged that "Mrs. Wylie celebrated the value of life at its richest, and for her the Puritan instinct disclosed richness in fundamental aspects of simple experience which, however she may have lived apart from them, won her envy and praise."[14] The decline in her poetic reputation followed the decline in Millay's and Bogan's, although she is arguably as fine and intellectually challenging a poet as either.

The great personal trauma of Elinor Wylie's life after about 1916 was her failure to bear a second child.[15] Completely estranged from the child of her first marriage, Philip Hichborn III, Wylie for several years invested all of her hopes for the restoration of legitimacy to her sexuality and marriage history, all of her hopes for future happiness, on the birth of another. But the chronic hypertension that gave her debilitating headaches and sapped her strength also at least four times prevented her from carrying a pregnancy to term, and one child died at one week of age. This often-renewed grief also contributed to her unhappiness and restless searching. Traumatic miscarriage is a common antecedent to the development of alcoholism in women, and excessive alcohol consumption in early pregnancy is now thought to cause miscarriage itself.[16]

The ideal mentor, guiding light, and perhaps obsession of Elinor Wylie's artistic and intellectual life was the poet Percy Bysshe Shelley.[17] Two of her novels, *The Orphan Angel* and *Mr. Hodge and Mr. Hazard*, are fictional accounts of what Shelley's life might have been like had he lived past the age of thirty. Her series of four sonnets, *A Red Carpet for Shelley*, laments her own inability to prepare a proper path, "a road for you to walk upon," for Shelley's return to the modern world. Hers was both a personal affinity and a serious scholarly pursuit that had begun, as she told it, when she was seven years old.

William Drake has noted the general affinity female poets felt with Shelley and the other Romantics, whose "sexually ambivalent sensibility combined creative masculine power with a feminine capacity to be in touch with emotion; and yet the effort was doomed by burnout or early death, reflecting the frustration women also felt in trying to assert the power of their unexpressed selves."[18] And it is not difficult to see how even the superficial facts of Shelley's life would have prompted Wylie's identification with him. The child of a prominent British family, Shelley had disgraced himself in their and the world's eyes by being expelled from Oxford for arguing in print that the existence of God could not be proven empirically. His subsequent marriage, at age eighteen, to the daughter of a merchant further alienated him from the social world in which he had grown up, as did his anguished abandonment of that first marriage for the love of Mary Wollstonecraft Godwin, the daughter of his mentor, philosopher William Godwin. The scandal of his marriages and unorthodox personal and sexual liaisons forced Shelley into exile in Italy in 1818, where in grief and despair over the loss of his two children from his first marriage and the deaths of two from his second, he produced most of his best-known work. Shelley's assertion of hope in the face of despair over personal unhappiness and social injustice, his rejection of orthodoxy in his ideas about love and marriage, his belief in poetry despite his lack of a consistent audience, his restlessness, his poor health, and even his small, frail, and almost ethereal physical self were all aspects with which Wylie herself could identify. As Farr has pointed out, Wylie first embraced Shelley as a comfort in the face of despair, and his idealism and belief in love as the redeemer of humankind's fallen moral nature gave her hope that her own conflicted existence might somehow be redeemed.[19] She devoted herself to his memory and image as one might to a saint, gathering as much information about him as she could and collecting "relics" of his life, imitating his habits and preferences (as when she attempted to adopt for herself his stated preference for white wine over whiskey or ale).[20] Knowing her own poetic gift as hopelessly inadequate next to Shelley's, she embraced him as an artistic model, as a better self, as an ideal lover, and as a divinely innocent figure whom she might defend against the world's summary judgments, in a way that she could not defend herself.[21] While other critics have argued that she worshipped a Shelley she created in her own image and had a merely "superficial" understanding of his work, she nonetheless imagined into being her own productive career based on his example.

In the last years of her life, Elinor Wylie lived in England, apart from her third husband, and was involved for a time in a painful affair with a man whose wife and family had befriended her. Her sonnet sequence, *One Person,* chronicles this relationship. When personal anecdotes about Wylie in this period do appear, they are often quite negative and describe behavior that is bizarre and unaccountable, although easily attributable to uninhibited drunkenness.[22] It is clear that Wylie was, even at the height of her literary power and fame, almost pathetically insecure. Many such anecdotes feature Wylie leaving an event or making a scene when she herself was not made the center of attention at it. She was evidently quite vain about her physical self—she was a famous beauty in the circles in which she moved and troubled by the inevitable changes in her appearance brought by age and years of poor health. Few of the tellers of these anecdotes are willing to say that Wylie was drinking too much at the time—most often they comment on her "hypersensitive" temperament—but the nature of the confrontations and their aftermath is often consistent with that explanation. Louise Bogan included Wylie in her list of notoriously heavy-drinking female poets, as if Wylie's problem had been common knowledge.[23] And it was Edna St. Vincent Millay who sympathetically reported that Wylie's health was in danger in particular from her refusal to give up drinking alcohol.[24]

Elinor Wylie suffered a fall downstairs in June 1928, likely the result of the first of a series of strokes that would soon kill her. She broke bones in her back and endured great pain for several weeks as a consequence. Suffering from depression as well, and contemplating the end of her marriage to Benét, Wylie seemed to her friends to be very ill. Although she was writing a great deal of poetry in her suffering, it grew clear that she could not continue to live as much alone as she was then living. In November 1928 she contracted what was diagnosed as Bell's palsy (but which was probably another stroke), which paralyzed one side of her face and increased her isolation and despair. Early in December she crossed the Atlantic to rejoin her husband in New York. On December 16th, after a week of debilitating headaches, during which she corrected the proofs of her final volume of poetry, she died of a major stroke, saying as she fell, "Is that all it is?" She was forty-three.

Wylie's poems, like those of nearly all the women in this study, reflect a profound ambivalence about the sensual body's interference with the mind's pursuit of intellectual beauty and clarity. Among the many things she admired in Shelley was his tendency to forget to attend to his physical needs, for food or sleep, for example, so involved was he in art and ideas.[25] And the whole course of her life, at least until she began to write in earnest in its last decade, had been determined by her vacillation between the lessons of her earliest training in how to be a wife and mother, how to "be art," and the ambition of her intellect and artistic sense. That she was an extraordinary beauty, by all accounts, only exacerbated this problem. Her porcelain white skin, amber eyes, black hair, and fey, ethereal beauty of form doomed her to a preoccupation with the physical when she would rather have effaced her physical self. The relationships she pursued inevitably disappointed her mind and spirit, and the ideal of a second child eluded her because her body failed to sustain the dream. Many of Wylie's poems enact this conflict between the gendered physical expectations of her social training and an ideal of mental freedom. Her dramatic monologue "Nebuchandnezzar" turns the Babylonian king's punishment for vanity and evil (to spend his life grazing in the field like an animal) into a self-chosen answer to the body–mind conflict:

> My body is weary to death of my mischievous brain;
> I am weary forever and ever of being brave;
> Therefore I crouch on my knees while the cool white rain
> Curves the clover over my head like a wave.
>
> The stem and the frosty seed of the grass are ripe;
> I have devoured their strength; I have drunk them deep;
> And the dandelion is gall in a thin green pipe,
> But the clover is honey and sun and the smell of sleep. (CPW 48)

Nebuchandnezzar imbibes unconsciousness from the field in which he grazes, and body and mind are reconciled. Thus the poem looks beyond the "flawed light of love and grief" that shone over Wylie's whole troubled history, toward a potent self-medicating solution. "This Corruptible" attempts a taxonomy of the vexed relations between personified "Body," "Mind," "Heart," and "Spirit" or "Soul." The situation, apparently, cannot be resolved, and all four parts are both vulnerable and dangerous.

> The Body, long oppressed
> And pierced, then prayed for rest
> (Being but apprenticed to the other Powers);
> And kneeling in that place
> Implored the thrust of grace
> Which makes the dust lie level with the flowers.
>
> Then did that fellowship
> Of three, the Body strip;
> Beheld his wounds, and none among them mortal;

> The Mind severe and cool;
> The Heart still half a fool;
> The fine-spun Soul, a beam of sun can startle. (CPW 204)

The body, suffering from physical exhaustion and illness, asks literally to die but is summoned back to a tenuous existence by "that fellowship / Of three": the detached and observing Mind, the besotted Heart, and the artist's shimmering Soul. The poem offers no relief to the body's real suffering, however; it is left to languish, gravely wounded.

At the time of her last love affair, Wylie held out some hope that body/mind/soul conflict might be resolved by love. The sixth sonnet of her *One Person* sequence admits the conflict in similar terms:

> I have believed that I prefer to live
> Preoccupied by a Platonic mind;
> I have believed me obdurate and blind
> To those sharp ecstasies the pulses give:
> The clever body five times sensitive
> I have never discovered to be kind
> As the poor soul, deceived and half-divined,
> Whose hopes are water in a witch's sieve. (CPW 177)

Now "both soul and body are unfit / to apprehend this miracle" of love, the poem concludes, and the relationship could not last—the soul's hopes drain away through that "witch's sieve" and she is left with the burden of the sensitive, but also cruel, body.

Wylie's poems construct a variety of masks and strategies for the protection of that vulnerable soul, whose physical body only exposes its vulnerability. It is from her poem "Let No Charitable Hope" that Cheryl Walker took the title of her important study of female poets in the Modernist period, *Masks Outrageous and Austere*. That these masks are constructed of jewels and crystals and precious stones, glass and porcelain, and glittering metals makes them uniquely Wylie's, and even when she attempted plainer disguise, her *Black Armour* glows with polish. In her 1923 essay "Jewelled Bindings," Wylie described her poetic craft in terms of lapidary arts, work "in metal and glass, in substances hard and brittle" on the way to creating the poem, a "'small jewelled receptacle' for a gilded bird."[26] Indeed, her poems constitute a study of ways to protect the self and soul from the scrutiny and censure of a hostile world. "The Tortoise in Eternity" celebrates his protected bed in a "house of patterned horn," which is "Tougher than hide or lozenged bark, / Snow-storm and thunder proof." "There is not one" human out there, he claims, "who owns / An armour to his need" (CPW 34). "A Proud Lady" is made of stone, carved and cut by "Hate in the world's hand." "What has it done, this world, / With hard finger-tips, / But sweetly chiselled and curled / Your inscrutable lips?" (CPW 32–33). Her "Sleeping Beauty" lies "imprisoned in the marble block. / . . . granite is her dress" (CPW 246). All of this armor, protection, and disguise enables the soul to rest, sometimes to the point of complete withdrawal, for

> When I am dead, or sleeping
> Without any pain,
> My soul will stop creeping
> Through my jewelled brain. (CPW 52)

Like those of most of the other poets in this study, only more so, the poems of Elinor Wylie continually explore and test the idea of withdrawal to unconsciousness and oblivion. In her early parable comparing "The Eagle and the Mole," she sides with the mole, that tenacious avoider of light:

> If you would keep your soul
> From spotted sight or sound,
> Live like the velvet mole;
> Go burrow underground.
>
> And there hold intercourse
> With roots of trees and stones,
> With rivers at their source,
> And disembodied bones. (CPW 4)

This founding utterance governs in theme much of the rest of Wylie's body of work in poetry. "Winter Sleep" contemplates the migration of birds to warmer climes, and longs for a retreat from the "wicked and cross and old" world. "It's not with them that I'd love to be, / But under the roots of the balsam tree." "It's there that I'd love to lie and sleep, / Soft, soft, soft, and deep, deep, deep!" (CPW 20–21). And "Prophecy" confidently predicts the speaker's safe withdrawal to protection and seclusion worthy of a fairy tale's somnolent princess.

> I shall lie hidden in a hut
> In the middle of an alder wood,
> With the back door blind and bolted shut,
> And the front door locked for good.
>
> I shall lie folded like a saint,
> Lapped in a scented linen sheet,
> On a bedstead striped with bright-blue paint,
> Narrow and cold and neat. (CPW 50)

Absent from this remarkably static image is the handsome prince, whose fairy-tale kiss typically awakens the young woman from her death/sleep, initiating her into both adult sexuality and "happily ever after." Farr's observation that Wylie feared sexual intimacy, as well as Wylie's unhappy experience with conventional marriage, may be reflected in this poem.[27]

The drinking metaphor is also well developed in Wylie's poems. Among her papers at the Library of Congress is a draft of an untitled poem, the refrain of which is a comparison: "I love you more than . . ." One stanza begins "I love you more than drink" and links the lover's attention to the "blessed relief" offered by wine. Her painful study of the last love triangle of her life sees the dilemma almost wholly in terms of alcohol. "The Loving Cup" passes between the lips of the poet, the wife, and the husband, whose lips pass "elixir" to both women as well. The poet contemplates the significance to her of the "draught" shared between the married couple.

> Should I not count me more unfortunate
> If from two cups you drank my single fate,
> Than now, when both of you set lips to one
> And from its sole brim drink division?
> For you have drunk me joy and she despair
> In the same wine, that served you share and share,
> But never share and share alike: the mood
> In which you drank transformed the wine to blood.

But love, and the poet's wishful thinking, undoes this jealous transubstantiation.

> Yet it is saved: your drop converts it all,
> And makes it holy and medicinal:

She drinks her health (who drank to me disease),
Long life, and happiness and more than these;
Moons in solution, flavours of the sun's:
The cup is loving, having kissed you once. (CPW 230–31)

The cup, however, fails to unite her with her beloved in the end, as the privileged bond of husband and wife supersedes her claims. The "holy and medicinal" wine ironically fails to heal the relationship, though the poet/speaker finds peace in it. In "To a Blackbird Singing," the poet promises the bird the soothing draught that Bacchus promised his poet-celebrants in ancient Greece,

Sing, and set your little foot
On golden grape and silver vine:
The Wine-God loves your song: the fruit
Will cool your lovely throat with wine. (CPW 101)

Very often drinking some "draught" or other is the means to the unconsciousness the poet seeks, as in "Nebuchandnezzar." The gentleness of rain "falls unheeded on the dead / Asleep; they have had deep peace to drink" ("Bells in the Rain," CPW 19). In her poem actually entitled "Sanctuary" she figures her retreat in those terms: "Full as a crystal cup with drink / Is my cell with dreams, quiet and cool . . ." but she protests to the figure building that cell, "Stop, old man! You must leave a chink; / How can I breathe?" "*You can't, you fool!*" he answers (CPW 14). This expression of the double-sided nature of the idea of sanctuary reflects the double nature of alcohol too; "blessed relief" can be suffocation or drowning as well.

As for Elizabeth Bishop and Louise Bogan, withdrawal in Wylie's work is often figured specifically in terms of submersion in ice-cold water, often to the point of drowning, an image Wylie may have derived from the circumstances of Shelley's famous death.[28] "Three Wishes" sees the descent beneath the waves to a liquid and anesthetizing alternative world in essentially positive terms:

Sink out of being and go down, go down,
Through the steep layers of emerald and jade
With the warm thin skin of turquoise overlaid,
Where the slow coral spins a ghostly town

Of tower and minaret and fretted crown,
Give up your breath in sleep's subaqueous shade,
Hold to oblivion: are you afraid
Of cold deep death? Are you afraid to drown? (CPW 49)

The beauty of the details in this poem indicates Wylie's interest in withdrawal from the ugly and familiar world to a place of beauty, often pictured in vague and romantic terms reminiscent of the alternative death-worlds of Edgar Allan Poe. Thomas Gray viewed this preference in Wylie negatively: "The self of the poems, the lyric speaker, did not find it easy to 'pretend' that she and the world were friends. The world was to her, most consistently, 'an unlighted kennel.' At best, it was rankly and grossly sensuous, and painfully overstimulating to a delicate sensibility. Her poems dramatize the reactions of a sensibility whose appetites are ethereal to an existence whose satisfactions are mundane. . . . The raging of the soul to attain a pure spiritual existence is only an extension of the preference for the finest, rarest, most nearly subliminal sensations and the desire to escape to an elegant, bauble-filled fantasy land."[29] But most of Wylie's plunges to the deep are presented in far more naturalistic terms, terms that recall the water so cold it burns, the "fire-water" of Bachelard, and of Elizabeth Bishop's poems about alcohol. Her sonnet "August" contrasts the dusty heat of a southern day with imagined depths suggesting death and its whitening, deadening effects. The sestet longs for "those white lilies, luminous and cool" found in a "hemlock-darkened northern stream" by swimmers, "diving where the sun / Scarce warms the surface of the deepest pool" (CPW 8). Peering into Somes's Pond in "Atavism," the poet sees that "A silent paddle moves below the water" and "Tall plumes surmount a painted mask of death" (CPW 10). "Spring Pastoral" envisions a kind of ultimate comfort brought by hands chilled to deathlike coldness in a spring freshet. "Dabble your hands, and steep them well," she asks "Liza." "Until those nails are pearly white" . . . "Then come to me at candlelight."

Lay your cold hands across my brows,
And I shall sleep, and I shall dream
Of silver-pointed willow boughs
Dipping their fingers in a stream. (CPW 39)

Sometimes, the poet sees liberation in her own suicidal submersion, as in her almost celebratory "Drowned Woman."

He shall be my jailer
Who sets me free
From shackles frailer
Than the wind-spun sea.

He shall be my teacher
Who cries "Be brave,"
To a weeping creature
In a glass-walled wave.

But he shall be my brother
Whose mocking despair
Dives headlong to smother
In the weeds of my hair. (CPW 53)

Such measures, and sympathetic understanding of them, are ironically necessary for spiritual survival. In the "Address to My Soul," she counsels: "Wear water, or a mask / Of unapparent cloud; / Be brave and never ask / A more defunctive shroud" (CPW 160). The "defunctive shroud" firmly associates the mask of water or cloud with death itself. Her late poem "Priest. XXth Dynasty" speculates on the mummified remains of an ancient dignitary, but sees his demise not in the desert waste of Shelley's "Ozymandias," but once again in terms of icy water.

Old Mortality's cold plunge
Laps your living throat and muzzle,
Saps the strength with which you lunge
Choking in this joke or puzzle
His ambiguous bones expunge.

Bones expunge and bones expound
Dust's equivocal composure;
Lithe and slippery life is drowned,
Stifled in an eyelid's closure,
Sealed in lips without a sound. (CPW 249)

The draught of forgetfulness and silence, of freedom and irresponsibility, is a trope well established in these poems—indeed, in the work of many a writer burdened with an overactive and oversensitive conscious mind. It is impossible to delineate such imagery in Wylie (or in Bogan and Bishop) without thinking of the poems of Sylvia Plath, a poet of two generations later, not known to be alcoholic, but launched on a path toward suicide from an early age. The wish for literal death—or so we say, given the posthumous publication of the famous *Ariel* poems—takes the place of the metaphoric withdrawal into the icy sea of the earlier poets. For Plath, the body-mind conflict is always resolved through the obliteration of the body in suicide, so that, as she put it in "Edge," "The woman is perfected."[30] That some of these poets imagine a place of sensationless peace that is specifically *not* death may link the imagery to their conflicted and troubled use of alcohol. And the use of alcohol is one among several strategies for survival—withdrawal, dissembling, disguise, self-protection—undertaken by women poets in this pioneering generation.[31]

Chapter 5

"Thought's End"

Léonie Adams and the Life of the Mind

Among the younger generation of female Modernist lyric poets, a list that generally includes Millay, Wylie, the later poems of Sara Teasdale,[1] Louise Bogan, and Léonie Adams, Adams (1899–1988) was long considered to be the most talented. Her arrival on the New York poetry scene coincided precisely in time with that of Bogan (and their careers are linked in a number of other ways)—although she pursued a far less circuitous route to get there. But after her highly praised second book, *High Falcon and Other Poems,* appeared in 1929, she fell silent as a lyric poet, her creative energies subsumed by those of her scholar-critic husband, William Troy, and in the social round of their academic lives that included, by all accounts, prodigious amounts of alcohol.

Wallace Fowlie taught with Adams and Troy at Bennington College in Vermont in the 1930s, and "Remembering Léonie Adams" in *The New Criterion* on the occasion of her death in 1988, he recalled a woman of formidable intellect and "spiritual power" clearly living within the confines of her husband's regard for her. "Bill [Troy], who often spoke in a somewhat pontifical manner, made a statement as if it were orthodox doctrine: 'We recognize great poetry by its genuineness, by its concreteness, and by its definiteness.' . . . Bill, at that moment turned to her—this was unusual because in public he often seemed to ignore her—and said: 'Léonie, your poems have those qualities.' It was an ecclesiastical nod of approval."[2] Louise Bogan recalled visiting Adams and her husband at about the same time, and leaving with a kind of a shudder, "I [am] more than ever convinced that a spinster's life is to be the future life for me. Wifehood is too damned full of hero-husband worship . . ." (WWL 127). Fowlie also remembered Adams reciting *Lycidas* from memory for a group of Bennington faculty friends, clearly enchanted by her intonation of Milton's lines. He noted that she alone was willing to correct her husband when he misquoted a line of poetry or mistook a biographical fact. And Fowlie quotes her from memory in this charming anecdote about alcohol:

> . . . I did almost no traveling that year [1928]. I enjoyed living in Paris, although I was very lonely there. Every afternoon, late in the day, I went to the one café I used, the Dôme in Montparnasse. I had a corner table that always seemed empty, and ordered the same drink day after day, from the same waiter. He was a friendly fellow who grew accustomed to my being there at the same time each day. He saved the table for me. I don't drink and had been told that vermouth was the mildest of drinks. So I ordered it each day. It seemed more sophisticated to me than a *citron pressé* or a cup of tea. The waiter and I always exchanged a few words. He was the only person with whom I spoke French. After two months of sitting at the Dôme and watching the people go by on the wide sidewalk, the waiter one day, when there were very few people seated at the café, said to me as he put the glass on my table, "Madame, do you order vermouth because you believe it to be a harmless drink?"
>
> "Yes, that is exactly why I take it."
>
> "But, Madame, it is far from being harmless. It is addictive. If you continue much longer ordering a glass of vermouth every day, you will

94

become an addict. Vermouth is from the absinthe plant. It is the substitute for absinthe because that drink is by law now forbidden in France."[3]

Fowlie leaves this story uncommented upon in his memoir, though I feel certain that he included it in part because of the coyness represented in Adams's statement "I don't drink" and in the discussion of the particularly addictive nature of the drink she is serving Fowlie in the scene he recalls. In fact, Adams drank a great deal—was even celebrated in her hard-drinking circle for her capacity to "hold her liquor." Although there is little if any evidence that Adams actually fell victim to alcohol addiction, she was a heavy drinker in a heavy-drinking generation, and she wrote about that drinking, its sources, its effects, and its motivations, in her poems—poems of breathtaking beauty and craft.

Léonie Adams was born in Brooklyn in December 1899, the fifth of six children of Charles Frederic Adams—who despite his high New England name and education had been born in Cuba to a Venezuelan mother and an American sugar executive. Léonie's mother, Henrietta Rozier, was of a Virginia family that claimed descent from original settlers of the seventeenth century. Léonie was raised Roman Catholic in a highly protective household (she remembered her father accompanying her on the subway even after she went to college). She attended Brooklyn public schools, then entered Barnard in 1918. In college, she was a truly outstanding academic student, and one of a select group of girls permitted to live in an apartment at 606 West 116th Street, outside the college's single dormitory, the evolution of a formal experiment in "cooperative living" designed in part to accommodate the wishes and eccentricities of these unusual young women. "The Ash Can Cats," as they eventually called themselves (thanks to their beloved theater professor Minor Latham, who chided Adams and others in her Southern drawl for "'sit[ting] up all night readin' poetry come to class lookin' like Ash Can Cats'"[4]), included the anthropologist Margaret Mead, who has written about this period in the life of the college and the group in her memoir, *Blackberry Winter*. In Adams's senior year (Mead was two years younger) the two women shared a room in the apartment, posting on the door a sign that announced, "We don't believe in private property, please keep yours out." Their motto came from Millay, whose *A Few Figs from Thistles* had given all unconventional and ambitious young women words to live by: "'Safe upon the solid rock the ugly houses stand: / Come and see my shining palace built upon the sand!'"[5] Mead reports that she devised a "kinship" system for the group, and that she and Léonie Adams were among the "parents."[6] The group was energetically literary and mildly political; they attended plays and performances, and demonstrated along with many others on behalf of Sacco and Vanzetti at the time of their trial in 1921. As editor of the *Barnard Bulletin*, Adams was moved to write an editorial entitled "Cheer up, Mr. Coolidge"—in response to the then vice president's worrying article in *Delineator*, asking "Are the 'Reds' Stalking Our College Women?"[7]

Adams was at first a "secret poet" at Barnard, but by her junior year, when her first poem appeared in print ("April Mortality" in *The New Republic*), Mead could say that "the most exciting events [of the apartment and its circle] centered around Léonie's poetry . . . we recognized that Léonie was a real poet, whereas none of the rest of us was a real anything as yet."[8]

> The presence of one highly gifted person whose talent is recognized has an enormous effect on everyone belonging to a group. It makes for a very different affirmation of the values that are being taught in courses and discussed by critics. It also affects one's estimation of one's own talents. . . . [W]e made a protective and enjoyable shield around Léonie and supported her in whatever she chose to do. This included editing *The Barnard Bulletin*. . . . It saddened us when Léonie failed to obtain the Caroline Duror Fellowship, Barnard's only graduate fellowship. . . .
>
> We were a happily captive audience for Léonie's long narrative anecdotes. . . . I saw myself as a kind of production manager, helping to keep our shifting groups organized around Léonie.[9]

"April Mortality" was in every way a characteristic beginning for Adams, as she would return over and over again in her work to the way the turn of seasons measures out human life. The shaping of natural description to the contours of a mental state or emotional condition would also be her dominant mode. Lest one be tempted to imagine that April's annual return brings any sort of permanence to our individual existence, "Be bitter still, remember how / Four petals, when a little breath / Of wind made stir the pear-tree bough, / Blew delicately down to death."[10] The poem is conventional in form, elevated in tone, and wise beyond its years—clearly the work of a "real poet." Many years later, the critic Harold Bloom included it in his version of *The Best Poems of the English Language,* and expressed his mystification at its author's disappearance from the canon.[11]

After her graduation from Barnard in 1922, Adams struggled to make a New York living on her own terms. Waitressing at a Waverly Place restaurant in 1923, she escaped again through the help of Margaret Mead. Mead was working as a research assistant to sociologist William Fielding Ogburn and, ever-protective of Léonie and her talent, brought Adams into the office too. Adams in turn helped to get Louise Bogan a similar job, as well as poet Louise Townsend Nicholl. Elizabeth Frank reports that "Ogburn enjoyed having an office full of working poets, and used to arrive in the morning with a ready supply of baseball jingles. 'See,' he would say, after reciting them, 'I can write poetry too!'[12] This lively crowd of literary newcomers, associated with *The Measure, The Nation,* and *The New Republic* (among other, smaller literary magazines) included not only Bogan, Nicholl, and Adams, but also the prodigious drinker Edmund Wilson (who pursued Adams romantically despite the fact that she informed him that she was determined to remain a virgin[13]), and anthropologists Mead and Ruth Benedict, both of whom also had poetic ambitions. The idealism represented in Adams's expressed wish to remain free of sexual entanglement—to remain free of the body's claims and demands—is also inscribed in her poems. Critic Cheryl Walker has suggested that this attempt to "retreat to the mind" was characteristic of this generation of female modernists.[14] Mead's memoir describes the remarkable self-possession of this second generation of "new women."

> We belonged to a generation of young women who felt extraordinarily free—free from the demand to marry unless we chose to do so, free to post-pone marriage while we did other things, free from the need to bargain and hedge that had burdened and restricted women of earlier generations. We laughed at the idea that a woman could be an old maid at the age of twenty-five. . . .
>
> We did not bargain with men. . . . At the same time we firmly established a style of relationships to other women. "Never break a date with a girl for a man" was one of our mottoes in a period when women's loyalty to women usually was . . . subordinate to their possible relationships to men. We learned loyalty to women, pleasure in conversation with women, and enjoyment of the way in which we complemented one another in terms of our differences in temperament . . .[15]

Hilary Lapsley, writing about Mead's relationship with the women in her circle, recognized the existence of lesbian relationships among them, and claims that Adams found "her own emotional interests troublesome as it became clear to her that she more readily fell in love with women than men" and that Adams later took pains to forget—and to have others forget—these episodes from her youth.[16] Adams eventually did have a brief sexual affair with Wilson (which both keenly regretted), but she was passionately attracted to Louise Bogan, who did not reciprocate. Lapsley reports Adams "struggling with a sexual identity she found more torturous than 'chic'" and that she traveled to Santa Fe in the summer of 1927 to be with Bogan. Bogan sent her home, accusing Adams of "arrested development." Mead was at this time collecting the dream narratives of her friends, and among her papers are several of Adams's dreams of sexual encounters with women and fear of sexual disapproval.[17] Mead allows that a growing awareness of sexuality did affect relationships in the group. "Sophisticated as we were," she writes, "we were still remarkably innocent about practical matters relating to sex. . . . But we knew about Freud. . . . We learned about homosexuality, [and] . . . we knew that repression was a bad thing. . . . We thought of ourselves as radicals—in terms of our sentiments rather than our adherence to any radical ideology."[18] Conflicted sexuality is common to nearly all the poets in this study, and an established antecedent to alcoholism in women generally. The relative freedoms of the 1920s permitted some women to express feelings they might have vigorously repressed in an earlier (or later) era. The disquiet underlying many of Adams's earliest poems may be traced in part to her discomfort with her own attraction to women.

But Adams, who remained single until 1933, derived much of her emotional sustenance from this group of remarkably talented, ambitious, and unconventional women: Bogan, Nicholl, Benedict, and Mead, and also Elizabeth Huling, Eda Lou Walton, and Genevieve "Jed" Taggard. Frank quotes Mead, a sophisticated psychoanalytic theorist in a time when they were all thinking in Freudian terms, on the way in which the dramas of their young lives figured in their poems. "Many of our poems grew out of our relationships to one another, and the intensities of the contemporary human plots were discussed and rediscussed against the background of the childhood and special temperament of each."[19] In her own memoir, Mead recalls the special day of April 30, 1925, when she learned that she'd won the fellowship that would enable her to travel for the first time to do research in Samoa, and the Ash Can Cats gathered to celebrate. Part of the plan was to hang May baskets (a holdover from Barnard traditions) on the doors of seven writers they admired, including Bogan and Ruth Benedict. Indeed they did, most notably placing a basket "woven of willow withes and filled with wild flowers, on the door-knob of Edna St. Vincent Millay's house in Greenwich Village. . . . Edna Millay called out to us from a high window . . . ran down the steep stairs and caught us and asked our names. 'Léonie Adams I know,' she said, holding out her hand, and Léonie tossed her glove over the garden wall." The May basket received notice in Franklin P. Adams's famous literary gossip column "The Conning Tower."[20]

Despite the fact that, or perhaps because, this was the era of Prohibition in the "City on a Still," the atmosphere of high seriousness and literary ambition was leavened with high spirits and socializing, lubricated by bootleg whiskey and gin. Part of the program of female self-determination included the right to drink in public and among men—Wilson among them. Like the much more self-conscious knights of the Algonquin Round Table a couple of miles uptown, this Greenwich Village crowd entertained itself with word games and literary gossip, and regarded itself as utterly alienated from middle-class American values. This Village circle is also notable because it was largely female. Whereas Dorothy Parker was a kind of mascot to the male drinkers at the Algonquin, these women partied and drank together. Louise Bogan claimed that she herself was likely to "go down in history as the heartiest drinker among the female poets," although Adams, she said, challenged her claim (WWL 144).

It was another college friend, Marian Smith, who took a sheaf of Adams's poems to editor Louis Untermeyer, and Adams got from him her most important encouragement to continue writing poems. Raymond Holden, then married to Bogan, took her first book manuscript to his friends at the Robert McBride publishing house, and *Those Not Elect* was accepted for publication. Adams claimed that Holden acted without her knowledge or permission, although she had always benefited from such interventions by friends. The book appeared, to very respectful reviews, in 1925. Holden's similar gesture, a couple of years earlier, had resulted in the appearance of Bogan's first book, *Body of This Death*, also from McBride, in 1923. When Adams's second book, *High Falcon*, appeared in 1929, it was dedicated to Bogan and Holden.

In the years following the publication of *Those Not Elect* in 1925, Adams supported herself as an editor, first at the Wilson Publishing Company, and then in the publications department of the Metropolitan Museum. She had grown to be a beautiful woman; her "'half-Latin-American prettiness and obvious purity of spirit'" attracted the attention of numerous would-be suitors,[21] but Adams had ambitious (and solitary) plans. In 1927, the same year that her again-roommate Mead's *Coming of Age in Samoa* was accepted for publication, Adams was awarded a Guggenheim Fellowship, one of the first ever awarded to a poet, and she used the money and the freedom to live abroad in 1928–29, primarily in Paris. She was living at the Hotel de Fleures in the company of the poet Allen Tate and his wife, novelist Caroline Gordon, when *High Falcon* appeared. Adams's Paris life was extended when her Guggenheim was, and through 1929 and 1930 she battled her loneliness by visiting the Dôme and the salon at Gertrude Stein's apartment, and by attending literary parties, most famously those given by novelist Ford Madox Ford. The period of Paris as a popular haven for American writers was coming to an end, and Adams was productive but restless and relatively solitary during her sojourn abroad in Paris and in England, where she did meet H. D. and Bryher (Winifred Ellerman Macpherson), as well as Robert McAlmon.

Adams returned to the United States a poet with a solid, even glowing reputation. On the strength of her books and her prizes, she secured her first teaching job, at Washington Square College of New York University. There she taught literature and poetry writing, and met and fell in love with scholar and critic William Troy. They were married in 1933, and Adams disciplined her unruly emotional life both in her husband's needs and in an increasingly observant Catholicism. She published that year a Borzoi chapbook version of her poem "The Measure," with illustrations by George Plank. But from then until 1954, Adams was virtually silent as a lyric poet. While the critical establishment remained respectful of her work—she was appointed poetry consultant to the Library of Congress (precursor to the present poet laureate role) in 1948–49, and, most significantly, was awarded, with Louise Bogan, the 1955 Bollingen Prize just after both their "selected poems" appeared—Adams's reputation became increasingly anachronistic, based on two slim volumes published in the 1920s. Bogan was somewhat defensive when the prize was announced, and wrote to Katharine White at the *New Yorker:* "I do think that both Léonie and I deserved it, if only for *hanging on*, over the years!" (WWL 295).

Adams shares the slimness of her output with almost all of the poets in this study. Certainly she shares with them, and with Bogan in particular, the "aesthetic of limitation," both self-imposed and enforced by the literary establishment, that demanded "impersonality" and the exclusion of open emotion in poetry by women.[22] Many female poets of this era tended to discipline emotion by the imposition of intricate and difficult form on their poems, and the influence of Marianne Moore is everywhere felt in them. The "masks outrageous and austere" of Elinor Wylie, which Cheryl Walker sees as a common defense among the younger female Modernists against accusations of emotionality or sentimentality, are both worn by the speakers of many of these poems and woven into their very language and form. Lee Upton has aptly called these strategies "defensive measures."

Adams herself was defensive when asked about her lyric silence. "I sometimes feel that poetry at present like other things is about to undergo the kind of variation that amounts to the leap to a new genus. I was first preoccupied with sound patterns—that took me to the seventeenth cen-tury—then I recognized the necessity for the more modern preoccupation with images which should not be gathered along the way of discourse or meditation, but assumed before starting out, like apparel, or entered into as a world. I have been silent a long time because I am now grappling with the limitations of the lyric."[23] The "limitations of the lyric" were being exploded and the form reinvented all around Adams, although the years of the Second World War caused many a poet to question the value of his or her work. Still, something silenced Adams, just as something silenced Bogan, and tried to silence Bishop, and separated Millay from the main thrust of her gift. Although Adams would continue teaching through the 1960s, at Columbia from 1947 until her retirement in 1968, and would be honored with a two-year appointment in creative writing at the University of Washington in 1968–70, she published almost nothing between 1954 and her death in 1988.

When *High Falcon* appeared in 1929, Bogan wrote to her editor, John Hall Wheelock, with considerable enthusiasm. "Have you seen Léonie Ad-ams' book, *High Falcon*? It is dedicated to Raymond and me. We are very proud. It is full of extraordinary loveliness—and a sharpness that I, for one, could not put a name to. She has the greatest talent in the really grand manner of anyone writing in America today. I wish it were not so near, and dependent on, the dreadful dream in her own heart" (WWL 48). This cryptic statement could have several reference points, the first of which might be the frightening (to her) passion Adams had felt for women, Bogan in particular. Bogan was firmly heterosexual herself, and rejected overtures from more than one woman in her lifetime; perhaps she would judge Adams's sexual ambivalence to be "dreadful." But whatever the dreadful dream was, it is clear that Adams—like Bishop, Millay, Wylie, and like Bogan herself—deadened its pain with alcohol.

William Troy died in 1962, and Adams, who saved every piece of writing her husband did (he published no books during his long academic career), helped his friend Stanley Edgar Hyman edit a *Selected Essays* volume, which appeared in 1967. Thereafter, she lived and taught from the home she and Troy had shared in New Milford, Connecticut. She died in 1988 at the age of eighty-nine.

Adams was a lyric poet in the "grand manner," as Bogan put it. Her poems are accessible on the surface, but ultimately refuse to resolve to "meaning" in the conventional sense. It is both Adams's sense of what a poem should be, and a psychic or temperamental instinct on her part, to distance and refine the raw material of a poem until "[i]ts meaning is its form."[24] "The first draft of each of these poems might have been a description. The final draft, now printed, is a system of allusions and correspondences, which gives forth a quality of intellectualized emotion and an atmosphere of enigma and secretiveness."[25] This alchemy, if you will, was certainly an artistic discipline for Adams. Fowlie says, "Adams is not interested in sentiments which have not been policed or deflated, which have not been recast in a form that purifies them."[26] Annie Finch insists, "Adams is a lush, sensual poet who directed her sensuality not towards other people but primarily towards the materials of poetry, towards syntax and symbol, diction and word-sound, in short, towards the language itself."[27] Elder Olson remarked that this transformative atmosphere can be confusing to readers and reminiscent of intoxication: "All things appear, whatever sense they appeal to, as they might to one in a drowsy fever, or between sleeping and waking, or fast in a spell."[28] The preoccupations of Adams's life and work, refined though they may be, are consistent within themselves (unusually so) and, often, with the work of other poets in this study.

Adams differs from these other poets in the remarkable absence in her work of poems and images concerned with water. The sea that burns and freezes Bishop; that is Millay's constant reference and a bower of possible refuge for Wylie; the flume that represents the flow of time and experience to Bogan, rarely appears in naturalistic or symbolic form for Adams. "The River in the Meadows" imagines a boat slipping beneath the surface of a river of "flowing silver," but the speaker is necessarily at a distance. "The

Figurehead" takes an "Ozymandias"-like look at a ship's decoration washed up on the beach, and imagines the violence of the storm that "swept us from our course," "Leaving the murderous tribute lodged in sand" (SPA 89). But Adams's imagination is fed most often by the woods, and the play of light and wind in trees, rather than by water.

The dominant metaphors in Adams's poetry are from the natural world, but she is not at all a "nature poet." Although very few people appear in her poems, nearly all the poems are about fundamental human questions—the meaning of time and mortality, the failure to connect with one another, the burden of consciousness. Her typical method is to describe a natural scene—and very often these are scenes of incipient transformation: the forest (quite often) on the cusp of transition, from night to day, or day to night; at solstice or equinox, or caught up in historical change. But these descriptions are shaped around a state of mind or emotional condition, so that the poem ends up being less about the natural world than about the feeling or memory generated by, or represented by, the moment or scene. The poems are startlingly impersonal on the surface; such personality as they express is deeply figured in the multivalent (and sometimes obscure) language and imagery she employs. Read with the conflicts of her life in mind—her ambivalent sexuality, her frustrated artistic life, and her struggle with alcohol—the poems open almost to eloquence in their expression of conflict and pain.

"Grapes Making" can serve as an example both of Adams's method and of such reading. One of Adams's best-known and most anthologized poems, "Grapes Making" is ostensibly a kind of time-lapse visual description of the progress to maturity of grape vines over the course of a season, particularly of the visual relationship between light, leaves, and swelling fruit. There can be no "scene" without a perceiving consciousness, of course, but in this case, the mind/eye/I presents itself only in the poem's imagery and detail.

> Noon beats down the leaf; the noon
> Of summer burns along the vine
> And thins the leaf with burning air,
> Till from the underleaf is fanned,
> And down the woven vine, the light.
> Still the pleached leaves drop layer upon layer
> To wind the sun on either hand,
> And echoes of the light are bound,

And hushed the blazing cheek of light,
The hurry of the breathless noon,
And from the thicket of the vine
The grape has pressed into its round. (SPA 15)

The considerable music of the form—tetrameter lines shaped around repeated words and sounds and punctuated with the exact rhyme of "bound"
and "round"—suggests both Adams's skill with poetic tools and the intricate
patterns of "woven vine" one finds in a grape arbor. Here we are "in the
field," as it were, looking directly at the vine and the leaves and the grapes
and the sun. By the third and final stanza, however, the autumn grape harvest has begun, and the poem becomes less visual and turns inward toward
a contemplation of both the passage of time and the natural association of
grapes with wine-making and a desirable unconsciousness.

Now shady sod at heel piles deep,
An overarching shade, the vine
Across the fall of noon is flung;
And here beneath the leaves is cast
A light to colour noonday sleep,
While cool, bemused the grape is swung
Beneath the eyelids of the vine;
And deepening like a tender thought
Green moves along the leaf, and bright
The leaf above, and leaf has caught,
The emerald pierces day, and last
The faint leaf vanishes to light. (SPA 16)

This deflected ("Beneath the eyelids of the vine") wish for unconsciousness
is expressed often enough in Adams's poems to link her with Bishop and
Bogan, and perhaps most directly with Elinor Wylie, whose poems are filled
with figures who slink away from care. Like Bishop, Adams contemplates
cusps of consciousness—falling asleep, waking slowly; and, like Wylie, she
imagines a "sanctuary" in sensationless and thoughtless oblivion. Like all of
these poets, she sees an inherent conflict between the mind—intellect, artistic
ambition, transcendence—and the female body, with its problematic desires
and demands. Babette Deutsch dryly remarked on the "conjugal quarrel
between body and soul" in Adams's work, which expresses this conflict in

many poems of ambivalence, both about intellect and about sexuality.[29] Typically, her metaphors are seasonal (rather than scientific, as in Bogan's "The Alchemist"), but the concern is the same:

THIS SEVERING

I turned as new resigned:
A summer gleaned, my business was within,
My charge the sober mind,
My care the wintry bin.

And found the boughs in stain,
Past-promise-hued. O not
Before, earnest as rich was yet so plain;
A harvest was ungot.

Beech drenching down my pathway goldenheart,
Ash, pensive light-cheek rose,
Both pluck the thought apart,
And meant you, heart, to close?

So fell the doomed farewells;
So, so looked forth a thing:
Regret, reproach, what else
Must baffle, vex, beguile this severing. (SPA 26)

The poem expresses both a similar resolve and a similar disappointment as "The Alchemist" and indeed the rhyme of "resigned" and "mind" in Adams's first stanza gently recalls the "I burned my life that I might find / A passion wholly of the mind" of Bogan's. The "severing" of which Adams speaks is both the resolve to turn away from pleasure to inner work typical of New Englanders in the late fall, and also the separation of heart from mind that female poets of Adams's generation regularly struggled with. The abundance of autumnal poems in Adams's oeuvre recalls the similar preoccupation of Emily Dickinson—"Words for the Raker of Leaves," "The Runner with the Lots," and "For Harvest" are among her greatest poems and express this ambivalence about putting away the body in favor of mind. They may also be included in the group of images expressing transitional states of consciousness or a wish for oblivion. The fact that the "severing," the resolve to reside in "the sober mind," costs the speaker her heart suggests that the choice might be fatal, that a balanced life may not be possible. "Send Forth the High Falcon," one of Adams's signature poems, also presents the mind in heroic, masculine terms and the heart as its "simple" and "unschooled"— perhaps feminine—nemesis.

> Send forth the high falcon flying after the mind
> Till it come toppling down from its cold cloud:
> The beak of the falcon to pierce it till it fall
> Where the simple heart is bowed.
> O in wild innocence it rides
> The rare ungovernable element,
> But once it sways to terror and descent,
> The marches of the wind are its abyss,
> No wind staying it upward of the breast—
> Let mind be proud for this,
> And ignorant from what fabulous cause it dropt,
> Or with how learned a gesture the unschooled heart
> Shall lull both terror and innocence to rest. (SPA 90)

Gerard Manley Hopkins's windhover is suggested here, whose "dapple-dawn-drawn falcon" soars and then "buckles" to a terrifying and beautiful dive. But Adams's falcon-mind crashes Icarus-like, valorized even as it falls, and submits to the ministrations of a mechanical heart that will "lull" it to unconsciousness. The mind must be protected from knowing from what heights it has fallen, by whatever means—and celebrated for having flown at all.

In "Quiet" Adams also considers the costs of banishing one aspect of the self (the opposite of "quiet," presumably) in favor of another. "Quiet" might be a disciplining of desire or of mind, or perhaps a chemical means of dulling pain. The discipline of form in the poem—a-b-c-b-c-a rhyme scheme, ritual repetitions, heavily alliterated diction—recall Hopkins's sonnet "Peace," and also suggest a willed effort toward "quiet."

> Since I took quiet to my breast
> My heart lies in me, heavier
> Than stone sunk fast in sluggish sand,
> That the sea's self may never stir,
> When she sweeps hungrily to land,
> Since I took quiet to my breast.

Strange quiet, when I made thee guest,
My heart had countless strings to fret
Under a least wind's fingering.
How could I know I would forget
To catch breath at a gull's curved wing,
Strange quiet, when I made thee guest?
Thou quiet, hast no gift of rest.
The pain that at thy healing fled
More dear was to my heart than pride.
Now for its loss my heart is dead,
And I keep horrid watch beside.
Thou, quiet, hast no gift of rest. (SPA 97)

The regret expressed here at the loss of feeling, of "heart," inherent in choosing "quiet," recalls Millay's resolve in "*Fontaine, Je Ne Bourai Pas De Ton Eau!*" not to choose the sheltered life, as well as the "cruel ease" of Bogan's "Come, Break with Time." Respite from the mind-body conflict can be found temporarily and unsatisfactorily in alcohol, as we have seen, which might be one form of chosen "quiet." But in fact the conflict cannot be resolved—"Thou, quiet," ironically, "hast no gift of rest." "How shall we forsake this angel and this devil?" Adams asks, in "Companions in the Morass." "We are weak earth, we run before the wind / By which our hearts were bowed" (SPA 115). In "Those Not Elect" the title and opening poem of her first book, she warns of the body's potentially escalating demands:

Never taste that fruit with the soul
Whereof the body may not eat,
Lest flesh at length lay waste the soul
In its sick heat. (SPA 96)

At the time this poem was written, Adams was troubled by her own sexual desire for women, Louise Bogan among them. The self-condemnation in these lines—in every way, she figures her desire as sinful and "sick"—reveals the particular intensity of the mind-body conflict for Adams.

Like the other poets in this study, Adams imagines escape from the tension of desire in terms of unconsciousness or oblivion. Adams is a much different poet than Bishop or Wylie, however; and in her imagining of that sanctuary—which is always related to or in danger of becoming death itself—she recalls no one so much as Emily Dickinson. "Thought's End" projects the speaker's journey beyond consciousness into undifferentiated space with Dickinsonian ambivalence:

> I'd watched the hills drink the last colour of light,
> All shapes grow bright and wane on the pale air,
> Till down the traitorous east there came the night
> And swept the circle of my seeing bare;
> Its intimate beauty like a wanton's veil
> Tore from the void as from an empty face.
> I felt at being's rim all being fail,
> And my one body pitted against space.
> O heart more frightened than a wild bird's wings
> Beating at green, now is no fiery mark
> Left on the quiet nothingness of things.
> Be self no more against the flooding dark;
> There thousandwise, sown in that cloudy blot,
> Stars that are worlds look out and see you not. (SPA 98)

"Thousandwise" recalls Hopkins as well, and the bleak realism of the final couplet suggests something of the dark religious doubt of his "terrible sonnets." But, like Dickinson, this speaker expresses curiosity at the idea that one might both cease to be and know the sensation of losing "self." Dickinson often imagined that loss of self in death, mostly famously in "I heard a fly buzz when I died" (#591) and "I felt a funeral in my brain" (#340). Adams here conflates the nightly descent into sleep—or other kinds of unconsciousness—with death, and the absence of fear and anxiety in that state is at least theoretically desirable. After a moment of panic at losing oneself "at being's rim," to be unseen can be ultimately comforting, safe. "Sundown" sees the violent colors of a sunset as evidence of "the immortal extinction, the priceless wound, / Not to be staunched" and the hour itself in terms of alcohol. The poem begins: "This is the time lean woods shall spend / A steeped-up twilight, and the pale evening drink, . . ." (SPA 62). In other poems, Adams describes nights of confused torment that resolve into the everyday reality of morning—poems like "Early Waking," "Sleeping to Waking," "Twilit Revelation," and "Fragmentary Stars." "Evening Sky" sees the sunset as the advent of torment—an "encounter [with] the damned god" (SPA 114).

Annie Finch has pointed out that nature in Adams's poems "is full of sounds that are profoundly meaningful but don't hold particular reference."[30] "To Unconscionable Sound" operates by way of a rich pun on "unconscionable." The sound is both immoral or heartless, and also imperceptible or unavailable to consciousness, without "reference." And it is also necessary for the act of creating poetry.

> Go, fill the bell of the wind
> With the sweet unconscionable sound;
> Do not breathe on the mind:
> It is an indifferent shell,
> Like whittled underwave,
> And had no timbre's form
> When the glittering wave withdrew
> But what its waters gave.
> Go twist the wind to a bell,
> Or let it whip and turn
> To any change you will
> The visionary cloud;
> They are innocent essence still.
> But not the brooding heart,
> A cloud that wraps about
> The tempest it outswept,
> And elemented then,
> When the cold fancy rose
> Which shakes off a heart like a dream
> In the hollow where it slept. (HF 36)

The sound, whatever it is, is wasted on the mind, which is substanceless like an "underwave" undone by the backward rush of the previous, larger ocean wave. The "visionary cloud," too, is an "innocent essence" unaffected by the sound. But "the brooding heart" takes in the sound, giving rise to "cold fancy," which then vanquishes the heart. The poem asks for inspiration, for sound, for poetry itself, which cannot be found in the mind or in ambition, but only in some alchemy of the heart that produces the dispassionate urge to create: cold fancy. The disciplining and distancing of emotion demanded of ambitious female poets is figured in Adams's complex metaphor.

"Death the Master" associates alcohol and death with the ultimate unconsciousness, although it is almost medieval in its conviction that death is the master of the feast of life itself. The setting evokes the innumerable "Last Supper" paintings in the Italian tradition, and the personification of death as a manipulative master of ceremonies also, of course, recalls Dickinson.

> Death is master at this feast,
> And our breath the fee to dine;
> Light as morning from the east,
> Feasting flesh from bone does twine.
> Come, skinny death, let now the priest
> By altar lambs be trimmed with vine.
> Death is master at this feast,
> And our breath the fee to dine.
> Then had death bemocked us least,
> So the jesting never ceased;
> Would rue like tender roses shine,
> And the poison go like wine.
>
> *Death is master at this feast.* (TNE 43)

Death does preside over all of nature and all of human life, and we are all obliged to drink the fatal draught in the end. The poison that flows like wine (or the wine that flows like poison) is designed to dull the pain of conflict and desire temporarily, but only Death himself can resolve it permanently. Léonie Adams's poems look toward that resolution, without actively seeking it.

Chapter 6

"Words from the
Piazza del Limbo"

Isabella Gardner as Fallen Woman

L ate in the 1960s, when her marriage to Allen Tate had fallen victim
to alcohol and another woman, Isabella Gardner (1915–1981) sat in
her room at New York's Chelsea Hotel and tried hard to take stock
of her life. Among her papers are numerous chronologies from this
period, with special attention to the places in which the major events of
her life had unfolded. "'38 *Nov. married Van*—Falsington / '39—sailed: London, Paris, Rome, Florence, Greece, Ville Franche, Cambridge. Sept—Rosy
born—Falsington." In the margins of these chronologies, she totaled and
retotaled the years of her four marriages, evaluating her success in what she
most valued: love.

4 Van
7 Seymour
8 Bob
8 *Allen*
24 years

Happiest *1939
1944, 1945, 1946, 1953 & 1955, *1960, 1961, 1962
8 *extremely* happy
6 happy

---

10 sad & painful[1]

Gardner might reasonably have concluded at this point that she had not been granted a fair portion of personal happiness in her life. Four failed marriages, the last especially heartbreaking, her daughter irretrievably brain-damaged from a heroin overdose; her son also a heroin addict and mysteriously lost at sea; her bright red hair, her beauty, and her health ravaged by time and alcohol and sadness; her poetic voice all but silenced. And yet, she lived on, and the impression one takes from even her own account of her life is of a spirit determined to live and love, to enjoy food and friends and good talk, and to make art.

Isabella Gardner was born in 1915 into several of the most prominent Boston families. She was niece to the eccentric and free-spirited art patron Isabella Stewart (Mrs. Jack) Gardner. Her mother was a Grosvenor (Rose Grosvenor Gardner) and her father a Peabody (George Peabody Gardner) and she was raised in an atmosphere of wealth and anxiety, of high social expectations and summers in Maine and Rhode Island, and also, through her father, of volubility, wit, and high spirits. A bright and imaginative red-headed child with a beautiful singing voice, she also stuttered and suffered from shyness, and she invented imaginary refuges from the rejection she felt from her mother. She wrote to a scholar late in her life, "I was born in a sort of sous cloche . . . with my brother George, 2 years younger than I. I could not have survived without him. My birth was a disaster for my mother. It was desperately important to her (because of another woman my father loved) to bear a son. I was the 2nd daughter. She has (but I love her) rejected me all the years of my life."[2] "Belle" and George had a kind of world of their own within the family, attended by their own nanny, and

Belle's most vivid recollection from that childhood is a particular utopian "home" that she imagined over and over again.

> I had a secret magical hallucinatory life from which George (to his *dismay)* was excluded. .... I called it Card Island (or Cod Island?) It was a tiny village on a hill beside an ocean harbor. The meeting house was lit with warm light. The people in the houses opened their doors & their arms to me, I was *theirs*, one of *them*. They gave me cookies and milk.
>
> They were more real to me than my family. Even my dear George could not go.
>
> I told my father about Card Island and when he would come to kiss me goodnight he always asked me to tell him what I'd done & whom I'd seen the night before on Card Island. We had an Irish laundress, who must have been a very sensitive and imaginative woman, because she would say that she too had been to Card Island.[3]

Gardner wrote several poems about her childhood (at least one about Card Island itself), most of them centered on the summers spent on Roque Island, Maine, and at Bristol, Rhode Island. She once called the ocean "my mother, my redemption, my passion, my element. I am fearless there. I am in the arms of the mother I never had."[4] It seems clear from the poems and letters she wrote about her childhood that she associated it with summer and the ocean, where she was away from the oppressive influence of her mother's disappointment. "Summers Ago," "Summer Remembered," "Summer Evening," "West of Childhood," and "Card Island or Cod Island?" all picture the child "in the arms" of the sea, and in the company of her brother and male cousins who encouraged her romantic and adventurous spirit.

Gardner said that she began to write poems as a child of seven, and that she was encouraged by "a doting aunt [who] put them into a bound leather book."[5] Her real passion, however, was for acting. At the Park School in Brookline she discovered that a script and an alternative persona could conquer her shyness and stammer, and she appeared in several productions and won a public speaking prize. At the Foxcroft School for Girls in Virginia, she was a prize poet as well as an actor and director and president of the Dramatic Club. After Foxcroft she elected not to go to college, but studied for a time with a private literature and writing tutor, which had the effect of embarrassing her to poetic silence. "I stopped writing *poetry* then because I felt I was too facile."[6]

Gardner threw herself wholeheartedly into acting after her formal schooling ended. She acted in local productions and helped to found, with friends, Boston's Studio Club, which sponsored plays and readings. By all accounts Gardner had considerable stage presence, and was excellent in particular at broad character comedy. At twenty-one she left Boston for East Hampton, Long Island, to study acting for the summer at the Leighton Rollins School of Acting, then moved to London for a year to attend the Embassy School of Acting. In both settings she was surrounded by extraordinarily talented actors and directors, many of whom became her lifelong friends. In her second summer at East Hampton, she married the new director of the Rollins company, Harold Van Kirk, and they lived for a time on a cottage farm in Falsington, England. The following year her daughter Rose was born, and she moved back to the United States and became a resident actor with the Bass Rocks Theater in Gloucester, Massachusetts. She developed a specialty playing comic characters with Irish brogues; one director memorably described her as "the perfect adorable silly ass."[7] Eventually she landed a significant role as the cockney maid in the Chicago production of Noel Coward's *Blithe Spirit,* but was fired from the company when the other actors complained that she stole their scenes. She continued to act for a time, but grew tired, she said, of playing other people. It is clear, too, that she was sharply wounded by her dismissal from the *Blithe Spirit* cast.

At about the same time, she divorced Van Kirk and married Seymour Shapiro, a theatrical photographer she'd met on the set of *Blithe Spirit.* A year later, in 1945, their son Daniel was born, and "Bellotschka" set about making a life for herself in the big, noisy community of Russian Jewish immigrants to Chicago, Shapiro's hometown. Her late poem "That Was Then" is dedicated to her niece, Riva Blevitsky.

> Union Pier Michigan. We called it Shapiro
> Shangri La. People said I needed a passport.
> I was the only Shicksa there Kolya Shura
> Manya Tanya and Sonya, Sulya Myra and
> Vera were there. And Riva a young girl then.
> Soda pop and ice cream parlors, no bars,
> Delicatessens but no liquor stores.
> They spoke fractured English fractured Yiddish
> and fractured Russian when they did not want
> their children to understand. Most husbands

drove down from Chicago fridays but mine
came to me thursdays bringing the squat green
bottles of Chilean white wine I drank
(he was angry if I forgot to buy
cucumbers) My daughter then five, now in
Bedlam, chased butterflies and thirty years
ago my infant son, now for some years
lost, was happy too.[8]

Among the pleasures of her sojourn among Shapiro's family was a redis-
covery of her need and desire to write poetry. "[O]ne day I wrote a poem.
And then another and another." A family friend brought the anthologist and
critic Oscar Williams to visit, who read Gardner's poems and encouraged her
to continue to refine her gift. "If it were not for his insistent encouragement
I doubt if I would have persisted," she said.[9] The more she wrote, and the
more beloved she became among her husband's family, the more jealous
her husband became. In 1949, she and Shapiro were divorced, and Gardner
soon married Robert Hall McCormick III, a successful Chicago real estate
developer and member of one of the city's most prominent families. It was,
she said, the only one of her marriages of which her family wholeheartedly
approved.

Bob McCormick was a genial recovering alcoholic (AA) and a patron
of the arts. Together he and Gardner commissioned a design from Mies van
der Rohe for the house at 299 South Prospect Street in Elmhurst, Illinois,
that they would occupy throughout their marriage. (The "McCormick
Mansion" has since been moved and is a permanent exhibit of the Elmhurst
Art Museum.) McCormick was delighted with his wife's literary ambitions
and encouraged her to send her poems out for publication, particularly to
Chicago's own *Poetry* magazine. In the summer of 1951, Gardner sent then-
editor Karl Shapiro a sheaf of seven poems, and he accepted five of them
and invited her to become a volunteer assistant editor at the magazine.
Although Shapiro doubtless saw the philanthropic possibilities of a positive alliance with a "Boston Brahmin beauty heiress poet" as well as the
McCormick family, he genuinely admired the freshness and originality of
Gardner's work.[10] "What made [her work] different from other poetry of
our time was that it was unobjectified—paint raw from the tube—without
being amateurish or offensive. It had the quality ... of being primitive, the
direct opposite of the modern, extremely fashionable baroque."[11]

Gardner devoted herself to *Poetry* for the next four years, coming into the office "religiously every day of the week, six hours a day" to keep ahead of the reams of incoming manuscripts.[12] She was soon promoted to unpaid associate editor and made it her practice to respond with real criticism and encouragement to nearly every submission. Gardner earned the everlasting gratitude and admiration of young poets such as Philip Booth, John Logan, and Galway Kinnell, all of whom achieved their first appearances in *Poetry* at Gardner's recommendation, not only for her eventual acceptance of their work, but also for the thoughtful and constructive rejection letters she sent them first. Gardner largely assembled the magazine's fortieth anniversary issue, which included poems by Elizabeth Bishop, e. e. cummings, Robert Graves, Randall Jarrell, Archibald MacLeish, Marianne Moore, Theodore Roethke, Wallace Stevens, and William Carlos Williams.[13] She also played an important role in the production of a special Dylan Thomas issue of the magazine, which included reproductions of several of Thomas's manuscripts.

Gardner's position at *Poetry* did not survive the change in editorship of the magazine from Shapiro to Henry Rago, and her editorial career was abruptly aborted.[14] But at the same time, her first collection of poems appeared, *Birthdays from the Ocean*, well published by Houghton Mifflin and a National Book Award nominee. Perhaps because of her position at *Poetry*, the book was widely reviewed and also widely praised for its originality of voice. Edith Sitwell noted, "Isabella Gardner is a very accomplished natural poet. Her poems have much charm; her technique is polished as well as natural, and inherent in the uses to which she puts it and in the material it shapes." With evident relief, she credits Gardner with masculine virtues, "There is no flopping, no untidy hanging about, none of that unfortunate mincing and teetering that is to be found in so many poems written by women."[15]

The praise must have seemed ironic to Gardner, who was determined to devote herself to her marriage to the point that she could announce to an interviewer "I am a woman first, and poet second." Living with McCormick and her children, Rosy and Dan, she tried to find stability and fulfillment in the role of wife and mother. But as her daughter began to suffer from mental illness and her relationship with McCormick became more distant, she took refuge in alcohol and eventually in another relationship (McCormick, to his credit, did not return to drinking under the strain). In July 1958 she met and fell in love with the man she understood to be her soul mate, poet Allen Tate.

Tate was among the most respected poets and men of letters of his generation, and apparently a compelling sexual partner to the many women with whom he is reported to have had affairs (including, among the poets in this study, Jean Garrigue). Although he and Gardner were drawn to each other to the point that each left a spouse so that they could marry (Gardner said, "Bob McCormick was a perfectly nice man. I suppose I could have gone on being married to him, but I wanted Allen Tate as my husband; and Bob understood"[16]), the relationship was stormy from the start, in part because of both people's heavy drinking. As was the case for many women of her generation, when Gardner sought medical help for anxiety and insomnia and "morning shakiness" during the difficult periods of her courtship and marriage to Tate, she was given Seconal and Dexamyl and "vitamin shots," and her drinking went unaddressed.[17] Although Gardner was in demand as a public reader of her poems during this period when readings attracted large and enthusiastic crowds (her stage training served her well in projecting her lines and overcoming her shyness and tendency to stutter), she saw herself as Tate's inferior in all things literary. She claimed she couldn't read without a couple of drinks beforehand, and their correspondence reflects both drunken writing and a constant concern with drinking. "No doubt both of us are drinking more than we should these days," she wrote just after Christmas in 1958, "But our patterns are very different. Mine is day-time & carefully spaced, solitary mostly, & *medicinal*—no gayety involved! . . . My way is less abusive physically & Kraus [her psychiatrist] says I should not worry at *all*. I think your current over-doing is very understandable. . . . I beg you to heed your doctor if he advises you to eschew what our friend Dahlberg calls "The Stygian Juice" entirely. I doubt if I shall but I will help you to & if you prefer me to I will—*No*—I take that back!!" (December 27, 1958). Here Gardner expresses the most common drinking pattern of female alcoholics—daytime, solitary, secret—and betrays a telling anxiety at the prospect of giving it up. She never found her way to lasting sobriety, and the pressures and disappointments of her marriage only exacerbated the problem.

Tate and Gardner (hereafter she called herself "Isabella Gardner Tate" and continued to do so even after they were divorced) conducted a strained literary partnership for a few years after their marriage in the summer of 1959, moving between Tate's appointment at the University of Minnesota (with summers in Wellfleet, Cape Cod) and extensive sojourns in Europe. The marriage faltered over Tate's unfaithfulness and tension between him

and Gardner's teenaged son, Daniel. At one point Gardner had been willing
to say to Tate that even in his philandering he gave each woman a great deal.
"I know that if I were never to see you again I would be blessed among
women" (July 23, 1958); by 1965 she would ask, "How can you be cruel on
top of betrayal?" (April 30, 1965). "Please realize that I must be concerned
with my children & the people I was involved with for twenty to thirty
years, that I must cook, & run the house, & be a 'hostess' & remind you to
write so & so & do my small chores and at the same time be a poet manqué"
(August 1, 1965).

Tate left Gardner during a visit to Italy in 1965, and they were divorced
in Mexico in March 1966. Thereafter Gardner ceased to maintain a permanent home, and divided her time between the artist colonies at Yaddo (Saratoga Springs, New York) and MacDowell (Peterborough, New Hampshire)
and New York's Chelsea Hotel. She continued to write for a time, publishing
a provisional "collected" poems, *West of Childhood: Poems 1950–1965* with
Houghton Mifflin in 1965. In the following years, her daughter and son both
foundered in the drug culture of the late 1960s; in 1974 Rose was judged
permanently brain-damaged as a result of a heroin overdose and Gardner's
father paid for her lifelong institutional care. Rose's son, born in 1970, was
raised by the Shapiro family. Gardner's son, Daniel, disappeared at sea off
the coast of Colombia, South America, in 1967. Daniel Shapiro had been
sharply critical (in print) of his mother's multiple marriages and alcoholism,
and they were sadly estranged at the time of his death.

Gardner's "home" at the Chelsea Hotel was the scene of large parties
and celebrations, as she conducted a highly alcoholic literary social life from
those legendary confines.[18] As her health deteriorated, she tried for a time to
live in California, associating herself with the Music and Arts Center at Ojai.
The experiment failed, including a relationship with a man there, and she
returned to New York and the Chelsea to live out her days. She published
a "new and selected" volume, *That Was Then*, in 1980. The small number
of deeply nostalgic new poems in that book articulate the implied second
phrase of the title, "and this is now." In 1981 she was belatedly named poet
laureate of the state of New York. She donated the $10,000 prize to Yaddo,
and on July 7, 1981, she died of a heart attack, alcohol undoubtedly an ag-
gravating cause.

Isabella Gardner's great gift as a poet was her innate and sparkling sense of rhythm. Her proponents praise her originality, above all, and also her moral and spiritual commitments. Ralph J. Mills, Jr., wrote of her "indisputable claim to natural gifts any poet would be proud to possess. . . . In Miss Gardner's work the rhythmic movement and the richness of language merge to fashion a sturdy but flexible musical idiom completely her own; and the poet is not afraid to permit it the utmost liberty of sensuous play."[19] Burton Robie claimed that "She rhapsodizes and takes startling liberties with words and forms that only a real poet would dare to do. . . . She is the musician and the magician."[20] But Gardner was forever exiled from the ranks of anointed poets of the so-called middle generation by their arbiter, Randall Jarrell, after the publication of her first volume. Always somewhat immune to mere pleasure in poetry, Jarrell saw little to praise in either Gardner's originality or her ear.

> Isabella Gardner is a fresh, individual, irregularly appealing poet with one great and several small faults. The great: she almost never, as yet, manages to write good poems. The small: she thinks random technical mannerisms (long intentionally lumbering doggerel lines, words split in two to form rhymes, sounding and insensible plays on words) personal form; she is extremely self-conscious; her poems are puddings full of raw suet, rhetorical zwieback, things too underdone or overdone to seem homogenous parts of one work of art; she is bewitched by all tricks, properties, allusions, gewgaws, doodads—any bright found object that can assure her that she too vividly and peculiarly exists.

And Jarrell was unable to restrain a gendered swipe at Gardner's personal manner and circumstances: "[T]o her the world is a costume-party for which she has just breathlessly overdressed herself, and these poems are her starry, tinsely, gold-leafy entrance into it."[21]

Gardner herself was somewhat embarrassed by the ease with which complex rhythms and rhyme schemes came to her, but she was serious about the moral commitments of her work. "If there is a theme with which I am particularly concerned, it is the contemporary failure of love . . . the love which is the specific and particular recognition of one human being by another," she wrote late in her life (CPG 162). From the beginning, she structured her work around Martin Buber's concept of "I-Thou" relations, and the success and failure of this idea in human interactions is her great subject. "That Craning of the Neck" is perhaps her best-regarded poem, and in it the poet recalls a ride on horseback through a desert landscape that startles a great blue heron.

> I followed him silently giving no quarter
> all that afternoon. He never flew far from me . . .
>   . . . I
> only wanted to stare myself into him to try
> and thou him till we recognized and became each
> other. We were both fishing. But I could not reach
> his eye. He fled in puzzled ponderous pain
> and I last rode home, conspicuous as Cain,
> yet ashamed of a resigned demeaning pity
> that denied us both. I returned to the city
> and visited the zoo, fished on a concrete shore,
> took children to aquariums, and rode no more.
> I found that the encyclopedia says "A
> gregarious bird . . ." No one spoke that desert day,
> not one word. That fisher who heaved to dodge my eye
> has damned himself an It and I shall never fly. (CPG 3–4)

The wistful and partly comic disappointment at the end of this poem may be the signature mood of Gardner's many poems about animals. Her more typical style involves considerable verbal dexterity, of the sort that so irritated Jarrell, a style ideally suited to the expression of a kind of ecstasy. Gardner's great subject was love, and she stands out among female poets of her generation in her willingness to treat the pleasures of sex, particularly of female sexual desire and fulfillment, in language that mimics the rise and fall of such pleasure. "Gimboling," for example, governs its volatile material with a conceit of dolphins and ocean, in an unwavering dactylic meter that allows the sensual play of both language and bodies:

> Nimble as dolphins to
> dive leap and gimble, sleek, supple
> as ripples to slip round each other to
> wander and fondle on under and into
> the seeking and coupling and swarming of water
> compliant as sea-plants to bend with the tide

unfolding and folding to frond and to flower
a winding and twining to melt and to merge
to rock upon billowing founder in surf
and a fathom's down drowning before the sweet waking
the floating ashore into sleep and to morning. (CPG 27)

Most of Gardner's ocean poems recall her childhood experiences at the
beach, though several, like this one, liken the buoyancy and flow of water
to sexual longing and satisfaction ("Letter from Slough Pond," for example).
They are notable in this group of poets for looking beyond "drowning" to
"sweet waking." There is a watery quality also to her poems that seem to
be about the effect of alcohol or the feeling of drunkenness. Her *Saloon
Suite* brings together three increasingly incoherent "songs" of revelry and
disintegration that draw on Gardner's own experiences and preoccupations.
The flow of "Waltz for Accordion" is followed by the "Jig for Harmonica,"
which mixes the Irish of Boston with the Jews of Chicago in, apparently, an
Italian café. Their toasts, like most, are about what has been or will be lost:

Murphy and company jig with Cohen
Shicker vie a Goy
Sing your slainthe landsmen
Lhude sing L'Chiam
Joy and joy and joy
and
Paesani Please It's time

The third song, "Tango for Zither" is a frank drunken reverie that begins
"Loving you Love loving you," and travels from fall to spring and from the
woods to the beach, and ends in a kind of ecstasy of longing:

Lost love-lost   love-lost
I am lost Love I am lost love-lost
Love lost.
Sail me sail me home
Sail me sail me sail me home
My sailor   sail me sail me home
Reef me   steer me. Navigate me
home   home   home   home
home. (CPG 57–58)

A considerable number of Gardner poems feature literal glasses of wine ("The Moth Happened," for example), as well as the feeling or experience of drunkenness without so naming it. Such poems, among the poets in this study, are quite rare. "On Looking in the Looking Glass," the title poem of her second volume (1961) captures the strangeness of perspective that alcohol brings, an opportunity that has attracted many artists to perception-altering substances. In this poem, the poet looks into the mirror and sees the familiar but strange apparition of her own face.

> Your small embattled eyes dispute a face
> that middle-aging sags and creases.
> Besieged, your eyes protest and plead,
> your wild little eyes are bright, and bleed.

The poet interrogates her face in the mirror, demanding to see "the child you were" and "the maker that you want / and aren't," then loses her courage and closes her eyes. "Gaze glare and flare and glint are buried by / my neutral eye- / lids. These island citadels are now surrendered / and with imagination's eye I see you dead" (CPG 54–55). The palpable self-loathing in these images is also striking. The image of the failed poet, however, connects it to some of Gardner's strongest poems, which are elegies and laments for the ruined lives of her artist friends. "When a Warlock Dies" for Dylan Thomas and "Writing Poetry" for James Wright lament the loss of poets and poems destroyed by alcohol in particular. "When a Warlock Dies" imagines the company of surviving poets as a society of "lemans, demons, fallen angels / and Familiars," who rush to elegize the dead "warlock" poet in forms that reflect Thomas's own distinctive rhythms. But this poet, an "apprentice witch" and "mere familiar of Familiars," knows that "not all the ink and drink and spunk from Wichita to Wales / will wake this cock" (CPG 44), who literally drank himself to death in New York City in 1953.

"Writing Poetry" she says, "is a game that no-one quits while he or she's ahead. The / stakes are steep." The poem is equally aware that the art of poetry is somehow occult, or so invested in the poet's own being, that it must cost him his life, one way or another. "Some [poets] are only kibitzers," she says,

> others play it safe
> (their chips are counterfeit) cheating, they may not come to grief,
> or so they hope, and hoping keep their places near the pot.

There are other gambits deployed to trick the croupier's hot
eye and hand. For some in terror for their reason and their rhyme
There's a disguise in style to rent or borrow or assume:
hair-shirts, brocaded waistcoats (the gilt is slightly tarnished)
sackcloth interlined, embroidered chasubles refurbished,
helmets turbans caps (with bells) wreaths high silk hats cockades . . .
and for women Quaker bonnets wimples coifs and sunshades,
long blue stockings hawking gloves a fan a hobnailed boot.
But it's the gamblers wearing their own hides who shoot
the moon rocketing on unprotected feet to outer space
where (out of pocket, having no sleeves up which to hide an ace)
they fall bankrupt or being down to their last chip are stran-
ded. No-one has pocketed the moon since the game began . . .
or . . . sooner than they did
they died. (CPG 77)

James Wright was a poetic "gambler" who bet his life in his poems, in Gardner's view, and died an alcoholic's death because of it. The women poets in
their "Quaker bonnets wimples coifs and sunshades, / long blue stockings"
occupy perhaps the most restrictive positions in this hierarchy, but are subject
to all the hazards of the practice of making art. In her verse meditation on
those hazards, "This Room Is Full of Clocks," written as her marriage to
Allen Tate disintegrated, Gardner named them frankly:

It is possible
that there should be a Forest Preserve for poets
each with his or her mate but I remind myself
that the poet is rumored to be less constant
than the swan. No the bard must do his best with book
and bed and booze and blunders of the heart and
bearing witness burying friends banning bombs
and using onomatopoeia with restraint. (CPG 87)

Apparent here is the blackish humor that characterizes much of Gardner's
most memorable work. In this she is closest in spirit to Dorothy Parker,
though she was a far more ambitious poet that Parker ever claimed to be.
Like nearly all of these poets, she wrote from a position of relative economic
privilege, and from a stormy and troubled personal life.

The fear and anxiety in that personal life is also well documented in Gardner's poems. "The Panic Vine" opens with a taxonomy of an anxiety attack, an occasion for self-medication on the part of many female drinkers, and also an unintended consequence of drinking too much:

> The panic vine quickens on the spine with the rise
> and fall of every breath; and blooms inside the eyes.
> A cold fruit bulges from the veins of wrists and arms
> to bleed a virus juice into our sueded palms. (CPG 35)

And the nightmares common to sleep troubled by alcohol also make their way into these poems, as the potential sanctuary of unconsciousness becomes frightening in itself. "Nightmare" unfolds with the inevitability and urgency of hallucination:

> A sleeping woman dreams she wakes
> Into a surging room of shrieks
> and shapes. In the frantic room a red
> haired woman looms . . . on her bent arm
> there sleeps a girl's carved wooden head
> A doll-sized nursing bottle nipples her huge palm
> Both head and bottle drop and leeringly she
> beckons. The dreamer screams her hatred
> of the leering shape. Scrabbling for safety
> the dreamer flounders on the floor.
> The leerer pounces from behind the door.
> The struggling dreamer stands
> The dreamer lifts and clenches both her hands
> The dreamer rips the red curls
> in handfuls from that hateful head and hurls
> the hairy gobbets at those manic eyes
> The leerer dreadfully diminishes in size
> She shrinks and shrinks into a little child.
> The screaming dreamer beats the dwindling child.
> The dreamer lifts a chair to smash that leering child.
> Nothing at all remains. Not hag nor child.
> No traces and no tokens.
> The red-haired dreamer wakens. (CPG 47)

Here is disturbingly frank autobiography, with imagery of self-loathing, regret, and sorrow about the failures of mothering in her life, an exhausting narrative of impotent rage directed against the psychic shadows and shapes of a too-realistic dream, whose "nursing bottle" suggests not only ironic motherhood, but her chosen antidote to such terror.

Gardner contemplates the idea of sanctuary in her poems and, as for the other poets in this study, a retreat to unconsciousness or even death is at least at times an attractive alternative to continued engagement. At various times, the poet envies a mummified Egyptian girl ("In the Museum") and contemplates a retreat into the woods and the "laurels" ("It Rained Last Night"). "Collage of Echoes" makes literary comedy of this wish for oblivion:

> I have no promises to keep
> Nor miles to go before I sleep.
> For miles of years I have made promises
> And (mostly) kept them.
> It's time I slept.
> Now I lay me down to sleep
> With no promises to keep.
> My sleeves are ravelled.
> I have travelled. (CP 117)

The cleverness and lightness of tone here deflects the deep sadness of a mother who has lost both her children, and a person who has lost, over and over again, at love. But Gardner's most complex and eloquent expression of the wish to withdraw—a desire expressed with varying degrees of urgency by all of the poets in this study—occurs in "'The Whole World's in a Terrible State of Chassis,'" a poem she published in the *Chicago Review* in 1954, and which remained uncollected until the *Complete Poems* was assembled after her death. The title is the last line of Sean O'Casey's 1924 play, *Juno and the Paycock*; it is the Paycock himself, Captain Boyle, who mispronounces the word "chaos" so memorably. Gardner's epigraph credits the play and explains the poem's central metaphor: "*Joxer said and the Paycock said "I'm puttin' on my moleskin trousers."* In the play, Joxer is the Paycock's friend; "Juno" is his wife. Gardner's use of the play recalls both her experience in the theater and her affinity for the Irish. *Juno and the Paycock* tells of the misadventures and tragedies of the Boyle family in the aftermath of the Easter Rebellion of 1916, and throughout the misery, Joxer and the Paycock are resoundingly drunk. "Moleskin trousers" were standard issue among the Irish lower classes in the early twentieth century; Joxer and the Paycock put them on primarily to head down to the pub. Thus the contemplation of withdrawal in the poem is explicitly associated with alcohol, though its protagonist is actually the mole.

> You burrow through dusty labyrinths of time
> rooting around or under the obstructing stone
> scrabbling for the buried bone of Fido (or an ancestor)
> never surfacing to be fractured by light
> stabbed by jade blades stoned by the wind's weight
> drowned in the sweet violent smells of dung roses seawater
> blasted by explosions of bird song and hilarious children.
> Your humped wake heaves a braille warning on the unguarded
> lawns and in the wild dazzling gardens overhead.
> You dare not burst through the earth's skin you are lonely
> not perceiving tear totem fist nor phallus of your own kin
> neither where you exist nor where the loud light lives. (CP 152)

Elinor Wylie's mole comes to mind, whom she prefers to the soaring eagle in "The Eagle and the Mole": "If you would keep your soul / From spotted sight or sound, / Live like the velvet mole; / Go burrow underground" (CPW 4). Gardner pursues her metaphor longer than does Wylie, but in the end, her mole is just as immured, receiving at a well-muffled distance the sounds above the "earth's skin." "The loud light" (of love and grief, perhaps) is death to the blind mole, and while Gardner's unconventional life choices were subject to a good deal less public scrutiny than Wylie's, the two women share the feeling that all told, it might be better to withdraw from the world's judgment on one's "fallen" state.

Gardner lived longer than Wylie, and was not as driven a writer. Thus she had time to reflect upon her status as a fallen woman, in poems both of self-blame and regret, and of black humor and irony. In 1965, at the end of her marriage to Allen Tate, and after a series of trips to Italy, Gardner wrote "A Word from the Piazza del Limbo" for her cousin Bill Congdon, one of her closest childhood friends. The real Piazza del Limbo is a tiny square on the Arno in central Florence, in medieval and Renaissance times the burial place for infants who died without being baptized. Thus the poem, with characteristic humor, locates the poet among those whose salvation remains in doubt and also with radical innocence. It opens complaining of the voluminous and self-righteous letters the poet has received recently from a born-again Christian friend, particularly their utter self-absorption:

> Indeed he declines to address himself to my
> distress. Although I have written him of
> various despairs he does not even
> upbraid me for Sloth, the sin with which
> I wake and eat, that monkey on my back.
> I realize that right this minute he may
> be praying for me (though fretfully, the
> way one writes a postponed letter, I MUST
> pray for Belle today) because being yet
> but a fresh-washed lamb he is bound to be
> nervous about wasting God's time, and of
> course his own which I can well understand.

This friend, after all may have business with God himself, "while I at present / lack even a genuflecting acquaintance. / Not God's fault God knows. I have avoided / Him since losing innocence." The poet recalls a time when "I believed," presumably in the possibility of salvation, but literally, she says, in her "own Omnipotence." She recovered, just in time, but at a cost:

> I lived too long a time in innocence,
> but not quite long enough to wholly make break or addle
> me. A critic wrote "the pilgrim for whom no chapel
> waits." But still I wear the scallop shell
> and shall till I go down the well
> Ding   Dong   Belle (CPG 88–89)

Isabella Gardner, like Elizabeth Bishop, lived well into the era of confessional poetry (and of AA and the medical establishment's growing understanding of the mechanisms of addiction). She is more openly autobiographical in her work than any of the other poets here. Her poems tell us of courage and humor in the face of disappointment and tragedy, and are relatively frank about her own dependence on "bed and booze and blunders of the heart" to keep herself alive and writing. Only a few years older, Elizabeth Bishop's "conspiracy of silence" was far more absolute.

Chapter 7

The Prodigal

Elizabeth Bishop's Exile

E lizabeth Bishop once attributed her alcoholism to her childhood experience of the famous Salem, Massachusetts, fire of 1914. In an unpublished poem entitled "A Drunkard," which dates from about 1960, Bishop remembered her three-year-old "amazement" at the fire's glow and being "terribly thirsty," but unable to capture the attention of her mother, a ghostly figure outside her window, giving coffee to refugees arriving on the beach in boats. The poem recalls a great many details of the fire: the red glow through the windows, cinders and ash in the air and on the beach, boards "shiny black like black feathers," furniture and clothes washed up with the tide. When, the next morning, the curious child picks

Photograph by Josef Breitenbach

up a woman's black cotton stocking from the rubble, she remembers her mother saying sharply "*Put that down!*"

> I remember clearly, clearly—
> But since that day, that reprimand . . .
> I have . . . suffered from abnormal thirst—
> I swear it's true—and by the age
> of twenty or twenty-one I had begun
> to drink, & drink—I can't get enough
> and, as you must have noticed,
> I'm half-drunk now . . .[1]

Bishop ended the draft with a half-hearted disclaimer: "And all I'm telling you may be a lie. . . ." But her description of the Salem fire corresponds perfectly with newspaper accounts of June 26, 1914 (when she *was* three years old), and her distant relationship with her mother in this scene is familiar from her descriptions in her memoir "In the Village" and in other unpublished poems and stories. Inadequate mothering, with consequent insecure attachment and low self-esteem, is a frequent common denominator among female alcoholics, and among the poets in this study.[2]

"Lucius," an autobiographical figure in Bishop's early stories about her childhood, fixes his grandfather rum toddies on winter evenings. But Bishop's first mention of her own drinking does place it at the "age / of twenty or twenty-one"—during her junior year of college at Vassar, just before the repeal of Prohibition, when she and her literary friends would sit discussing politics and books in a local speakeasy, drinking bad wine out of teacups. In the summers, they brought bottles of Scotch and bourbon as "house presents" to one another, and drinking figures large in their chronicle of activities. Bishop drank destructively from this time forward, and the burden of concealing such a social liability on the small Vassar campus made her a solitary figure there. By about 1939, her life was dominated by her need for alcohol, and by the effects of heavy drinking on her body, on her mind, and on her relationships. Guilt and shame attached to her abuse of alcohol made it impossible for her to live her life comfortably, and alcoholism fed her sense of homelessness.

Elizabeth Bishop drank destructively because she was an alcoholic, and she was an alcoholic for a number of possible reasons. She may have inherited the tendency; her memoirs of her family reveal that there were alcoholics on both sides; as Bishop said "Father had to stop [drinking], and his father, and three uncles. It can be done" (OA 211). Alcoholism responds to environmental triggers as well. Not all children of alcoholics are affected by the condition; some event or series of events leads the potential problem drinker—who may have inherited a faulty alcohol-processing enzyme, or a tendency to fear strong emotion or direct confrontation—to her nemesis. In the lives of writers, as we have seen, those triggers might include the romantic notion of the drinking writer, the solitary and undefined nature of a writer's "work," or that belief that a writer needs to be free of ties to the mundane world in order to create.

Why Elizabeth Bishop in particular developed alcoholism, we may never know. But why she drank at all is a more interesting question, and is as individual to a writer as her education or personal background. The answer posited in "A Drunkard" is comprehensive: many users of alcohol report drinking to fill a perceived void, and the ache at the heart of that poem is the distance between the child in her crib and the mother on the lawn, and the harsh words that are their only exchange. There was a void at the center of Elizabeth Bishop's life: her father had died when she was eight months old, her mother was mentally ill and permanently institutionalized when Elizabeth was five, and her daughter never saw her again. Raised in the homes of relatives in Massachusetts and Nova Scotia, Bishop never acquired the knack of homemaking; that is, of finding a permanent place to call home, or of feeling at home where she lived. Bishop was aware of this void, but she was poorly suited by temperament and training to confront it, mourn for it, heal it. She chastised herself for lapses in her restraint (she once compared herself unfavorably to the dolls of her childhood: "Their stoicism I never mastered / their smiling phrase for every occasion") (EAPJ 102). In a nature so reticent, which kept painful memory and personal anguish even from itself, alcohol provided license to talk, to cry, to stop being the stoical New Englander she'd been raised to be. But Bishop's friends reported that her most painful self-revelations often occurred in alcohol-induced "blackouts," and she would not remember having made them at all.

Elizabeth Bishop was troubled throughout her life by the physical sensation of the passage of time. She said she could feel, even hear time rushing past, and this worry finds its way into all her work—from letters and journals to published poems. In the prose version of the events also described in the poem "In the Waiting Room," the terrible anxiety that six-year-old

Elizabeth feels that day at the dentist's with her aunt is more explicitly associated with a rush to maturity, represented in the poem by her aunt, and the "awful hanging breasts" she sees in *National Geographic*. Unable to comfort herself with a precise reckoning of time ("In a few days it would be my seventh birthday"), she is caught in its unstoppable flow. "It was like coasting downhill, this thought, only much worse, and it quickly smashed into a tree. *Why* was I a human being?" (CPR 33). In her most cogent and persuasive statements about her use of alcohol, she said she drank in order to lose that dizzying sense of time rushing by. But the stepping out of time that being very drunk seemed to allow was itself frightening. When Robert Lowell in 1960 sent her a draft of his poem, "The Drinker," which begins, "The man is killing time—there's nothing else," she responded with empathy, identifying first with the man's falling out of time. "The sense of time is terrifying—have hours gone by, or one awful moment?—How long have the cars been parked?" She commended the "sense of release" of the poem's ending, "a sense . . . that only the poem, or another fifth of Bourbon, could produce" (OA 386). Bishop found brief respites from her anxiety about time by escaping New York for the easygoing tropical south—Mexico, Key West—finally settling for fifteen years in Brazil.

Bishop's nature was as fearlessly observant as it was reticent, and she also drank to escape the tyranny of that observing consciousness. Several times she complained in letters about the burden that her "famous eye" placed on her, and her autobiographical Robinson Crusoe laments in "Crusoe in England" that his nightmares are of

> other islands
> stretching away from mine, infinities
> of islands, islands spawning islands,
> like frogs' eggs turning into polliwogs
> of islands, knowing that I had to live
> on each and every one, eventually,
> for ages, registering their flora,
> their fauna, their geography. (CPO 165)

He then ferments his island's one kind of berry and makes home brew.

Hemingway's oft-quoted point about drinking in order to stop writing when he had done his day's work is useful, although by middle age Hemingway was combining alcohol with work to the detriment of both his health and his art. Bishop herself, like all of the women in this study, could not write productively and drink heavily at the same times in her life, and her long fallow periods often correspond to times when her drinking fell out of control. This separates her from still other writers, mostly male, who argue that because poets are inhibited by the world, they must drink in order to escape it, to free themselves to write. Bishop could write only when she was firmly "in" the world.

Bishop may also have fallen victim to an "environmental trigger" akin to the mythos of the "drinking writer" that had developed so forcefully in the generation just older than hers; in Bogan and Millay, for example. Studying the surrealists in France in 1936 and 1937, she would have imbibed along with Pernod, the highly romantic notion of the suffering artist. She never claimed a wish for a place in such a fellowship, but certainly the model of the tormented and troubled poet was attractive to her, and to others of her own generation.

The progress of alcoholism through Bishop's life was both idiosyncratic and typical. She began drinking in college in response to social pressure and the need to free herself from personal shyness. She believed in dreams and the unconscious as sources of creative power, and the release that alcohol provided her was intensely interesting to her. She was accompanied in her use of alcohol by her college friends, although by the end, she was beginning to be embarrassed and secretive in her drinking. As she finished college, several conditions under which Bishop would live her adult life became clear to her: she had no home to return to from college, and would wander the world in search of one; she would be uncomfortable being alone even for brief periods of time; she would continue to suffer, as she had since childhood, from debilitating asthma and allergies, and from serious depression; she had fallen in love with her college roommate and would endure a long struggle to come to terms with the fact that her romantic passion would be for women; and she would try to make a life in a most solitary, competitive, and uncertain vocation—as a writer. All of these conditions embarrassed her to silence, and required consolation from time to time. And they tended to encourage Bishop in the consumption of that cheap and readily available anesthetic, alcohol. She drank bourbon by choice, but is seen in her own descriptions of her travels sampling the national beverages wherever she goes: Newfoundland rum, Irish whiskey, the fiery sugarcane liquors brewed in tropical climates.

In the long period between her graduation from college in 1934 and the publication of her first book, *North & South*, in 1946, Bishop established the drinking pattern of a classic dipsomaniac—that is, she was sober for long periods of time, but was liable to alcoholic binges lasting several days. These binges made her ill, tended to bring on attacks of asthma that required hospitalization, and yet also permitted her the only release of emotion and misery that she was capable of at the time. She often used the long-distance telephone when drunk, calling friends and talking of her difficulties; sometimes she told her stories to those nearer at hand. Almost invariably, she would not later remember the conversations, and full of shame and self-loathing, issued apologies all around, and resolved to reform. In 1946, she consulted a psychiatrist, Dr. Ruth Foster, in part in hopes of finding a way to stop drinking destructively.

The pain and uncertainty of these post-college years cast a pall over Bishop's gifts and ambitions as a poet so formidable that not even the warm reception of *North & South* could dispel it. And the book's reviewers located within the poems a moral vision, a firm sense of right and wrong, of control, that Bishop could hardly have recognized in herself. For example, Randall Jarrell praised her poems in specifically moral terms: "Instead of crying, with justice, 'This is a world in which no one can get along,' Miss Bishop's poems show that it is barely but perfectly possible—has been, that is, for her . . . [her poems tell us] that morality, for the individual, is usually a small, personal, statistical, but heartbreaking or heartwarming affair of omissions and commissions the greatest of which will seem infinitesimal, ludicrously beneath notice, to those who govern, rationalize, and deplore."[3] This praise may have been sweet to Bishop, but it must also have seemed nonsensical, so much was her life at this time a slippery moral struggle to "do well," as she saw it—in her relationships both sexual and platonic, in the eternal dilemma of "work," and with alcohol.

The slough of depression into which Bishop had fallen deepened over the next four years, as the alcohol binges became separated by fewer and fewer periods of sobriety. In June 1949, she checked herself into a private sanitarium in Blythewood, Connecticut, where she spent two months under the care of doctors and psychologists. She spent the following year as the poetry consultant to the Library of Congress, her first nine-to-five job, and she missed many days and weeks of work because of asthma attacks and alcoholic illness. At the Yaddo artists' retreat in Saratoga Springs in both 1949 and in the fall of 1950, she suffered so acutely from loneliness and shyness, and from the implicit competitiveness among the guests, that she retreated often to the oblivion of drunkenness for consolation. In the small (but generally tolerant) community of the colony, Bishop's troubles with alcohol were well known, and this deepened her sense of shame and isolation.

In the fall of 1950 at Yaddo, Bishop was caught up in what she called a "brainstorm" of writing and drinking that yielded late in November an awful moment of self-awareness. On the night that a hurricane raged through New York and New England (November 25), Bishop felt she had reached bottom. She wrote to her doctor, Anny Baumann, on the morning after:

> I'm going to write you a letter that I'll probably not send but maybe I'll re-read it every day as a reminder to myself. I've been having a sort of brainstorm ever since I got here, just can't stop writing, can't sleep, and although at the time I wrote before I had managed not to drink for a stretch, I've certainly made up for it since & made a damn fool of myself & got into a peck of troubles.—& made a very good friend of mine here very unhappy.
>
> Well, last night as the trees came crashing down all around me and I felt like death, it seemed a sort of natural phenomenon equal to the brainstorms and I suddenly made up my mind. I will *not* drink. I've been stalling along now for years & it's absolutely absurd. Dr. Foster said: "Well, go ahead, then—ruin your life"—and I almost have. I also know I'll go insane if I keep it up. I *cannot* drink and I know it. . . .
>
> I shake so I can't sign my name. (OA 210–11)

Later Bishop discovered that the "trouble" she had assumed had not materialized, and she lost her resolve. The link she draws here between creative inspiration (the "brainstorm") and heavy drinking is common to the experience of many alcoholic artists, but rare in Bishop's life. After a three-weeklong binge, she spent Christmas week, 1950, in the Saratoga Hospital, one of many holiday seasons she would spend in or near hospitals.

Bishop wandered around New York and New England for another year, before Anny Baumann insisted that she leave the scenes of her acutest misery. On November 10, 1951, she left New York harbor on the S.S. Bowplate, headed for Brazil and a trip around the world.

The first stop on the freighter trip was Santos, Brazil, and there Bishop disembarked in order to visit friends from the United States then living in Rio de Janeiro. Pearl Kazin was there with her husband Victor Kraft, and Bishop also wanted to visit two women she had met briefly ten years earlier in New York, Brazilian Lota de Macedo Soares, and her American friend,

Mary Stearns Morse. Within two months, Bishop had fallen in love with Lota Soares, and had decided to make her home, for the time being, with Lota in Brazil. Thus began the only extended period of personal happiness in Bishop's adult life, and she also began, with Soares's formidable help, to regain control of her drinking.

Bishop suffered from very serious asthma attacks in her first months in Brazil, not surprising among the tropical molds and mildews and the menagerie of animals in Lota's mountain home outside the resort town of Petrópolis, Brazil. In mid-1952, Anny Baumann prescribed from long distance a course of oral and injected cortisone, the first such treatment Bishop had received. At first, her response to the cortisone was euphoric—she could breathe for the first time in months. But cortisone's common side effects include nervousness and sleeplessness. For a while Bishop enjoyed the wakefulness; she wrote, for the first time, long pieces of autobiographical prose, the strongest of which, "In the Village," she said she wrote right on the typewriter, on "a combination of cortisone and the gin and tonic I had in the middle of the night."[4] When the nervousness became intolerable, she began to medicate herself with alcohol. Because she was an alcoholic, she was unable to control the drinking on her own. At Lota's insistence, in early 1953 Bishop entered a hospital to dry out and there began aversion therapy for the first time, in the form of Antabuse (disulfiram). New on the market in the early 1950s, Antabuse was designed to make the drinker violently ill when he or she consumed alcohol, and was hailed as a possible cure for the disease of alcoholism at the time.

Bishop maintained her use of Antabuse and kept her drinking under control for nearly ten happy years in Brazil. She wrote well—her poems about Brazil are among her very best—and she also, in this period of clarity, gained almost total recall of her childhood in Nova Scotia and Boston, and wrote much about that as well. Not until 1961, when Lota Soares took a more-than-full-time job with the government of Rio de Janeiro and Bishop was left alone much of the time did she again fall into a pattern of destructive drinking. Bishop said she felt less guilty about her drinking in Brazil and that this freedom from the self-hatred and shame she had always associated with her alcoholism made it easier for her to drink moderately, and, with the help of Soares and of Antabuse, not to drink at all.

Lota Soares suffered a mental breakdown beginning in about 1964. In 1967 she committed suicide, and Bishop returned to the United States to live. In the face of this tragedy, Bishop's classic dipsomaniac pattern of alcoholism became more and more a pattern of continuous and excessive drinking. Grieving and feeling guilty over Soares's death, and unable to be alone even for short periods, Bishop was so much under the control of alcohol between 1968 and 1970 that she later could not contemplate these years without exquisite shame, both for her own degradation and for the pain she had caused those around her.

Through the intercession of her friend Robert Lowell, Bishop was hired to teach at Harvard University in the fall of 1970, and there she began to right her life. She did not stop drinking, but with the help of her new friend and lover Alice Methfessel, she was able to meet her classes and maintain her friendships, and even to write some of her greatest poems. They are collected in the slim volume called *Geography III*, published in 1976, and four more strong poems, "Santarém," "Pink Dog," "North Haven," and "Sonnet," followed between 1976 and her death in 1979. She felt less urgency about her drinking and was impatient with her friends' attempts to get her to stop. In a particularly bad time she wrote to Anny Baumann, with whom she had an appointment,

> . . . I'll be there—and sober. Please don't worry about that! [I am full of Antib [Antabuse]—at the moment—& couldn't possibly take a drink before Thursday, even if I wanted to. . . .]
>
> What I'm writing to ask you is this—*please* don't just discuss drinking with me, or scold me for any past lapses, *please*. There were two or three bad days about two weeks ago now—and I have talked & talked with Dr. Wacker (head of the Harvard Med. services) about this—OF COURSE I know I shouldn't drink, and I try hard not to. I have missed only one class in five years because of this and I have NEVER taken a drink before a class. . . . I feel I can't bear to be made to feel guilty *one more time* about the drinking. There *are* things that are worse, I think, and I hope you can help me with them. (OA 600)[5]

In this textbook alcoholic's denial, Bishop conceals the fact that she did miss numerous classes for reasons certainly related to drinking—hangovers, asthma attacks brought on by drinking, physical injuries incurred while she was drunk. And her careful calculation of the length of Antabuse's effectiveness ("before Thursday") belies her "even if I wanted to." But the self-possession in this voice was new to her, as if she had accepted the conditions under which she would live out her life, and had accepted responsibility for the consequences.

In fact, by this time the long periods of heavy drinking had begun seriously to affect Bishop's health, and she suffered almost continuously from associated illnesses and injuries. Her death in October 1979 from a cerebral aneurysm is a common one for lifelong alcoholics, as alcohol tends over time to thin the blood vessels of the brain. Her ability to write and to function as well as she did in the last years of her life is a result of both her own resilience of spirit and the steadfast caretaking of her friends.

Elizabeth Bishop published only one poem explicitly about alcoholism. Entitled "The Prodigal," the poem was written during the darkest period of the years just before she left for Brazil and a fresh start, appearing in the March 17, 1951, issue of the *New Yorker*. Bishop distanced herself from the poem's events by saying that its method was like "that spiritual exercise of the Jesuits—when they try to think in detail how the thing must have happened," and by identifying the poem's inspiration as her response when "one of my aunt's stepsons offered me a drink of rum, in the pigsties, at about nine in the morning," on her trip to Nova Scotia in 1946 (OA 479). But the poem is also a self-conscious presentation of her own solitary battle with alcohol between 1948 and 1950, perhaps the darkest period of that lifelong struggle.

> The brown enormous odor he lived by
> was too close, with its breathing and thick hair,
> for him to judge. The floor was rotten; the sty
> was plastered halfway up with glass-smooth dung.
> Light-lashed, self-righteous, above moving snouts,
> the pigs' eyes followed him, a cheerful stare—
> even to the sow that always ate her young—
> till, sickening, he leaned to scratch her head.
> But sometimes mornings after drinking bouts
> (he hid the pints behind a two-by-four),
> the sunrise glazed the barnyard mud with red;
> the burning puddles seemed to reassure.
> And then he thought he almost might endure
> his exile yet another year or more.

The physical description of alcoholic queasiness in this poem, attributed to the sow who eats her young and later to the staggering flight of bats in the barn, is compelling; but what links it most to Bishop's own self-described experience of alcoholism is its presentation of a person exiled from normal human relationships, from "home," by his own bestial behavior.[6] Living among pigs, he is at times inured to the smell, the mud, the dung, but Bishop insists that his exile is at least in part a matter of will—the prodigal, the wastrel, not yet having decided to return to be forgiven, need only decide and he may return.

> Carrying a bucket along a slimy board,
> he felt the bats' uncertain staggering flight,
> his shuddering insights, beyond his control,
> touching him. But it took him a long time
> finally to make his mind up to go home. (CPO 71)

Bishop's prodigal must "make his mind up to go home" (her syntax puts curious emphasis on the "up," as if it had moral significance, or as if he needed to make his mind up, to invent it, in the absence of a firm identity) and he is at times aware, "his shuddering insights, beyond his control," of what is required of him. The vaguely hopeful ending, suggesting that although he took a long time to make his mind up he eventually went home, leaves the emphasis on willpower, and echoes Bishop's belief at the time that self-discipline would be the cure to her lifelong (or adult lifelong) drinking problem. Although Bishop saw no clear "home" from which she was exiled, the picture of her relative removed from the home of her favorite aunt (who lived in the favorite home of Bishop's childhood, Great Village, Nova Scotia) out to the pigsty behind the barn is a fitting analog to her own experience of shame and isolation.

Had Bishop been born only a few years later (and with a somewhat less reticent character) she might have written more poems explicitly about alcoholism, might even have finished and published "A Drunkard." But trained as she was in the Modernist mode of impersonality in poetry—as Louise Bogan herself had articulated them for female poets—and conditioned as she was as a woman to be ashamed of the real circumstances of her life (and perhaps having made an aesthetic judgment about the lack of inherent interest in poems about drunkenness), she did not. In contrast to poets only slightly younger than herself—Robert Lowell, John Berryman,

W. D. Snodgrass, and, indeed, Isabella Gardner—Bishop actively objected to the confessional mode ("You just wish they'd keep some of these things to themselves," she memorably told *Time* magazine[7]), and so invested her profound emotion and personal struggle deep in the objects and places that serve as images in her poems. These "objective correlatives" are not rigid one-to-one correspondences, but fluid and developing personal metaphors. Examining these metaphors closely across Bishop's poetry and prose, one discovers that the story of her struggle with alcohol, as well as the story of the rest of her life, is told in her work, in her own reticent way. As with most of the other poets in this study, that imagery begins with the sea.

In a little parable written in 1937 called "The Sea and Its Shore," Bishop invented a loosely autobiographical character called Edwin Boomer (Bishop's mother's family was named Boomer). Boomer's job is to clean the litter off the beach at night and to burn it. He quickly becomes caught in a confusion of interpretation. Unwilling to believe that the information printed on the trash he collects is random or insignificant, he attempts to organize it. Overwhelmed by the flow of information and the necessity to judge, Boomer drinks, and when he drinks, the distinction between printed word and real world of sea and sand is lost—everything seems to be composed of type—and the ocean becomes an extension of Boomer's alcohol- and word-sodden world: "On nights that Boomer was most drunk, the sea was of gasoline, terribly dangerous. He glanced at it fearfully over his shoulder between every sentence he read, and built his fire far back on the beach. It was brilliant, oily, and explosive. He was foolish enough then to think that it might ignite and destroy his only means of making a living" (CPR 174).

The man alone among trash, discarded words, seeking the truth about language, recalls Wallace Stevens's "The Man on the Dump," whose "days pass like papers from a press."[8] The man on the dump is not apparently alcoholic, but he is homeless, even exiled, and the little poke at Keats that Stevens makes in the final stanza of his poem ("Did the nightingale torture the ear, / Pack the heart and scratch the mind?") raises the subject obliquely by reminding us that Keats's ode is in part a hymn in praise of the partial death, potentially restful, that is available to the hypothetical drinker. Keats's speaker is ambivalent about this oblivion (and alcohol is itself a metaphor in the ode) and the man on the dump comes to his "purifying change" stone-cold sober. But for Bishop, the flirtation with unconsciousness persisted, often with the specific goal of escaping the obligation "to see."

The image of water that is flammable, dangerous, about to explode re-curs frequently in Bishop's poems, recalling Bachelard's association of "the water that flames" with poetic inspiration in *The Psychoanalysis of Fire.*[9] The image occurs most often in Bishop's most self-reflective poems, poems whose composition corresponds in time with her most difficult negotiations with alcohol. This is not to say that those poems are "really" about alcoholism; only that when Bishop assesses herself in her poems, she is extraordinarily honest in that assessment.

The best-known fiery body of water occurs in Bishop's great poem "At the Fishhouses" (1948). Conceived during her trip "home" to Nova Scotia in 1946, the same trip that produced "The Moose" and the inspiration for "The Prodigal," the poem records a visit by the poet with an old fisherman "netting, / his net, in the gloaming almost invisible" outside the fishhouses of a small port. After nearly fifty lines of luminous description of the physi-cal scene, the poet is tempted to personal or philosophical speculation, but retreats from it:

> Cold dark deep and absolutely clear,
> element bearable to no mortal,
> to fish and to seals . . . One seal particularly
> I have seen here evening after evening.

She goes on to describe her humorous encounters with the seal, but is drawn again to the meaning of the scene, only again to retreat: "Cold dark deep and absolutely clear, / the clear gray icy water . . . Back, behind us, / the dignified tall firs begin." And then, unable to avoid the pull of the water any longer, she mentally plunges in:

> I have seen it over and over, the same sea, the same,
> slightly, indifferently swinging above the stones,
> icily free above the stones,
> above the stones and then the world.
> If you should dip your hand in,
> your wrist would ache immediately,
> your bones would begin to ache and your hand would burn
> as if the water were a transmutation of fire
> that feeds on stones and burns with a dark gray flame.
> If you tasted it, it would first taste bitter,

then briny, then surely burn your tongue.
It is like what we imagine knowledge to be:
dark, salt, clear, moving, utterly free,
drawn from the cold hard mouth
of the world, derived from the rocky breasts
forever, flowing and drawn, and since
our knowledge is historical, flowing, and flown. (CPO 65–66)

The water so cold it burns is first, of course, a physical description of
the icy-cold water of the North Atlantic. But at the same time, in a poem in
which Bishop is considering her origins—on her first visit to her mother's
home since her death there in 1934—the cold water both reflects the absence of maternal warmth in her life and perhaps the drug with which she
medicated that sense of loss. The shifting sea of knowledge is both general
and communal ("It is like what *we* imagine knowledge to be"), and highly
personal, as the startling image of rocky breasts makes her speculations suddenly physical again. The fleeting nature of both kinds of knowledge remind
one of the "shuddering insights, beyond his control" of "The Prodigal," and
we see that this is another exiled figure, trying to make her mind up about
her place in the world. Here she contemplates the choice between the impoverished but beautiful land and the tempting oblivion of the paradoxical, and
alcohol-like, sea—cold but burning; like knowledge, but promising death.

The fiery water returns a couple of years later in "The Bight," also a
poem of reticent self-examination. The subtitle, "[*On my birthday*]," ("Thirty-
seven and far from heaven," she noted elsewhere), guides our reading of the
apparently "objective" description of excavations underway in the harbor
(the Key West Bight) in Key West in 1948. The poem begins by describing
the water:

At low tide like this how sheer the water is.
White, crumbling ribs of marl protrude and glare
and the boats are dry, the pilings dry as matches.
Absorbing, rather than being absorbed,
the water in the bight doesn't wet anything,
the color of the gas flame turned as low as possible.
One can smell it turning to gas; if one were Baudelaire
one could probably hear it turning to marimba music. (CPO 60)

The juxtaposition of pilings dry as matches and water turning to gas both recalls the flammable water of "The Sea and Its Shore," and sets the uneasy tone of the rest of the poem. It is about metaphor—correspondences—and the metaphors are expressed in terms of potential violence. Pelicans crash into the water like pickaxes; man-of-war birds have tails like scissors; shark tails are sharp like plowshares; the boats "lie on their sides, stove in, / and not yet salvaged, if they ever will be, from the last bad storm." It is a poem about disorder, and the subtitle suggests a "correspondence" between the disorder without and the disorder within.

The mention of Baudelaire recalls both the French poet's idea of *correspondance,* which is the poem's apparent subject, and his decadent, inebriated reputation, which is its implicit subject. The comparison between the unsalvaged boats and "torn open, unanswered letters" first appeared in a letter from Bishop to Robert Lowell from January 1948. Describing the same bight, she wrote, "The water looks like blue gas—the harbor is always a mess, here, junky little boats all piled up, some hung with sponges and always a few half sunk or splintered from the most recent hurricane—it reminds me a little of my desk" (OA 154). The poem's central pun derives from this: "The bight is littered with old correspondences." This in turn recalls Stevens's man on the dump's matter-of-fact statement: "The dump is full / Of images."[10] Like Bishop's bight, Stevens's dump was real, as was the man; Stevens walked by them often near his home in Hartford, and like the bight the dump represents a reality that cannot be softened through poetry. Perched upon his pile of images and worn-out poetic tropes, the man on the dump is also testing the legitimacy of metaphoric language that has lost its necessary connection to the real: "The moon is creeping up. / The sun is a corbeil of flowers the moon Blanche / Places there, a bouquet / Ho-ho." Or, "the floweriest flowers dewed with the dewiest dew." The man on the dump's tentative resolution comes when the moon finally creeps above the pile of images upon which he sits, on its own: "the moon comes up as the moon," he says, into an "empty sky." It seems likely that Bishop nods at Stevens here, although her subject is finally quite different, shifting from Stevens's concern with how to *say* reality to her own with how to *see* it. This is "The Bight"'s major subject and a major concern in Bishop's poems—in "The Armadillo," for example, where the reality of a hillside fire asserts itself against the poet's romanticizing vision. And in "Anaphora," her poem about sunset in Key West—Stevens's territory, of course—Bishop refines this idea by having the revelation about the sun's "endless / endless assent" occur not to the "drift of bodies" gathered for the view, but to "the beggar in the park," "without lamp or book"—like Stevens's willfully unlettered man who is able, momentarily anyway, to see the moon for what it is.[11]

The famous last lines of Bishop's poem, "All the untidy activity continues, / awful but cheerful," took some time for her to discover. The drafts of "The Bight" offer numerous alternatives to the two adjectives, among them a pair that strongly suggest that she was also thinking about alcohol as she wrote the poem: the phrase "poisonous but relaxing" is penned in the margin of one of the drafts.[12] It is of course impossible to know what Bishop's intentions for the phrase might have been; but the two-sidedness of alcohol's effect in her life is certainly reflected in it. The final version of the ending Bishop recalled a couple of weeks after the poem appeared in February 1949. The spring of 1949 was one of the most difficult of Bishop's life and alcohol played no small part in her misery. She wrote with apologies to Anny Baumann in March,

> . . . a day or so after I got back everything just seemed to blow up. It was all aggravated by worrying about this "job" [at the Library of Congress] (still uncertain) and a couple of other problems that I really can't do anything about at all.
> . . . I am hoping . . . that this last sad business I put my friends and myself through may mark the beginning of some sort of metamorphosis.
> Everyone has been unbelievably kind. You know I'm sorry so I won't say that. I'm taking the pills and at least feel sane again and thank you once more for your help. . . .
> ps: I think I'll enclose a poem about Key West that was in *The New Yorker* a few weeks ago. . . . if I can just keep the last line ["awful but cheerful"] in mind, everything may still turn out all right. (OA 184)[13]

Clearly, Bishop devised the description in the "The Bight" to reflect her current circumstances, as well as her poetic concerns. Despite its "objective" tone, it is one of her most personal poems, reflecting the "mess" of her life at the time.

One sees imagery related to fiery water in a few other poems of this period; but the image all but disappears from Bishop's poetry during her happy years in Brazil, and by the time she came to write the poems of *Geography*

III in the early 1970s, the cultural revolutions of the 1960s had made it possible for even Elizabeth Bishop to make explicit reference to drinking in her poems. "Crusoe in England"'s home brew comes to mind, as does the *grog à l'américaine* of "The End of March." But several critics have noted the startling and ubiquitous presence of volcanoes and lavalike substances in the poems of *Geography III,* and we are once again in the realm of "firewater"—in the deeply self-assessing "In the Waiting Room" (1971), "Crusoe in England," and "The Moose" (1972), at least. But in the cryptic late poem "Night City," the firewater returns explicitly and again the personal connection is compelling. On its first level a faux-naive description of the view of a city from a plane at night, the poem's metaphors are characteristic:

> No foot could endure it,
> shoes are too thin.
> Broken glass, broken bottles,
> heaps of them burn.
>
> Over those fires
> no one could walk:
> those flaring acids
> and variegated bloods.
>
> The city burns tears.
> A gathered lake
> of aquamarine
> begins to smoke.
>
> The city burns guilt.
> —For guilt-disposal
> the central heat
> must be this intense.
>
> Diaphanous lymph,
> bright turgid blood,
> spatter outward
> in clots of gold
>
> to where run, molten,
> in the dark environs

green and luminous
silicate rivers.

In its surrealism, its preference for the intense visual image over the predominantly narrative impulse of most of her other late poems, "Night City" has more in common with the poems of *North & South* than with those of *Geography III*. For this reason, the return of the burning water image suggests a figured presentation of alcoholism once again. Just back from Brazil to a northern city in 1971, when the poem was written, Bishop revisited the scenes of her early misery. Even the fanciful surrealism of her description here is expressed in terms familiar from elsewhere in Bishop's thinking about her life. She often described herself as "born guilty," for as long as she could remember convinced of her own vague but terrible responsibility, possibly the result of her mother's illness and disappearance. An anxious and free-floating guilt is also the emotional milieu of the alcoholic, along with the related feeling of shame, especially for women.[14] The poem "Five Flights Up," the final poem in *Geography III,* speaks directly to this shame; there the speaker contrasts her own guilt-burdened mornings to the carefree innocence of birds and dogs. For Bishop, the fact that "The city burns tears" and "The city burns guilt" makes it almost necessarily a figure for her psychological and emotional life as it related to alcohol. The final image of the "careful" creature overhead, presumably the plane itself, walking in a rhythm measured by the blinking lights on its wings, "green, red; green, red," offers a hope of transcendence, or at least of tenuous control, perhaps in the form of measured language, or poetry.

Readers have pointed out other kinds of water imagery in Bishop's poems, in particular the figure of the ocean wave in its tension-release, expand-extinguish, or advance-retreat pattern. Robert Lowell observed it first in his review of *North & South* in 1947, recognizing that Bishop's poems typically presented "two opposing factors": "The first is something in motion, weary but persisting, almost always failing and on the point of disintegrating, and yet, for the most part, stoically maintained. . . . The second factor is a terminus: rest, sleep, fulfillment or death."[15] This kind of imagery occurs very often in Bishop's early poems, beginning with "The Wave," which she wrote while in high school. While it is tempting to think of the local oblivion that occurs every time a wave meets the shore (ripples "extinguish themselves / against the walls" in "Quai d'Orleans") as figuring the oblivion that drunkenness offers as well, the imagery belongs first to the natural environment of a poet who lived all her life on the Atlantic coast, as well as to a broad theme of retreat and withdrawal that occurs throughout Bishop's work, from the "Sonnet" of 1928 to "The End of March" (1974) and "Santarém" (1978). The impulse to drink may be psychologically related to the impulse to retreat, and the two are explicitly linked in "The End of March."

Almost equally ubiquitous in Bishop's work is the semiconscious figure, half awake or half asleep, dreaming or daydreaming or barely thinking at all. The image also characterizes Bishop's way of thinking—like Léonie Adams, she was fascinated by those margins of consciousness and interested in dreams as a source of unconscious material for poems. (She specifically identified "Varick Street" and "In the Waiting Room" as having substantial dream-derived content.) Many times she described in journals the phenomenon of opening her eyes in the morning and viewing familiar objects and furniture from the reclining angle. The same sensation is described in her poem "Sleeping Standing Up," one of several she wrote specifically about dreaming:

> As we lie down to sleep the world turns half away
> through ninety dark degrees;
> the bureau lies on the wall
> and thoughts that were recumbent in the day
> rise as the others fall,
> stand up and make a forest of thick-set trees. (CPO 30)[16]

And yet, other versions of semiconsciousness seem more specifically linked to the use of alcohol. Bishop dedicated "Little Exercise" (1946) to her friend and perhaps lover Tom Wanning, who also suffered from alcoholism. The poem describes an electrical storm in Florida, and what is interesting is that the poem's ostensible subject is unaware of the storm at all. The speaker directs us, and perhaps him, to picture the scene:

> Think of the storm roaming the sky uneasily
> like a dog looking for a place to sleep in,
> listen to it growling. . . .
>
> Think of the boulevard and the little palm trees
> all stuck in rows, suddenly revealed
> as fistfuls of limp fish-skeletons.

It is raining there. The boulevard
and its broken sidewalks with weeds in every crack
are relieved to be wet, the sea to be freshened.

Now the storm goes away again in a series
of small, badly lit battle-scenes,
each in "Another part of the field."

Think of someone sleeping in the bottom of a row-boat
tied to a mangrove root or the pile of a bridge;
think of him as uninjured, barely disturbed. (CPO 41)

This image of someone sleeping through a thunderstorm and missing the transformations wrought by lightning and rain seems harmless enough, until one places the poem in the context of Bishop's other work. The Florida thunderstorm is the central image of several other Bishop poems, notably the unpublished "It is marvellous to wake up together" (EAPJ 44) and "Rain Towards Morning" (1950).[17] Both of these are love poems. Although the meaning of the electricity generated by the storm and in the relationships is ambiguous, in both cases the storm is carefully observed and described. This poem, set in the same scene, dedicated to a lover, and describing both the storm itself and the subject's unnatural unconsciousness of the electricity in the air, suggests the sadness of what is missed by the drinker who has (safely) withdrawn from the emotional field.

"Love Lies Sleeping" (1938) identifies for the only time in Bishop's published work the moment of waking up with the effects of an alcoholic hangover. Set in New York, the troubled emotional territory of poems like "Varick Street" and "The Man-Moth," it prefigures "Night City" in the surrealism of its imagery:

Earliest morning, switching all the tracks
that cross the sky from cinder star to star,
coupling the ends of streets
to trains of light,

now draw us into daylight in our beds;
and clear away what presses on the brain:
put out the neon shapes
that float and swell and glare

down the gray avenue between the eyes
in pinks and yellows, letters and twitching signs.
Hang-over moons, wane, wane!

Two-thirds of the way through the poem, after describing "the immense city, carefully revealed," the speaker identifies herself as "I": "I hear the day-springs of the morning strike," and then, omniscient above the urban world, where even love is cruel, she issues a wish or a prayer:

Scourge them with roses only,
be light as helium,

for always to one, or several, morning comes,
whose head has fallen over the edge of his bed,
whose face is turned
so that the image of
the city grows down into his open eyes
inverted and distorted. No. I mean
distorted and revealed,
if he sees it at all. (CPO 16–17)

Bishop once told an interviewer that "the man" at the end of this poem was dead. That seems to me the least interesting way to read the poem, and Bishop was notoriously unwilling to help critics interpret her. The figure is hungover, the poem all but tells us, a subject Bishop would have been unhappy discussing with an interviewer, which may also account for the careful separation of the poem's author and speaker, by gender and person, from the man himself. But the image asks the hard question: how much of the surrealism, of the fascination with altered perspective, of the transforma-tion of ordinary objects into things beautiful and strange in Bishop's poetry had to do with the poet's use of alcohol? This is impossible to know, and unpleasant to ask. Unlike Lewis Hyde, who in an essay for the *American Poetry Review* in 1975, argued that it was booze, and not John Berryman, that wrote *The Dream Songs*.[18] Bishop—and all the poets in this book—were artists before they were alcoholics. And Bishop was an extraordinarily tenacious reviser of her own work, more concerned with craft than with publishing promptly; no drunken inspiration would pass from her hand unedited. But their dependence on alcohol throughout their poetic careers suggests that, almost of necessity, alcohol will sometimes be a subject in these poets' work, will sometimes be represented in their imagery. As Bishop expresses it here, if the drinker/poet is lucky, the drug she uses distorts the world, but revelation is the compensation. If she is not, she is hopelessly cut off from the world, unable to see it at all. It is probable that alcohol worked both of these ways in Elizabeth Bishop's life, as in the lives of all of these poets.

Chapter 8

Jean Garrigue

An Epilogue

he small body of biographical writing about Jean Garrigue (1912–1972) describes her in terms that suggest that she struggled with alcohol. J. D. McClatchy, in his introduction to her *Selected Poems* (1992), noted her "metaphysical drive toward excess" and her "passionate life," "fraught with . . . obsessions."[1] Her friend Stanley Kunitz called her "our one lyric poet who made ecstasy her home,"[2] and others refer to her "Dionysian temperament." On the face of it, her solitary, childless life, her numerous medical problems, and her growing melancholy resemble those of the other poets in this study, poets whose lives came to be dominated by alcohol dependence. Garrigue's poet contemporaries (she was a near-exact contemporary of John Berryman, Randall Jarrell, and Elizabeth Bishop),

Courtesy Virginia Hermann

who were enormously respectful of her work, spoke of her life with a kind of pitying condescension that I have come to associate with the unspoken disapproval with which female heavy drinkers are regarded. When I first planned this study, I had Garrigue penciled in among its subjects.

On the advice of Lee Upton, author of a lovely book-length critical study of Garrigue's poems, I wrote to Garrigue's friend, poet Jane Mayhall, and asked what she knew about Jean's drinking habits. Mayhall responded immediately and directly: "If alcoholism is the subject of your book, Jean Garrigue is not a candidate. . . . Jean Garrigue was *not* an alcoholic. [S]he was intoxicated on life, and didn't go for booze or drugs."[3] And so I put Jean Garrigue temporarily aside. A couple of years later, I wrote to Aileen Ward, executor of Garrigue's estate, to ask if a biography of Garrigue was in the works and if I might consult the biographer. Ward graciously met with me, and eventually I decided to embark on the daunting task of writing a critical biography myself, telling the story of Garrigue's remarkable life alongside the story of her work.

Thousands of pages of letters, journals, notebooks, and archival materials later, I have come to agree with Mayhall's assessment. Jean Garrigue certainly drank—as a young woman she drank heavily and regularly and apparently with the studied aim of achieving various kinds of ecstasy—but she was not an alcoholic; that is, she never became physically dependent on alcohol, never found drinking to be a problem, in itself, in her life. In this she was blessed—by temperament, by heredity, or by self-discipline she was able to make use of alcohol in the ways all of these poets sought to make use of it, without becoming addicted. She probably *was* what we think of as an addictive personality, prone to obsessions and literally addicted to cigarettes and coffee, for example, but she was not an alcoholic. Her use of alcohol, however, and its relationship to her work makes her an instructive counterpoint to the other poets in this study.

Jean Garrigue was born Gertrude Louise Garrigus, on December 8, 1912, in Evansville, Indiana. A child of her mother's middle age, "Louise" was raised for the most part by her beloved older sister Marjorie, born in 1901. Values in the household were solidly midwestern, but the family possessed a strain of artists as well. Louise's father, Allan C. Garrigus, had published more than a dozen short stories in local newspapers before giving it up to become a successful inspector for the U.S. Postal Service. Her older brother, Ross (born in 1894), was a newspaper editor and columnist in Vincennes, Indiana; and Marjorie was an accomplished concert pianist, a gifted interpreter of Chopin.

This idealistic, artistic tendency expressed itself most purely in young Louise. From the start, she was an imaginative, impulsive, and spirited child, given in school to calculated rebellions and floutings of rules (on the order of walking down the right side of the school staircase rather than the mandated left, persisting in this to the point of being suspended from high school. In later life, her niece remembers her sitting under the no-smoking sign on the Coney Island Ferry, puffing away.) She was passionate and romantic, prone to crushes on teachers and classmates at Shortridge High School in Indianapolis, in love with the feeling of being in love. Her family was concerned. When Marjorie married in 1924, they formalized the established arrangement, and put Louise under the special care and training of Marjorie's husband, Fred Smith, who was also managing the concert career of his wife.

Fred Smith was a writer and novelist himself, founder of the well-known radio program *March of Time* and an editor in *Time* magazine's radio division. He was also a fanatical idealist, conservative almost to the point of fascism (he later toured Nazi Germany and expressed his "admiration" for Hitler) and he sought to shape his sister-in-law according to his own ideals. First from afar (his letters to her are nearly all preserved in the carbons he carefully kept), and then when Louise moved in with them after high school, he attempted to dictate every aspect of Louise's development as a woman and a writer, above all to quash her romantic tendencies and what he saw as her self-indulgence. He was generous: he and Marjorie took Louise to France with them for extended stays in 1931 and 1932, easily the most important events of her adolescence; he took Louise's work seriously and responded carefully to every piece she sent him. He was also hard, opinionated, disapproving, and dictatorial. Soon after their second trip to Europe, Louise rejected the arrangement and returned home to Indianapolis to attend Butler College. A year later, she launched herself by transferring to the University of Chicago, changing her name to Jean (signing her letters home with a single initial formed by joining J and L back to back). She completed her bachelor's of arts degree in English in 1937, and stayed on for a year with the idea of completing a master's degree, but left without writing the required thesis. Her close friends there included the poet/critic Stephen Stepanchev and novelist/poets Ruth Herschberger (*Adam's Rib*) and Marguerite Young. She was a central figure in the famous Poetry Club, and a passionate admirer of Edna St. Vincent Millay—her life and reputation more than her poems. Dreaming of New York and Europe, lack of funds forced her instead to make her way back to Indianapolis after college, where she became editor of the *North Side Topics,* a local news-and-shopping weekly, a compromise she hoped never to have to repeat.

"Jean Garrigus," as she signed herself in the *Topics,* wrote serious, imaginative, and lively copy for the newspaper, two signed columns each week and a great deal of the rest of the paper. These pieces comprised the "stringbook" she hoped would land her a job in New York. Ultimately, however, she just went. With no job and no regular family support, she lived from day to day on the kindness of friends and the occasional check from home. Never interested in material possessions, Jean needed money only for the barest necessities, and for her fondest dream: to return to Europe. In New York, briefly on the Upper West Side, and then, for the next thirty years, in the West Village, she set out to make herself a poet and to have the kind of experiences that would generate poems, to live unfettered by the need for a remunerative career, taking small editing and writing jobs when she had to. By nature and inclination a love poet, Jean sought her material in intense and passionate encounters with "beauty" in the form of men and women, regardless of their marital status or availability. The real intimacy in her life was with women, but she sought with energy intense and uncommitted liaisons with brilliant men. Among her lovers in the 1940s were Alfred Kazin, Delmore Schwartz, Richard Blackmur, and Allen Tate. The women she loved and with whom she had more lasting sexual and emotional relationships were also brilliant but ultimately less well known.

The 1940s in Greenwich Village was a heavy-drinking time and place. New York solidified its reputation as an alcohol production and consumption capital during the 1920s and Prohibition, and in the years leading up to World War II this reputation only increased. Garrigue used alcohol as it has always been used by human beings, to lubricate social encounters, to liberate herself from the inhibiting influence of her family's conservative values, to make herself more open to experiencing whatever the night might bring. A night owl since childhood, Garrigue habitually viewed the world from the point of view Elizabeth Bishop called "that world inverted / where left is always right, / where the shadows are really the body, / where we stay awake all night" (CPO 70). Alcohol helped to provide this sense of an alternative, bohemian world, night after night in the low-rent clubs and bars and dingy apartments and studios of the West Village. This was precisely the world from which Bishop ran in panic, to Key West and eventually to

Brazil (Bishop's Village apartment was on King Street, just south of West Houston), but Garrigue made it her home base for nearly all of her adult life. She rarely endured summers in New York, spending weeks and even months in the country homes of friends, and at the Yaddo and MacDowell artist retreats. Whenever she could afford it, she traveled in Europe. But for nearly twenty-five years she listed her permanent address as 4 Jones Street, New York.

Garrigue's letters during the 1940s are filled with references to drinking and nightlife, with unself-conscious apologies for what was said, done, or forgotten under the influence of alcohol the night before. The Village bohemians of Garrigue's generation—like those of Millay's generation before—made a studied effort to free themselves from what they saw as the lingering puritanical ethos in America, and drinking a lot and often was both a part of that effort and evidence of its success. For Garrigue, the free consumption of alcohol was a small piece of a much larger program for her life: she would seek out the most intense, romantic, unconventional experiences she could find, and she would continue to do so until her death in 1972 at the age of sixty. She would not marry, she would not involve herself in a monogamous, long-term relationship with any man or woman, she would not bear children (her several abortions attest to this determination), and she would never have a job lasting more than one academic year. Above all she would remain free of ties and open to experience, an uncompromising idealist in pursuit of material for poems. In the ferocity of her defense of this ideal life, she resembles no one in her family so much as her brother-in-law Fred Smith, with his opposite obsessions and idealisms.

Garrigue's determined idealism extended to her poetic practice, and I have come to see that the pitying manner with which some of her fellow poets referred to her had less to do with any aspect of her personal life (except perhaps her self-enforced solitude) and more to do with her stubborn refusal to give up her sense of how a poem should work and mean, in the face of changing fashions, editorial advice, and declining reputation. As the confessional mode, looser meters, open forms, and free verse came to dominate American poetry in the postwar years, Garrigue gave up an initial capital letter on every line of every poem only in her posthumous volume, *Studies for an Actress*, and never really abandoned her preference for strict meter, dense language, and complex and extended metaphor over direct, personal revelation. She thought of her poems as objects of art rather than acts of communication, and she defended that practice to the end.

Garrigue's one major concession to economic necessity was to force herself to live for a year in Iowa City, 1942–43, and earn a master's degree in English as one of the early graduates of what would come to be called the Iowa Writer's Workshop. Founded in 1936, the master's program in creative writing drew from the start some of the country's most talented young people as students and some of its best-known writers as faculty. Poet Paul Engle directed the program for twenty-five years beginning in 1941 and is responsible for its development into the most important MFA writing program in the country. Garrigue, and her friend and lover Marguerite Young, were among the first class of students he admitted. Garrigue studied literature for the most part at Iowa, and was a teaching assistant for Engle. She briefly considered staying on to earn a doctorate, but failed her half-hearted attempt at the qualifying examination. In any case the master's degree enabled her to teach literature and writing at the college and university level. Adjunct positions in English and creative writing programs were her economic fallback throughout her life, and she took real pleasure in helping young poets to find their voices. She lived on grants and prizes when she could, and taught when she had to (at first, grinding schedules of multiple composition sections at Bard and Queens Colleges in New York, later more reasonable appointments at Smith College, the University of Connecticut, and the University of Washington, as well as at writer's conferences).

Falling in love and escaping from love are the major dramas in Garrigue's personal life, and, as in the life of Edna Millay, they occur over and over again. A small, intense, beautiful, and charismatic young woman, Garrigue made it a conscious practice to attract men, "make them fall in love" with her, then reject them as soon as marriage threatened. She was often involved in dramatic and painful love triangles, usually involving herself and another woman and a man, but not in the common heterosexual configuration. The man was typically in love with Garrigue, Garrigue in love, or wanting to be, with both the man and the other woman, or the man and the woman both in love with Garrigue. This dynamic occurred several times in her life, most significantly in 1952–54, when she was in love simultaneously with novelist Josephine Herbst and poet Stanley Kunitz, both of whom were devoted to her. She came as close as she would ever come to marrying with Kunitz, and genuinely loved him, but in the end she chose to maintain her independence and her constant but nonmonogamous relationship with Herbst, which had been threatened by the liaison with Kunitz, and which ultimately lasted until Herbst's death in 1969. Garrigue's letters and journal entries are preoccupied with the extreme emotions of a love affair—from her first real crush on a high school classmate, Nan Reasoner, to the very end of her life, Garrigue loved to write about sexual and emotional ecstasy and misery to the point that the relationships seemed concocted to occasion the anguished notes, letters, and journal entries—and ultimately poems—that resulted. Real misery was involved (particularly on the part of the men and women Garrigue loved and rejected), but the point for Garrigue seems to have been the emotion itself and the writing she was moved to do in the face of it. Over and over again her disillusioned lovers accuse her of loving the anguish and the uncertainty; of insisting, whenever a relationship became comfortable or familiar, on returning to the painful, anxious stage by whatever means possible. Indeed, her love letters are very often tortured and torturing, selfish and self-indulgent at the same time as they are rich, eloquent, and full of beauty and drama.

This enthusiasm for tortured love affairs was like an addiction for Garrigue, and as she grew older and unhealthy and less able to attract lovers at will, she became depressed. Perhaps most people at that stage would settle however grudgingly into a comfortable, monogamous relationship, but Garrigue did not. She continued to have love relationships, particularly with women, to the end of her life, and continued to dream of meeting the person whose soul and spirit would be equal to her own. And insofar as Garrigue has a reputation today, it is as a love poet. The last editorial project of her life, completed by her friend, poet Nancy Sullivan, was the anthology *Love's Aspects: The World's Great Love Poems.* Sullivan wrote in her introduction to the volume: "Jean Garrigue's great physical beauty was matched by her ability to translate into words the pleasurable essence of bliss. Her own love poems are brilliant exercises in tension, studies in the inevitability of passion, 'Love stamps its foot but cannot slip the knot.' They sing the brilliant mystery of first discovery, 'When everything had excellence at once,' and the waning afterlight, 'The nothing else can equal after it.' . . . [and] she knew so well about the joy and disappointment of love, 'And though the smoke is gone there is some fire / in saying so.'"[4] That she could summon and inspire these extremes of feeling right to the very end of her life is perhaps her most distinctive personal and poetic characteristic.

Garrigue's poems show literally none of the typical imagery of alcohol and the wish for unconsciousness that the poems of Bishop, Bogan, Wylie, and, in counterargument, Millay, show. If Wylie's "highest form of existence

[was] sensationless,"[5] that was Garrigue's greatest fear. The poems don't discuss the questions of engagement and withdrawal so common to the other poets. Instead they present a vivid and fully engaged consciousness, seeking out the extremes of feeling and thought that the other poets dream of numbing. Like them, she has poems specifically about alcohol—in fact she seems to have felt no pressure other than her own aesthetic standards to disguise or figure her poems about alcohol at all. She doesn't say "I am drunk" in a poem, but she has numerous poems about the sensation of literal intoxication. Her poem called "The Drunk" condemns him for his loss of control, but almost celebrates his freed spirit: "Gone to the state of childishness or evil / The drunk feels free now to do everything, / Give him a tree and he will be an ape, / A gun and he will murder like an infantry / Or dance or fornicate or puke or sing."[6] At least twenty-five of Garrigue's 170 poems use the words "wine," "liquor," or "alcohol" in a literal sense. And, like the other poets, she is also inclined to use metaphors of intoxication with reference to beauty and art. But she did not write a "sanctuary poem," there is a comparative absence of sleeping or otherwise unconscious figures in her poems, and she did not contemplate fountains, rivers, or the sea half-wishing to drown in them. The fires about to ignite in her poems are not on bodies of water, but in the poet's soul and spirit. Even less than most writers, perhaps, Garrigue avoided comfort and domestic security, and when the poems seek beauty in nature, the point is not to sink into it and expire.

It is difficult to demonstrate an absence of imagery, but it is possible to see in Garrigue's work evidence of a woman writer who has made her peace with the conflicts and contradictions of the role. Her poems about alcohol are for the most part also about ecstasy, "The Drunk" being a notable exception. In "Incantatory Poem" (1957), the speaker awaits the arrival of "you," a lover, in an ecstasy of sexual anticipation, fueled by and figured as wine intoxication:

> Hearing that you would come who by my love
> Have dreamed me into your head these lost long days
> I have caught birds and freed their essential blaze
> For still I am as always my heart's hungering slave
> And thus but dream life into its beat form
> Singing up voices out of the wine-gay blood.

Water and wine being the elements
I was big with cliffs and water-wracking rocks
And huger than I my heart hearing your own
Racing thus to come nearest home with cloud
Under its rain-bearing leaves that were your name
Meaning waif of the tribe of cloud and rain,
Hearing that you would come, blood climbed on bone.

Hearing that you would come in the green cold days
Neither good nor great, my wine-flown blood
Got up incanting sleep's towers to the moon . . .

Continuing to desire and wait, the speaker sinks not into oblivion or un-consciousness but into art, into poetry:

Hearing that you would come . . .

I make a poem I shape upon a prayer
To this all-fathering dark now come to flower,
When day was broken and we lie
Crossed with birds out of your name
I stole by watches of the griefless dream
In the element of the wine-transfiguring world.[7]

Garrigue's typically difficult syntax renders this ending of the poem obscure, but what is clear is that the transformation the speaker seeks is abetted by wine, and that it is wholly positive. Garrigue liked "Incantatory Poem" best among her own love poems, and the poem speaks both to her love for Josephine Herbst (who was in this case returning from a long sojourn in Europe) and her view of wine as a spur to both love and art.

The sociable connection of alcohol with intimacy and creativity is continually enforced in Garrigue's work. "For Jenny and Roger (Firenze)" begins, for example,

Drunk on your gaiety,
Your charm and crazy grace,
And drunk upon the blitheness of your words,
I talked with you all night
And now I am spent.[8]

This weariness is not death or the desire for death, but has the sense of ful-fillment that Susan Glaspell tried to describe as "'a rarefied sense of being something nearer pure spirit'" following "a violent encounter with life," and that Upton Sinclair dismissed so archly: "I cannot recall ever having read a greater piece of nonsense from the pen of a modern emancipated woman."[9] It was a state that Garrigue actively sought and it was through love—and alcohol—that she most often found her way there.

Similarly, Garrigue found herself, in 1953, in the famous gardens of the Villa d'Este in Tivoli outside Rome, a Renaissance palace with an astonish-ing display of allegorical fountains, formed by channeling the river Aniene into a system of hydraulics unique in its time. Contemplating the ferns and mosses of the grottoes and the pools with dragons and gargoyles spewing jets of water from their mouths, and especially the spectacular plumes and falls of the giant, multilayered "Organ Fountain," she imagines herself im-mersed in the water of the fountain she thirstily contemplates, not drowned or struggling, but a part of the joyfully ejaculating element itself. This is the central stanza of "For the Fountains and Fountaineers of the Villa d'Este":

> Shield of the water and water wall,
> Water roots, tentacles, bars,
> Spears of water and bolts,
> I know nothing here but the sense
> In this downflowing fall
> Of the wilderness of eternity.
> And I am flailed to earth.
> I am dank as a river god
> Scallop on scallop of the primeval flat water leaf
> With no roots but in water, taking its substance from liquid,
> Coats me and jackets me over.
> I am dense as lichen,
> Primordial as fern,
> Or, like that tree split at its base,
> Covert for winter creatures and water-retreated life,
> Tip with my boughs very serpent green,
> Or in a grand spirit of play
> Spurt water out of my nostrils. (GSP 65–66)

This is water as elemental as Bishop's icy Atlantic, as potentially annihilating as for Millay's swimmer enmeshed in weeds, and the poem briefly contemplates the plunge of the water down into the mossy depths. But the poet will not retire there, literally gathering moss under the water or within the cave formed by the "tree split at its base." Instead she is a jet or a dragon or a laughing gargoyle, shooting the water back into the air.

Afterword

Cheryl Walker, in noting the prevalence of "Sanctuary" poems among the nineteenth-century "nightingale" poets, also noted the relative absence of such poems among male poets in the same period. Of course, Keats had imagined his temporary withdrawal in "Ode to Autumn" and Whitman heard his "whispers of the heavenly Death" in "Out of the Cradle Endlessly Rocking," but the specific extinction of self sought by the nightingales appears among male poets of the period only rarely.[1] My own study proceeds from the idea that male poets of this era found their subject matter less proscribed, so that if they were so inclined, poems about the kind of withdrawal afforded by alcohol and drinking appeared readily in their work. It is neither useful nor desirable to essentialize differences between male and female poets, or between drinking and nondrinking poets. And it is certainly the case that after the Beat poets of the 1950s and the turn toward the "confessional" mode in even "academic" American poetry of the 1960s and beyond, poets wrote and published poems about their own alcoholism and other addictions, about mental illness and criminal behavior, among other formerly submerged or absent subjects. Alcoholism was nothing short of a scourge in the generations of poets, both male and female, born between 1900 and 1918 or so, but the female poets by and large never made the transition to the confessional mode.[2] Although their self assessments are extraordinarily honest and self-aware, the discussion of alcohol in their work is distilled and figured, made both resonant and safe.

Even a cursory look at the work of male poets whose alcoholism was both acknowledged and discussed in their lifetimes reveals the relative openness of their representations of drinking experience and alcohol's effects. *The Dream Songs* of John Berryman (born 1914) are almost too easy a case and have already been much discussed in this regard. As Lewis Hyde pointed out, "Dream Song 29" ("There sat down, once, a thing on Henry's heart") can only be, in its last stanza, describing the guilt that preys on the alcoholic prone to blackouts:[3]

> But never did Henry, as he thought he did,
> end anyone and hacks her body up
> and hide the pieces, where they may be found.
> He knows: he went over everyone, & nobody's missing.
> Often he reckons, in the dawn, them up.
> Nobody is ever missing. (33)

Berryman's compelling humor aside here, the experience of a blackout, of a piece of time mysteriously gone missing, happened to all of the poets in this study at one time or another. Confessing so, however, was far too risky.

Similarly, no female poet—with the exception of Isabella Gardner, arguably—was content to appear drunk, herself, in a poem. Berryman's "Dream Song 5" offers a fine counterexample. Constructed in three movements, in this case stanzas, the poem has Henry drink his way through an airplane trip, from "Henry sats in de bar & was odd" to "Henry sats in de plane & was gay," where he gets up, presumably to use the restroom, during a bit of turbulence. After a vision of the Virgin in the clouds out the window, "his thoughts made pockets & the plane buckt," and he apparently jostles another passenger: "'Parm me, lady.'" Later, presumably on the ground, he is hungover and visionary again:

> Henry lay in de netting, wild,
> while the brainfever bird did scales;

Mr. Heartbreak, the New Man,
come to farm a crazy land;
an image of the dead on the fingernail
of a newborn child. (7)

This record of a whole drinking episode, from the first drinks in the airport bar to the stumbling embarrassment on the plane to the painful hangover, needless to say, appears nowhere in the work of the female poets of this generation. Although the final image of the poem is obscure (it has been identified as a reference to a legend mentioned by Cervantes), the poem characteristically makes reference to Henry's own death, imagined throughout the *Dream Songs*, but here from within the misery of his hangover.[4]

Robert Lowell's (born 1917) struggle with bipolar illness and alcohol is well recorded in his voluminous *Collected Poems,* particularly in the late sonnets that have done so much to obscure his reputation as a brilliant lyric poet. But his most explicit expression of the experience of alcoholism dates from 1960 and is practically a litany of the "life problems" by which male alcoholism is nowadays diagnosed. "The Drinker" begins, though, with the blackout experience Berryman described so memorably. "The man is killing time—there's nothing else." And there is "No help now from the fifth of Bourbon . . . // No help from his body, the whale's / warm-hearted blubber . . ."

Once she was close to him
as water to the dead metal.

He looks at her engagements inked on her calendar.
A list of indictments.
At the numbers in her thumbed black telephone book.
A quiver full of arrows.

Her absence hisses like steam,
the pipes sing . . .
even corroded metal somehow functions. [. . .]

The cheese wilts in the rat-trap,
the milk turns to junket in the cornflakes bowl,
car keys and razor blades
shine in an ashtray. (116–17)

The speaker of Lowell's poem is familiar from his work after *Life Studies*: a despairing man in upper-middle-class circumstances, in this case alienated from what had been the comfort of those circumstances by an alcoholic binge, or many. The poem's frankness about the losses attributable to alcoholism—time, in particular—is startling, beyond even that of Berryman.

Theodore Roethke (born 1908, thus closer in age to Bishop than to Lowell) was widely known during his lifetime to suffer from both bipolar illness and alcoholism. His manic periods and drinking binges were often extreme, and he wrote frankly about the necessity of his periodic plunges to the "depths" of the fire, his need to free himself from disciplined consciousness, to move from "knowing" to "not-knowing." His "mixed sequence" titled "The Abyss" contemplates an entire episode of such alcohol-fed mania, beginning with the anticipatory "aura":

> Is the stair here?
> Where's the stair?
> "The stair's right there,
> But it goes nowhere."
>
> And the abyss? the abyss?
> "The abyss you can't miss:
> It's right where you are—
> A step down the stair."

Then the poem moves through madness to the stillness beyond:

> Too much reality can be a dazzle, a surfeit;
> Too close immediacy an exhaustion:[...]
>
> So the abyss—
> The slippery cold heights,
> After the blinding misery,
> The climbing, the endless turning,
> Strike like a fire,
> A terrible violence of creation,
> A flash into the burning heart of the abominable;
> Yet if we wait, unafraid, beyond the fearful instant,
> The burning lake turns into a forest pool,

> The fire subsides into rings of water,
> A sunlit silence. (219, 220–21)

"Do we move toward God, or merely another condition?" the poet asks, as so many of the poets of this generation felt called upon to ask. For the male poets, there seems to have been some satisfaction, or some atonement, in writing frankly about the condition of drunkenness and the experience of alcoholism. For women of this generation, such "confession" would have cost too much, it seemed: their reputations as women and their aspirations to be taken seriously as poets in the Modernist moment.

Notes

Preface

1. Hecht, "The Points of Her Compass," 6.
2. *The Collected Poems of Edna St. Vincent Millay*, 591. Further references to Millay's poems will be to this volume and included in the text, marked "CPM."
3. Ransom, "The Poet as Woman," 797, 801.
4. Ibid., 802, 804.
5. *The Blue Estuaries*, 15. Further references to Bogan's poems will be to this volume, and will be cited in the text as "BE."
6. Walker, *The Nightingale's Burden*, 41.

Introduction: Women Poets and Alcohol

1. Meade, in *Bobbed Hair and Bathtub Gin*, takes on female drinking writers specifically if sensationalistically: Parker, Millay, Zelda Fitzgerald, and Edna Ferber.
2. Room and Collins, *Alcohol and Disinhibition*, 542. Roe, "Alcohol and Creative Work," also found no abstainers and many steady drinkers among the painters she studied, all born between the late 1870s and 1907.
3. Hamill, *Drinking Life*, 107, 182–83.
4. Grant, "Drinking and Creativity," 88.

5. Hyde, "Alcohol and Poetry" and "Berryman Revisited," both in Kelly and Lathrop, *Recovering Berryman,* 205–28 and 269–72, respectively; Mariani, *Dream Song.*

6. Jersild, *Happy Hours,* 45. Lukas, writing in the *New York Times Book Review* in 1985, did include Bogan, Jane Bowles, Lillian Hellman, Carson McCullers, Millay, Parker, Katherine Anne Porter, and Jean Stafford in his list of sixty-three American "literary scrooders" (26).

7. Notable among these studies are Drake, *First Wave*; Erkkila, *Wicked Sisters*; Gilbert and Gubar, *Shakespeare's Sisters*; Juhasz, *Naked and Fiery Forms*; Ostriker, *Stealing the Language*; and Walker, *Masks Outrageous and Austere.*

8. The gender bias in these measures has been noted. For example, women drinkers are far less likely than men to be arrested for drunkenness or to encounter problems at work as a result of drinking, both of which appear on most diagnostic lists. See Vaillant, *Natural History of Alcoholism,* 27; Jersild, *Happy Hours,* 227–28.

9. The heritability of the tendency toward alcoholism has been demonstrated in so-called adoption studies in which twin boys, separated at birth and raised separately, showed a four times greater chance of developing alcoholism if one biological parent was alcoholic, regardless of the drinking habits of the adoptive family. Curiously, studies on twin girls do not show the same correlation; girls are thought to be more influenced toward drinking than boys by alcoholism in family members with whom they live. See Vaillant, *Natural History of Alcoholism,* 66 and 123, for summaries of the research.

10. Ibid., 45.

11. Ibid., 164.

12. American Psychiatric Association, *Diagnostic and Statistical Manual of Mental Disorders,* 181.

13. Juda, "Relationship between Highest Mental Capacity and Psychic Abnormalities," 307.

14. Andreason, "Creativity and Mental Illness," 1292.

15. Lang et al., "Drinking and Creativity," 393.

16. See, for example, "Booze and the Writer," 30.

17. Hajcak, *Effects of Alcohol on Creativity,* 6381.

18. Quoted in "Liquor Is Quicker," 91.

19. Bachelard, *Psychoanalysis of Fire,* 83.

20. Ibid., 87.

21. Lyu, *Sun within a Sun,* 15.

22. Quoted in "Booze and the Writer," 26.

23. Berryman, *Dream Songs,* 74.

24. Kazin, "'The Giant Killer,'" 44, 50.

25. Ibid., 50.

26. Dardis, *Thirsty Muse,* 46.

27. Lyu, *Sun within a Sun*, 10.
28. Ibid., 15.
29. Taylor, "Literature and Addiction," 9.
30. Wilson, *American Earthquake*, 89–90.
31. Day and Smith, "Literary and Biographical Perspectives on Substance Use," 63.
32. Storr, *Dynamics of Creation*, xii.
33. Bachelard, *Psychoanalysis of Fire*, 92–93, italics in the original.
34. Leonard, *Witness to the Fire*, 233.
35. Wilsnack and Beckman, *Alcohol Problems in Women*, 117.
36. Ibid., 128–29.
37. Ibid., 143.
38. Potter-Efron and Potter-Efron, *Treatment of Shame and Guilt in Alcoholism Counseling*, 140–41.
39. Wilsnack and Beckman, *Alcohol Problems in Women*, 251.
40. London, *John Barleycorn*, 42–43, 50.
41. Wilsnack and Beckman, *Alcohol Problems in Women*, 254, 355.
42. Rhys, *Good Morning, Midnight*, 107.
43. Wilsnack and Beckman, *Alcohol Problems in Women*, 12; Jersild, *Happy Hours*, 45.
44. Quoted in Wilsnack and Beckman, *Alcohol Problems in Women*, 13.
45. Kingree, "Understanding Gender Differences," 267.
46. Wilsnack and Beckman, *Alcohol Problems in Women*, 13; Jersild, *Happy Hours*, 43.
47. VanAmberg, "Study of Fifty Women Patients," 247.
48. Curran, "Personality Studies in Alcoholic Women," 649, 653.
49. Wall, "Study of Alcoholism in Women," 944.
50. Ibid., 945.
51. Karpman, *Alcoholic Woman*, vii–viii.
52. Ibid., x.
53. Wilsnack and Beckman, *Alcohol Problems in Women*, 351. And, indeed, contemporary research has ratified and furthered many of the observations of these early studies (for example, that women's heavy drinking most often follows a specific life event such as a divorce or a miscarriage). My intent here is not to dismiss this research, only to show the assumptions from which much of it proceeded.
54. Sandmaier, *Invisible Alcoholics*; McConville, *Women under the Influence*; Jersild, *Happy Hours*.
55. Drowne, *Spirits of Defiance*, 34.
56. The "disease" concept of alcoholism had been understood in the nineteenth century, but had faded in the debate over Prohibition, which had a distinctly moral tone (see Levine, "Discovery of Addiction," 155).

57. Crothers, "Is Alcoholism Increasing among American Women?" 734.

58. Alcohol consumption in the United States peaked in the decade 1820 to 1830 (at more than three times the current average), before temperance became a favorite cause of the Age of Reform, but Rorabaugh says that although women drank in this period, they were prevented from drinking their share by "gender ideals" and were prevented from reporting their drinking by "delicacy"; *Alcoholic Republic,* 12.

59. Johnstone's work points out the paradox of AA's conceptualization of alcoholism as a disease that is immune to a medical cure—and argues that "disease metaphor" is a more accurate description than "disease entity." The paradox is to be tolerated because the concept is effective in freeing individuals from alcohol dependence; "Literature and Addiction," 10–15.

60. Travisano and Hamilton, 696.

61. The back flap of the Penguin USA 2006 edition of *The Portable Dorothy Parker* presents a comic strip–style digest of Parker's biography—"Born," "Mother dies," "Suicide attempt," "Miscarriage," "Enlarged liver," etc.—the panels of which could represent moments in nearly all of these poets' lives.

Chapter 1: Dorothy Parker

1. *The Portable Dorothy Parker,* 82. Further references to Parker's work will be to this edition, and will be included in the text, marked "PDP."

2. Douglas, *Terrible Honesty,* 24.

3. Wilsnack and Beckman, *Alcohol Problems in Women,* 351.

4. Sinclair, *Era of Excess,* 233, 236.

5. Wilsnack and Beckman, *Alcohol Problems in Women,* 247.

6. None of the "collected works" volumes of these poets contains the work that the poets themselves took less seriously, but was nonetheless a part of their lifetime production. For Bishop, this would include a few finished and numerous unfinished poems and prose pieces and thousands of letters; for Bogan, the product of more than thirty-five years of writing criticism and reviews for *The New Yorker* and other publications; for Millay, her plays and pseudonymous prose sketches; and for Wylie, her lengthy and well-researched novels. Nonetheless, all of these poets, with the exception of Wylie, lamented her own lack of production in the genre she most valued, and more than one of them attributed that lack of production to struggles with alcohol.

7. See Keats, *You Might as Well Live*; Frewin, *The Late Mrs. Dorothy Parker*; and Meade, *Dorothy Parker.*

8. All three biographers are quite respectful of Parker's success as a writer, in particular her innovations in the short story genre. None of the three, however, is

careful to distinguish the emotions and actions of the characters in her stories from her own.

9. Meade, *Dorothy Parker,* 16.
10. Ibid., 43.
11. Ibid., 59.
12. Ibid., 75.
13. Ibid., 76.
14. Millier, *Elizabeth Bishop,* 38.
15. Meade, *Dorothy Parker,* 94.
16. Ibid.
17. Ibid., 95.
18. Ibid., 132.
19. Keats, *You Might as Well Live,* 113.
20. Meade, *Dorothy Parker,* 109.
21. Douglas, *Terrible Honesty,* 252–53.
22. Frewin, *The Late Mrs. Dorothy Parker,* 105.
23. Meade, *Dorothy Parker,* 161.
24. Frewin, *The Late Mrs. Dorothy Parker,* 116.
25. Keats, *You Might as Well Live,* 127; Frewin, *The Late Mrs. Dorothy Parker,* 144.
26. Keats, *You Might as Well Live,* 125.
27. Ibid., 161.
28. Ibid.
29. Parker and d'Usseau, *Ladies of the Corridor,* 43.
30. Quoted in Kinney, *Dorothy Parker,* 97.

Chapter 2: Louise Bogan

1. Frank, *Louise Bogan,* xvi.
2. Bowles, *Louise Bogan's Aesthetic of Limitation,* 137.
3. Frank, *Louise Bogan,* 414.
4. Louise Bogan's letters are collected in *What the Woman Lived: Selected Letters of Louise Bogan* (Ruth Limmer, ed.) (WWL). Her poems are collected in *The Blue Estuaries* (BE), and journals and other autobiographical material are collected in *Journey Around My Room* (JAMR). Further references to these books will be included in the text.
5. Quoted in Bowles, *Louise Bogan's Aesthetic of Limitation,* 55–56.
6. Wilsnack and Beckman, *Alcohol Problems in Women,* 251.
7. Bauer, *Alcoholism and Women,* 102; Knight, "Dynamics and Treatment of Chronic Alcohol Addiction," 236; Parkhurst, "Drinking and Alcoholism," 160.
8. Frank, *Louise Bogan,* xv.

9. Bogan, "Poetesses in the Parlor," 45.
10. Ostriker, *Stealing the Language,* 88–89.
11. Frank, *Louise Bogan,* 137–41.
12. Bogan, *Poet's Prose,* 54.
13. The piece was used by Ruth Limmer, Bogan's first literary executor, as the backbone of her "mosaic" of Bogan's autobiography, also titled *Journey Around My Room.*
14. Wall's demographic summary of patients included in the study leaves room for Bogan—two of the women were writers, twelve were Catholic, thirteen were the product of unhappy marriages, and there were numerous women of about Bogan's age.
15. Frank, *Louise Bogan,* 192.
16. Ibid., 195.
17. Quoted in ibid., 285.
18. Quoted in Seager, *Glass House,* 109.
19. Box 24, Folder 4, Louise Bogan Papers, Amherst College Library, Amherst, Massachusetts; hereafter cited (ACL Box#:Folder#). Quoted with permission of the library and of Mary Kinzie, executor of Bogan's literary estate.
20. Frank, *Louise Bogan,* 284–86.
21. Quoted in ibid., 286.
22. Quoted in ibid.
23. Quoted in ibid., 328.
24. Quoted in Bowles, *Louise Bogan's Aesthetic of Limitation,* 136.
25. Meredith, "Poems of a Human Being," 4.
26. Bogan was taking Librium, a drug also often prescribed at the time to ease the symptoms of alcoholic withdrawal.
27. Frank, *Louise Bogan,* 413–14.
28. Quoted in ibid., 416–17.
29. Bowles, *Louise Bogan's Aesthetic of Limitation,* 136.
30. Middlebrook, "Problem of the Woman Artist," in Bloom, *American Women Poets.*
31. Sandra Cookson noted the prevalence and significance of wasteland imagery in "Putting to Sea" and "Psychiatrist's Song"; "'The Repressed Becomes the Poem.'"
32. Frank, *Louise Bogan,* 108.
33. Cookson, "'The Repressed Becomes the Poem,'" 158.
34. Bogan's imagery, language, and stanza form here are echoed by Elizabeth Bishop in "The Moose," a poem published in 1972 but begun twenty-five years earlier.

Chapter 3: Edna St. Vincent Millay

1. Sinclair, *Cup of Fury,* 90.
2. Gould, *Poet and Her Book,* 255–56.
3. Sinclair, *Cup of Fury,* 85.
4. Cowley, in *Exile's Return,* has given the definitive account of life among the Greenwich Village artists in the '20s; see especially "The Greenwich Village Idea," 61–76.
5. Douglas, *Terrible Honesty,* 24.
6. Cowley, *Exile's Return,* 56.
7. Norman Brittin lists the following writers and artists as Millay's Village associates: Malcolm Cowley, Theodore Dreiser, Alfred Kreymborg, Kenneth Burke, Dorothy Day, Paul Robeson, e. e. cummings, Hart Crane, Llewelyn Powys, John Sloan, Wallace Stevens, Susan Glaspell, Eugene O'Neill, Djuna Barnes, Edmund Wilson, and John Peale Bishop; Brittin, *Edna St. Vincent Millay,* 9. Of these, Dreiser, cummings, Crane, Stevens, O'Neill, Barnes, and Wilson all came to suffer from alcoholism.
8. Floyd Dell, Millay's Provincetown Players associate, wrote in his memoir, *Homecoming,* in 1933 that he had been glad for the arrival of Prohibition, for he "thought the saloon a bore," and he condemned the "petty law-breaking" of the masses (337). Millay responded with a fierce defense of the lawbreaking as a morally necessary stand against unjust oppression; Millay to Dell, 13 December 1933, *Letters,* 255.
9. Boyd, *Distressing Dialogues,* 29–37.
10. Quoted in Sinclair, *Cup of Fury,* 88.
11. Ibid., 89. See, for example, Cowley, *Exile's Return,* 69–71. Upton Sinclair is similarly dismissive of H. L. Mencken's campaign against Prohibition, conducted in the pages of the *American Mercury:* "'Was any more poisonous nonsense ever penned by an intellectual man?'" (97).
12. Eastman, *Great Companions,* 78.
13. Dash, *Life of One's Own,* 142–43.
14. Quoted in Rittenhouse, *House of My Life,* 253.
15. Nancy Milford confirms that Millay had several equally ambivalent romantic relationships with women, from her college days forward.
16. Cowley, *Exile's Return,* 84.
17. Milford, *Savage Beauty,* 239.
18. Ibid., 249–51. Joan Dash also gives a thorough account of the supportive nature of the Millay-Boissevain marriage; see *Life of One's Own,* 160–227.
19. The precise nature of Millay's physical illness has not been discovered. Milford describes the surgery Millay had on July 18, 1923, as an attempt both to remove

her appendix and to straighten "a prenatal twist in her intestine"; see Milford, *Savage Beauty,* 254–56.

20. Dash, *Life of One's Own,* 171; Gould, *Poet and Her Book,* 162.
21. For example, Millay to her family on July 28, 1925: "We have very little gin left. It takes about all we can get from day to day to keep Crosby laying brick. . . . One is to be congratulated that Kline, who sold us this excellent applejack— he makes it himself—is himself a teetotler"; *Letters,* 196. Joan Dash remarks that "Edna certainly did" drink too much during this time; *Life of One's Own,* 187.
22. It is apparent that the marriage between Millay and Boissevain permitted each to participate in other sexual relationships as well. See, for example, Dash, *Life of One's Own,* 171; Brittin, *Edna St. Vincent Millay,* 23; and Milford, *Savage Beauty,* 351–61.
23. Milford, *Savage Beauty,* 438–40.
24. Eastman, *Great Companions,* 102–3.
25. Ibid., 101–2.
26. Ibid., 103–4.
27. Milford, *Savage Beauty,* 473–75.
28. Wilson, *Shores of Light,* 787–88.
29. Milford, *Savage Beauty,* 508.
30. Atkins, *Edna St. Vincent Millay and Her Times,* 61.
31. Gray, *Elinor Wylie,* 66.
32. Walker, *Nightingale's Burden,* 145–46.
33. Walker notes this tendency in several early twentieth-century female poets, including Millay, Bogan, H. D., and Sara Teasdale; see *Masks Outrageous and Austere,* 10.

Chapter 4: Elinor Wylie

1. Gould, *Poet and Her Book,* 181.
2. Ibid., 180–81.
3. Benét, *Prose and Poetry of Elinor Wylie,* 4.
4. Farr, *Life and Art of Elinor Wylie,* 24.
5. Edmund Wilson remembered Wylie's vivid life in an obituary essay. See "The Death of Elinor Wylie," in *Shores of Light,* 392–96. There are at least twenty-five published first-person memoirs of Millay available now.
6. Olson, *Elinor Wylie,* 20.
7. Ibid., 166.
8. Ibid., 313.
9. Ibid., 189.

10. Wylie, *Collected Poems of Elinor Wylie*, 277. Further references to this edition will be included in the text and marked "CPW."

11. Olson, *Elinor Wylie*, 144; Benét, *Prose and Poetry of Elinor Wylie*, 7–8.

12. Gregory and Zaturenska quote an 1854 essay by Englishman George Bethune, lamenting the "prominent fault of female poetical writers."

13. Gregory and Zaturenska, *History of American Poetry*, 298.

14. Zabel, "Pattern of the Atmosphere," 275.

15. Olson, *Elinor Wylie*, 318.

16. Wilsnack and Beckman, *Alcohol Problems in Women*, 93.

17. Farr's chapter, "The Chosen Image," is the best and most sympathetic account of Wylie's relationship with the poetry and life of Shelley; Farr, *Life and Art of Elinor Wylie*.

18. Drake, *First Wave*, 175.

19. Farr, *Life and Art of Elinor Wylie*, 116.

20. Ibid., 125, 137.

21. Ibid., 120–21.

22. See, for example, Olson, *Elinor Wylie*, 320–21; Gould, *Poet and Her Book*, 181.

23. Bogan, *Letters*, 144.

24. Gould, *Poet and Her Book*, 181.

25. Farr, *Life and Art of Elinor Wylie*, 123.

26. Wright, "Elinor Wylie," 16.

27. Farr, *Life and Art of Elinor Wylie*, 24.

28. Ibid., 121.

29. Gray, *Elinor Wylie*, 61, 67.

30. Plath, *Ariel*, 84.

31. Ostriker identified "duplicity," employed with such richness by Emily Dickinson, as an enduring strategy among female poets; *Stealing the Language*. Cheryl Walker, in her *Masks Outrageous and Austere*, explored the "mask" and "armor" strategies in depth.

Chapter 5: Léonie Adams

1. The trajectory of Sara Teasdale's life—from problematic mothering to troubled marriage, abiding depression, childlessness, and dependent relationships with "caretaker" figures—resembles those of the poets in this study, and her poems express the same wish for sanctuary or oblivion as well. This intrigued me, and I wrote to her biographer, William Drake, asking him what he knew about her drinking habits. He replied that Teasdale had been a teetotaler—but was so obsessive about it that her very abstemiousness was "like an addiction" (personal correspondence). Drake's book says nothing about Teasdale's drinking habits,

although he does mention the "sleeping pills" and tranquilizers with which she medicated her depression and anxiety; *First Wave,* 290–92.

2. Fowlie, "Remembering Léonie Adams," 18.
3. Ibid., 20.
4. Howard, *Margaret Mead,* 43.
5. Mead, *Blackberry Winter,* 106.
6. Ibid.
7. Ibid., 107.
8. Ibid.
9. Ibid., 107–8.
10. Adams, *Those Not Elect,* 44. Adams's poems appear in two volumes, *Those Not Elect* (TNE) and *High Falcon and Other Poems* (HF). *Poems: A Selection* (SPA) appeared in 1954. Citations to Adams's poems will be to these editions, and noted in the text.
11. Bloom, *Best Poems of the English Language,* 936.
12. Frank, *Louise Bogan,* 75.
13. Ibid.
14. Walker, *Masks Outrageous and Austere,* 176.
15. Mead, *Blackberry Winter,* 108–9.
16. Lapsley, *Margaret Mead and Ruth Benedict,* 30.
17. Ibid., 181.
18. Mead, *Blackberry Winter,* 103–5.
19. Quoted in Frank, *Louise Bogan,* 88.
20. Mead, *Blackberry Winter,* 132–33; Howard, *Margaret Mead,* 71–72.
21. Quoted in Howard, *Margaret Mead,* 102.
22. Bowles, *Louise Bogan's Aesthetic of Limitation.*
23. Quoted in Millett, *Contemporary American Authors,* 213.
24. Fowlie, "Poetry of Léonie Adams," 226.
25. Ibid., 225.
26. Ibid.
27. Finch, "Léonie Adams."
28. Olson, *Elinor Wylie,* 81.
29. Deutsch, *Poetry in Our Time,* 236.
30. Finch, "Léonie Adams."

Chapter 6: Isabella Gardner

1. Isabella Gardner Papers, Washington University Library Manuscript Collection, St. Louis. Quoted with permission of the library and of Robert Gardner.
2. Letter from Gardner to Judy Bartholomay, February 9, 1974. Washington Uni-

versity Library, St. Louis. Quoted with permission of the library and of Robert Gardner.

3. Ibid.
4. Ibid.
5. Ibid.
6. Ibid.
7. Ibid.
8. Gardner, *Collected Poems*, 120. Further references will be included in the text and marked "CPG."
9. Letter from Gardner to Judy Bartholomay, February 9, 1974.
10. Quoted in Janssen, "Postillion for Pegasus," in Bak, *Uneasy Alliance,* 200.
11. Shapiro, "Voices," 4.
12. Janssen, "Postillion for Pegasus," in Bak, *Uneasy Alliance,* 201.
13. Ibid., 205.
14. Ibid., 209.
15. Sitwell, "Tidy, Natural Taste," 14.
16. Quoted in Gould, *Modern American Women Poets,* 276.
17. Isabella Gardner's letters to Allen Tate are among her papers at the Washington University Library. This information is from a letter dated December 15, 1958. Quoted with permission of the library and of Robert Gardner.
18. Gould, *Modern American Women Poets,* 281.
19. Mills, *Essays on Poetry,* 186.
20. Robie, "Poetry," 3286.
21. Jarrell, "Recent Poetry," 122.

Chapter 7: Elizabeth Bishop

1. Most of Bishop's previously unpublished poems, drafts, and fragments have been collected by Alice Quinn, in *Edgar Allan Poe and the Juke-Box*, hereafter "EAPJ." "A Drunkard" appears on pages 150–51 of that book. Her selected letters are published in *One Art,* edited by Robert Giroux; hereafter "OA." Her prose writings—short stories and journalism—can be found in *Elizabeth Bishop: Collected Prose,* hereafter "CPR." And her published poems appear in *Collected Poems 1927–1979,* hereafter "CPO."
2. Gomberg, "Female Alcoholic," in Tartar and Sugarman, *Alcoholism,* 629.
3. Jarrell, *Poetry and the Age,* 235.
4. Spires, "Afternoon with Elizabeth Bishop," 7.
5. The bracketed sentence appears in the original of Bishop's letter (November 29, 1975, in Elizabeth Bishop Papers, Vassar College Library, Poughkeepsie, New York), but has been edited out of the published version. Quoted with permission of the library.

6. Mike Figgis's 1995 film, *Leaving Las Vegas*, tells the story of an alcoholic's suicide by drinking and portrays vividly this sense of exile. Homelessness and rejection are the film's leitmotif: "Don't ever contact me again"; "Don't come in here again"; "We don't want your kind around here"; "I'm going to have to ask you to leave"; "I never want to see you again."

7. Schwartz and Estress, *Elizabeth Bishop and Her Art,* 303.

8. Stevens, *Collected Poems,* 201.

9. Bachelard, *Psychoanalysis of Fire,* 83.

10. Stevens, *Collected Poems,* 201.

11. Bishop could not have read Stevens's poem at the time she wrote her story, although Stevens may have seen "The Sea and Its Shore" in the Winter 1937 issue of *Life and Letters Today.*

12. Elizabeth Bishop Papers, Vassar College Library, Poughkeepsie, New York. Quoted with permission of the library and Farrar, Straus, and Giroux.

13. According to Fountain and Brazeau's "oral biography," *Remembering Elizabeth Bishop,* Bishop was hospitalized on this occasion after drinking rubbing alcohol when no other alcohol was available (112).

14. Potter-Efron and Potter-Efron, *Treatment of Shame and Guilt in Alcoholism Counseling,* 7, 140.

15. Lowell, "Thomas, Bishop, and Williams," 497.

16. See also "The Weed," "Sunday, 4 a.m." and "A Summer's Dream."

17. Bishop's poem "Electrical Storm" is set in Brazil.

18. Hyde, "Alcohol and Poetry," 215. Hyde later moderated this radical claim; see Hyde, "Berryman Revisited," in Kelly and Lathrop, *Recovering Berryman,* 269–72.

Chapter 8: Jean Garrigue

1. McClatchy, "Introduction," in Garrigue, *Selected Poems of Jean Garrigue,* xii.

2. Kunitz, *Kind of Order,* 256.

3. Personal correspondence, June 27, 1998.

4. Sullivan, "Introduction," in Garrigue, *Love's Aspects,* xl.

5. Gray, *Elinor Wylie,* 66.

6. Garrigue, *Ego and the Centaur,* 66.

7. Garrigue, *Selected Poems,* 57–58.

8. Garrigue, *Studies for an Actress,* 34.

9. Sinclair, *Cup of Fury,* 89.

Afterword

1. Walker, *Nightingale's Burden,* 53–54.
2. Half a generation later, everything had, of course, changed. Anne Sexton was born, for example, in 1928 and Sylvia Plath in 1932.
3. Hyde, "Alcohol and Poetry," in Kelly and Lathrop, *Recovering Berryman,* 217.
4. Haffenden, *Life of John Berryman,* 83–84.

Bibliography

Abraham, Karl. "The Psychological Relations between Sexuality and Alcohol." *International Journal of Psycho-Analysis* 7 (January 1926): 2–10.

Adams, Léonie. *High Falcon and Other Poems.* New York: John Day, 1929. (HF)

———. *Poems: A Selection.* New York: Noonday, 1954. (SPA)

———. *Those Not Elect.* New York: McBride, 1925. (TNE)

Alcoholics Anonymous: The Story of How Many Thousands of Men and Women Have Recovered From Alcoholism. 3rd ed. New York: Alcoholics Anonymous World Services, 1976.

American Psychiatric Association. *Diagnostic and Statistical Manual of Mental Disorders.* 4th ed. Washington, D.C.: American Psychiatric Association, 1994.

Anderson, Dwight. *The Other Side of the Bottle.* New York: A. A. Wyn, 1950.

Andreasen, Nancy C. "Creativity and Mental Illness: Prevalence Rates in Writers and Their First-Degree Relatives." *American Journal of Psychiatry* 144, no. 10 (October 1987): 1288–92.

Asbury, Herbert. *The Great Illusion: An Informal History of Prohibition.* Garden City, N.Y.: Doubleday, 1950.

Atkins, Elizabeth. *Edna St. Vincent Millay and Her Times.* Chicago: University of Chicago Press, 1936.

Bibliography

Bachelard, Gaston. *The Poetics of Reverie,* translated by Daniel Russell. Boston: Beacon Press, 1969.

———. *The Psychoanalysis of Fire*, translated by Alan C. M. Ross. Boston: Beacon Press, 1964.

Baudelaire, Charles. *Les Fleurs du Mal,* translated by Richard Howard. Boston: Godine, 1982.

———. "Get Drunk". *Paris Spleen*, translated by Louise Varese. New York: New Directions, 1970 (1869).

Bauer, Jan. *Alcoholism and Women: The Background and the Psychology.* Toronto: Inner City Books, 1982.

Benét, William Rose. *Prose and Poetry of Elinor Wylie*. Norton, Mass.: Wheaton College Press, 1934.

Bergler, Edmund. "Contributions to the Psychogenesis of Alcohol Addiction." *Quarterly Journal of Studies on Alcohol* 5 (December 1944): 434–49.

———. *The Writer and Psychoanalysis*. Garden City, N.Y.: Doubleday, 1950.

Berryman, John. *The Dream Songs*. New York: Farrar, Straus, and Giroux, 1969.

———. *Recovery*. New York: Farrar, Straus, and Giroux, 1973.

Bishop, Elizabeth. *Collected Prose*. New York: Farrar, Straus, and Giroux, 1984. (CPR)

———. *Complete Poems 1927–1979*. New York: Farrar, Straus, and Giroux, 1983. (CPO)

———. *Edgar Allan Poe and the Jukebox*, edited by Alice Quinn. New York: Farrar, Straus, and Giroux, 2006. (EAPJ)

———. *One Art* (Letters), edited by Robert Giroux. New York: Farrar, Straus, and Giroux, 1994. (OA)

Blocker, Jack S. *American Temperance Movements: Cycles of Reform*. Boston: Twayne Books, 1989.

Bloom, Harold, ed. *American Women Poets*. New York: Chelsea House, 1986.

———, ed. *The Best Poems of the English Language: From Chaucer through Robert Frost*. New York: HarperCollins, 2004.

Bogan, Louise. *The Blue Estuaries*. New York: Farrar, Straus, and Giroux, 1968. (Reprint Ecco Press, 1977). (BE)

———. *Journey Around My Room: The Autobiography of Louise Bogan,* edited by Ruth Limmer. New York: Viking, 1980. (JAMR)

———. "Poetesses in the Parlor." *New Yorker* 12 (5 December 1936): 42–56.

———. *A Poet's Prose: Selected Writings of Louise Bogan,* edited by Mary Kinzie. Athens, Ohio: Swallow Press/Ohio State University Press, 2005.

———. *What the Woman Lived: Selected Letters of Louise Bogan,* edited by Ruth Limmer. New York: Harcourt, Brace, Jovanovich, 1973. (WWL)

Boler, Kelly. *A Drinking Companion: Alcohol and the Lives of Writers*. New York: Union Square Publishing, 2004.

"Booze and the Writer." *Writer's Digest* 58 (October 1978): 25–33.

Bowers, John M. "'Dronkenesse Is Ful of Stryving': Alcoholism and Ritual Violence in Chaucer's *Pardoner's Tale*." *English Literary History* 57 (1990): 757–84.

Bowles, Gloria. *Louise Bogan's Aesthetic of Limitation*. Bloomington: Indiana University Press, 1987.

Boyd, Nancy [Edna St. Vincent Millay]. *Distressing Dialogues*. New York: Harper and Brothers, 1924.

Boyle, Helen. "A Note on the Psychology of the Inebriate Woman." *British Journal of Inebriety* 24 (April 1927): 182–85.

Brittin, Norman. *Edna St. Vincent Millay* (rev. ed.). Boston: Twayne, 1982.

Broyard, Anatole. *Kafka Was the Rage: A Greenwich Village Memoir*. New York: Vintage, 1997 (1993).

Cameron, Sharon. *Lyric Time: Dickinson and the Limits of Genre*. Baltimore: Johns Hopkins University Press, 1979.

Caramagno, Thomas C. *The Flight of the Mind: Virginia Woolf's Art and Manic Depressive Illness*. Berkeley: University of California Press, 1992.

Carpenter, Margaret Haley. *Sara Teasdale: A Biography*. New York: Schulte, 1960.

Conrad, Barnaby. "Genius and Intemperance." *Horizon* 23 (December 1980): 32–40.

Cookson, Sandra. "'The Repressed Becomes the Poem': Landscape and Quest in Two Poems by Louise Bogan," in Bloom, *American Woman Poets*, 151–59.

Cowley, Malcolm. *Exile's Return: A Narrative of Ideas*. New York: Norton, 1934.

———. "Three Poets." *The New Republic* 105, no. 19 (10 November 1941): 625.

Crothers, T. D. "Is Alcoholism Increasing among American Women?" *North American Review* 155 (1892): 731–36.

Crowley, John W. *The White Logic: Alcoholism and Gender in American Modernist Fiction*. Amherst: University of Massachusetts Press, 1994.

Curran, Frank J. "Personality Studies in Alcoholic Women." *Journal of Nervous and Mental Disease* 86, no. 6 (1937): 645–67.

Curry, Renee. "A Thirst for Reverie: Alcohol, Despair, and Dream Space in Elizabeth Bishop's Poetry." *Literature and Medicine* 18, no. 1 (Spring 1999): 101–13.

Dabney, Lewis. *Edmund Wilson: A Life in Literature*. New York: Farrar, Straus, and Giroux, 2005.

Dardis, Thomas. *The Thirsty Muse: Alcohol and the American Writer*. New York: Ticknor and Fields, 1989.

Dash, Joan. *A Life of One's Own: Three Gifted Women and the Men They Married*. New York: Harper and Row, 1973.

Day, Ed, and Iain Smith. "Literary and Biographical Perspectives on Substance Use." *Advances in Psychiatric Treatment* 9 (2003): 62–68.

Dell, Floyd. *Homecoming*. New York: Farrar and Rinehart, 1933.

Deutsch, Babette. *Poetry in Our Time*. New York: Holt, 1952.

Dickinson, Emily. *The Poems of Emily Dickinson,* edited by R. W. Franklin. Cambridge, Mass.: Harvard University Press, 1998.

Dodd, Elizabeth C. *The Veiled Mirror and the Woman Poet: H. D., Louise Bogan, Elizabeth Bishop, and Louise Glück.* Columbia: University of Missouri Press, 1992.

Donaldson, Scott. "Writers and Drinking in America." *Sewanee Review* 98, no. 2 (Spring 1990): 312–24.

Douglas, Ann. *Terrible Honesty: Mongrel Manhattan in the 1920s.* New York: Farrar, Straus, and Giroux, 1995.

Drake, William, *The First Wave: Women Poets in America 1915–1945.* New York: Macmillan, 1987.

———. *Sara Teasdale: Woman and Poet.* Knoxville: University of Tennessee Press, 1979.

Drowne, Kathleen. *Spirits of Defiance: National Prohibition and Jazz Age Literature.* Columbus: Ohio State University Press, 2005.

Dunham, Bob. "The Curse of the Writing Class." *Saturday Review* 10 (January–February 1984): 27–30.

Eastman, Max. *Great Companions: Critical Memoirs of Some Famous Friends.* New York: Farrar, Straus, and Cudahy, 1959.

Erkkila, Betsy. *The Wicked Sisters: Women Poets, Literary History, and Discord.* New York: Oxford University Press, 1992.

Farr, Judith. *The Life and Art of Elinor Wylie.* Baton Rouge: Louisiana State University Press, 1983.

Farrar, John, ed. *The Literary Spotlight.* New York: Doubleday, 1924.

Finch, Annie. "Léonie Adams." WOMPO: Women's Poetry Listserv. http://www.usm .maine.edu/wompo/Leonie-Adams.html.

Fleming, Alice. *Alcohol: The Delightful Poison.* New York: Dell, 1979 (1975).

Forseth, Roger. "Alcohol and the Writer: Some Biographical and Critical Issues (Hemingway)." *Contemporary Drug Problems* 13 (Summer 1986): 361–86.

Fountain, Gary, and Peter Brazeau. *Remembering Elizabeth Bishop: An Oral Biography.* Amherst: University of Massachusetts Press, 1994.

Fowlie, Wallace. "The Poetry of Léonie Adams." *Commonweal* 61 (26 November 1954): 24–26.

———. "Remembering Léonie Adams." *The New Criterion* 7, no. 2 (October 1988): 224–26.

Frank, Elizabeth. *Louise Bogan: A Portrait.* New York: Knopf, 1985.

Freedman, Diane, ed. *Millay at 100: A Critical Reappraisal.* Carbondale: Southern Illinois University Press, 1995.

Frewin, Leslie. *The Late Mrs. Dorothy Parker.* New York: Macmillan, 1986.

Gardner, Isabella. *The Collected Poems.* Brockport, N.Y.: BOAEditions, 1990. (CPG)

Garrigue, Jean. *The Ego and the Centaur.* New York: New Directions, 1947. (EC)

———. *Selected Poems*. Urbana: University of Illinois Press, 1992. (GSP)

———. *Studies for an Actress and Other Poems*. New York: Macmillan, 1973. (SA)

Gilbert, Sandra M., and Susan Gubar. *No Man's Land: The Place of the Woman Writer in the Twentieth Century; Vol. I: The War of the Words*. New Haven, Conn.: Yale University Press, 1988.

———, eds. *Shakespeare's Sisters: Feminist Essays on Women Poets*. Bloomington: Indiana University Press, 1979.

Gilmore, Thomas. *Equivocal Spirits: Alcohol and Drinking in Twentieth-Century American Literature*. Chapel Hill: University of North Carolina Press, 1987.

Gomberg, Edith S. "The Female Alcoholic." In *Alcoholism: Interdisciplinary Approaches to an Enduring Problem,* edited by Ralph E. Tartar and A. Arthur Sugarman, 603–36. Reading, Mass.: Addison-Wesley, 1976.

Goodwin, Donald W. *Alcohol and the Writer*. Kansas City: Andrews McMeel, 1988.

Gould, Jean. *Modern American Women Poets*. New York: Dodd Mead, 1984.

———. *The Poet and Her Book: A Biography of Edna St. Vincent Millay*. New York: Dodd Mead, 1969.

Grant, Marcus. "Drinking and Creativity: A Review of the Alcoholism Literature." *British Journal on Alcohol and Alcoholism* 16, no. 2 (1981): 88–93.

Gray, Thomas A. *Elinor Wylie*. New York: Twayne, 1969.

Gregory, Horace, and Marya Zaturenska. *A History of American Poetry 1900–1940*. New York: Harcourt Brace, 1946.

Gurko, Miriam. *Restless Spirit: The Life of Edna St. Vincent Millay*. New York: Thomas Y. Crowell, 1962.

Haffenden, John. *The Life of John Berryman*. Boston: Routledge Kegan Paul, 1982.

Hajcak, Francis J. *The Effects of Alcohol on Creativity*. Ph.D. diss., Temple University, 1975. *Dissertation Abstracts International,* 36, 6380B–6381B.

Hamill, Pete. *A Drinking Life*. Boston: Little, Brown, 1994.

Hayter, Alethea. *Opium and the Romantic Imagination*. London: Faber and Faber, 1968.

Hecht, Anthony. "The Points of Her Compass." *Washington Post Book World,* 21 March 1993, 6.

Hirsch, Edward. *The Demon and the Angel: Searching for the Source of Artistic Inspiration*. New York: Harcourt, 2002.

Hirsch, W. *Genius and Degeneration*. New York: Appleton, 1896.

Howard, Jane. *Margaret Mead: A Life*. New York: Simon and Schuster, 1984.

Hoyt, Nancy. *Elinor Wylie: Portrait of an Unknown Lady*. New York: Greenwood Press, 1977 (1935).

Hyde, Lewis. "Alcohol and Poetry: John Berryman and the Booze Talking." In Kelly and Lathrop, *Recovering Berryman,* 205–28.

———. "Berryman Revisited: A Response." In Kelly and Lathrop, *Recovering Berryman,* 269–72.

Bibliography

Irwin, Julie. "F. Scott Fitzgerald's Little Drinking Problem." *American Scholar* 56 (Summer 1987): 415–27.

Jackson, Charles. *The Lost Weekend*. New York: Farrar and Rinehart, 1944.

Janssen, Marian. "Postillion for Pegasus: Isabella Gardner and *Poetry*." In *Uneasy Alliance: Twentieth-Century American Literature, Culture, and Biography*, edited by Hans Bak, 199–214. New York and Amsterdam: Editions Rodopi B.V., 2004.

Jarrell, Randall. *Poetry and the Age*. New York: Knopf, 1953.

———. "Recent Poetry." *Yale Review* 45, no. 1 (Fall 1955): 122–35.

Jellinek, E. Morton. *The Disease Concept of Alcoholism*. New Brunswick, N.J.: Hillhouse Press, 1960.

Jersild, Devon. *Happy Hours: Alcohol in a Woman's Life*. New York: HarperCollins, 2001.

Johnstone, Rosemarie. "Literature and Addiction: Critical and Ideological Issues: A Symposium." *Dionysos* 5, no. 3 (Winter 1994): 10–15.

Juda, Adele. "The Relationship between Highest Mental Capacity and Psychic Abnormalities." *American Journal of Psychiatry* 106 (October 1949): 296–307.

Juhasz, Suzanne. *Naked and Fiery Forms: Modern Poetry by Women, a New Tradition*. New York: Octagon Books, 1976.

Kalant, Oriana Josseau, ed. *Alcohol and Drug Problems in Women: Research Advances in Alcohol and Drug Problems*. Vol. 5. New York: Plenum Press, 1980.

Karpman, Benjamin. *The Alcoholic Woman: Case Studies in the Psychodynamics of Alcoholism*. Washington, D.C.: Linacre Press, 1948.

———. *Hangover: A Critical Study in the Psychodynamics of Alcoholism*. Springfield, Ill.: Thomas, 1957.

Kazin, Alfred. "'The Giant Killer': Drink and the American Writer. *Commentary* 61 (March 1976): 44–50.

———. *A Walker in the City*. New York: Harcourt, 1951.

Keats, John. *You Might as Well Live: The Life and Times of Dorothy Parker*. New York: Simon and Schuster, 1970.

Kelly, Richard J., and Alan Lathrop, eds. *Recovering Berryman*. Ann Arbor: University of Michigan Press, 1993.

Kingree, J. B. "Understanding Gender Differences in Psychosocial Functioning and Treatment Retention." *American Journal of Drug and Alcohol Abuse* 21, no. 2 (1995): 267–81.

Kinney, Arthur. *Dorothy Parker*. Boston: Twayne, 1978, revised 1998.

Knapp, Caroline. *Drinking: A Love Story*. New York: Dell, 1996.

Knight, Robert P. "The Dynamics and Treatment of Chronic Alcohol Addiction," *Bulletin of the Menninger Clinic* 1, no. 7 (September 1937): 233–50.

Kunitz, Stanley. *A Kind of Order, a Kind of Folly*. Boston: Little, Brown, 1975.

Landis, Carney. "Theories of the Alcoholic Personality." In *Alcohol, Science, and Society: Twenty-nine Lectures with Discussions as Given at the Yale Summer School of Alcohol*

Studies, edited by Howard W. Haggard, 129–42. New Haven, Conn.: Quarterly Journal of Studies on Alcohol, 1945.

Lang, R. Alan, Laurie D. Verret, and Carolyn Watt. "Drinking and Creativity: Objective and Subjective Effects." *Addictive Behaviors* 9 (1984): 395–99.

Lapsley, Hilary. *Margaret Mead and Ruth Benedict: The Kinship of Women.* Amherst: University of Massachusetts Press, 1999.

Lender, Mark Edward, and Karen R. Karnchanapee. "'Temperance Tales': Antiliquor Fiction and American Attitudes toward Alcoholics in the Late Nineteenth and Early Twentieth Centuries." *Journal of Studies on Alcohol* 38 (July 1977): 1347–70.

———, and James Martin. *Drinking in America: A History.* New York: Free Press, 1982.

Leonard, Linda Schierse. *Witness to the Fire: Creativity and the Veil of Addiction.* Boston: Shambala, 1990.

Levine, Harry Gene. "The Discovery of Addiction: Changing Conceptions of Habitual Drunkenness in America," *Journal of Studies on Alcohol* 39, no. 1 (January 1978): 143–74.

"Liquor Is Quicker." *Economist* (13 February 1993), p. 91.

London, Jack. *John Barleycorn.* New York: Appleton Century, 1943 (1913).

Lowell, Robert. *Collected Poems.* New York: Farrar, Straus, and Giroux, 2003.

———. "Thomas, Bishop, and Williams." *Sewanee Review* 55 (July–September 1947): 497–99.

Lukas, J. Anthony. "One Too Many for the Muse." *New York Times Book Review,* December 1, 1985, 1, 26–30.

Lyu, Claire Chi-ah. *A Sun within a Sun: The Power and Elegance of Poetry.* Pittsburgh: University of Pittsburgh Press, 2006.

Mariani, Paul. *Dream Song: The Life of John Berryman.* New York: Morrow, 1990.

Marks, Jeanette. *Genius and Disaster.* Port Washington, N.Y.: Kennikat Press, 1926.

McClatchy, J. D. "Introduction." *Selected Poems of Jean Garrigue.* Urbana: University of Illinois Press, 1992.

McConville, Brigid. *Women under the Influence: Alcohol and Its Impact.* New York: Pandora Books, 1995.

Mead, Margaret. *Blackberry Winter.* New York: William Morrow, 1972.

Meade, Marion. *Bobbed Hair and Bathtub Gin: Writers Running Wild in the Twenties.* New York: Harcourt, 2004.

———. *Dorothy Parker: What Fresh Hell Is This?* New York: Random House, 1987.

Mendelson, Jack H., and Nancy Mello. *The Diagnosis and Treatment of Alcoholism.* New York: McGraw-Hill, 1985.

Meredith, William. "Poems of a Human Being." *New York Times Book Review,* October 13, 1968, 4.

Meyers, Jeffrey. *Manic Power: Robert Lowell and His Circle.* London: Macmillan, 1987.

Middlebrook, Diane Wood. *Anne Sexton*. Boston: Houghton Mifflin, 1991.

———. "The Problem of the Woman Artist: Louise Bogan, 'The Alchemist.'" in Bloom, *American Women Poets*, 145–50.

Milford, Nancy. *Savage Beauty: The Life of Edna St. Vincent Millay*. New York: Random House, 2001.

Millay, Edna St. Vincent. *Collected Poems of Edna St. Vincent Millay*. New York: Harper and Row, 1956. (CPM)

———. *Letters*. Allan Ross Macdougall, ed. New York: Harper and Brothers, 1952.

Miller, Nina. *Making Love Modern: The Intimate Public Worlds of New York's Literary Women*. New York and Oxford: Oxford University Press, 1998.

Millett, Fred B. *Contemporary American Authors*. New York: Harcourt Brace, 1943.

Millier, Brett C. *Elizabeth Bishop: Life and the Memory of It*. Berkeley: University of California Press, 1993.

Mills, Ralph Jr. *Essays on Poetry*. Normal, Ill.: Dalkey Archive Press, 2003.

Nardin, Jane. "'As Soon as I Sober Up I Start Again': Alcohol and the Will in Jean Rhy's Pre-War Novels." *Papers on Language and Literature* 42, no. 1 (Winter 2006): 46–72.

Newlove, Donald. *Those Drinking Days: Myself and Other Writers*. New York: Horizon Press, 1981.

O'Brien, John. *Leaving Las Vegas*. New York: Grove Press, 1990.

Olson, Elder. "Louise Bogan and Léonie Adams." *Chicago Review* 8, no. 3 (1954): 70–87.

Olson, Stanley. *Elinor Wylie: A Life Apart*. New York: Dial Press, 1979.

Ostriker, Alicia Suskin. *Stealing the Language: The Emergence of Women's Poetry in America*. Boston: Beacon Press, 1986.

Panter, Barry, et al., eds. *Creativity and Madness: Psychological Studies of Art and Artists*. Burbank, Calif.: AIMEDPress, 1995.

Parker, Dorothy. *The Portable Dorothy Parker*, edited by Marion Meade. New York: Penguin, 2006. (PDP)

———, and Arnaud d'Usseau. *The Ladies of the Corridor: A Drama in Two Acts*. New York: Samuel French, 1954.

Parkhurst, Genvieve. "Drinking and Alcoholism." *Harper's Monthly Magazine* 177 (July 1938): 158–66.

Perry, Constance. "A Woman Writing Under the Influence: Djuna Barnes and *Nightwood*." *Dionysos* 4, no. 2 (Fall 1992): 3–14.

Pickering, George White. *Creative Malady*. New York: Oxford University Press, 1974.

Plant, Moira. *Women and Alcohol*. London: Free Association Books, 1997.

Plath, Sylvia. *Ariel*. New York: Harper and Row, 1965.

Potter-Efron, Ronald T., and Patricia S. Potter-Efron, eds. *The Treatment of Shame and Guilt in Alcoholism Counseling*. New York: Haworth Press, 1988.

Ransom, John Crowe. "The Poet as Woman." *Southern Review* 2 (1936–37): 783–806.

Reiman, Donald H. *Percy Bysshe Shelley*. New York: Twayne, 1969.

Rhys, Jean. *Good Morning, Midnight*. New York: W. W. Norton, 1986 (1938).

Ridgeway, Jacqueline. *Louise Bogan*. Boston: Twayne, 1984.

Ridlon, Florence V. *A Fallen Angel: The Status Insularity of the Female Alcoholic*. Lewisburg, Pa.: Bucknell University Press, 1988.

Riley, John W., and Charles F. Marden. "The Social Pattern of Alcoholic Drinking." *Quarterly Journal of Studies on Alcohol* 8 (1947): 265–73.

Rittenhouse, Jessie. *The House of My Life: Vivid Impressions of American Poets and American Poetry*. Boston: Houghton Mifflin, 1934.

Robe, Lucy Barry. *Co-Starring: Famous Women and Alcohol*. Minneapolis: CompCare Publications, 1986.

Robie, Burton A. "Poetry." *Library Journal* 86 (1 October 1961): 3286.

Roe, Anne. "Alcohol and Creative Work I: Painters." *Quarterly Journal of Studies on Alcohol* 6 (1946): 415–67.

Roethke, Theodore. *Collected Poems*. Garden City, N.Y.: Doubleday, 1966.

Room, Robin. "A 'Reverence for Strong Drink': The Lost Generation and the Elevation of Alcohol in American Culture." *Journal of Studies on Alcohol* 45 (November 1984): 540–46.

Room, Robin, and Gary Collins, eds. *Alcohol and Disinhibition: The Nature and Meaning of the Link*. Research Monograph No. 12, U.S. Department of Health and Human Services. Washington, D.C.: U.S. Government Printing Office, 1983.

Rorabaugh, William J. *The Alcoholic Republic: An American Tradition*. New York: Oxford University Press, 1979.

Rose, Kenneth. *American Women and the Repeal of Prohibition*. New York: New York University Press, 1996.

Roth, Marty. "'Anacreon' and Drink Poetry; or, the Art of Feeling Very Very Good." *Texas Studies in Language and Literature* 43, no. 3 (Fall 2003): 314–45.

Sandler, Merton. *Psychopharmacology of Alcohol*. New York: Raven Press, 1980.

Sandmaier, Marian. *The Invisible Alcoholics: Women and Alcohol,* 2nd ed. Blue Ridge Summit, Pa.: Tab Books, 1992.

Schoen, Carol B. *Sara Teasdale*. Boston: G. K. Hall, 1986.

Schwartz, Lloyd, and Sybil P. Estess, eds. *Elizabeth Bishop and Her Art*. Ann Arbor: University of Michigan Press, 1983.

Seager, Allan. *The Glass House: The Life of Theodore Roethke*. Ann Arbor: University of Michigan Press, 1991 (1968).

Shapiro, Karl. "Voices." *New York Times Book Review,* December 24, 1961, 4.

Simon, Clea. "Diagnosing the Muse." *Boston Globe Magazine,* April 3, 1994, 10 ff.

Sinclair, Andrew. *Era of Excess: A Social History of the Prohibition Movement*. New York: Harper and Row, 1964 (1962).

Sinclair, Upton. *The Cup of Fury*. Great Neck, N.Y.: Channel Press, 1956.

Bibliography

Sitwell, Edith. "A Tidy, Natural Taste." *Saturday Review* 38 (9 July 1955): 14.

Spaulding, Frances. *Stevie Smith: A Biography.* New York: W. W. Norton, 1988.

Spires, Elizabeth. "An Afternoon with Elizabeth Bishop." *Vassar Quarterly* (Winter 1976): 7–8.

Stevens, Wallace. *Collected Poems.* New York: Knopf, 1954.

Storr, Anthony. *The Dynamics of Creation.* New York: Ballantine, 1993 (1972).

Sullivan, Nancy. "Introduction." *Love's Aspects: The World's Great Love Poems*, edited by Jean Garrigue, xxxv–xxxvii. Garden City, N.Y.: Doubleday, 1975.

Symons, Arthur. *The Symbolist Movement in Literature.* London: A. Constable, 1909.

Tate, T. O. "The Longest Goodbye: Raymond Chandler and the Poetry of Alcohol." *Armchair Detective* 18, no. 4 (Fall 1985): 392–406.

Taylor, Anya. "Coleridge and Alcohol." *Texas Studies in Literature and Language* 33, no. 3 (Fall 1991): 355–72.

———. "Coleridge, Keats, Lamb, and Seventeenth-Century Drinking Songs." In *Milton, the Metaphysicals, and Romanticism*, edited by Lisa Low and Anthony John Harding, 221–40. Cambridge: Cambridge University Press, 1994.

———. "Literature and Addiction: Critical and Ideological Issues: A Symposium." *Dionysos* 5:3 (Winter 1994): 9.

Thesing, William B., ed. *Critical Essays on Edna St. Vincent Millay.* New York: G. K. Hall, 1993.

Travisano, Thomas with Saskia Hamilton, eds. *Words in Air: The Complete Correspondence Between Elizabeth Bishop and Robert Lowell.* New York: Farrar, Straus and Giroux, 2008.

Tyrell, Ian. *Sobering Up: From Temperance to Prohibition in Antebellum America, 1800–1860.* Westport, Conn.: Greenwood Press, 1979.

Upton, Lee. *Defensive Measures: The Poetry of Niedecker, Bishop, Glück, and Carson.* Lewisburg, Pa.: Bucknell University Press, 2005.

———. *Jean Garrigue: A Poetics of Plenitude.* Rutherford, N.J.: Fairleigh Dickinson University Press, 1991.

———. *Obsession and Release: Rereading the Poetry of Louise Bogan.* Lewisburg, Pa.: Bucknell University Press, 1996.

Vaillant, George. *The Natural History of Alcoholism Revisited.* Cambridge, Mass.: Harvard University Press, 1995.

Van Amberg, Robert J. "A Study of Fifty Women Patients Hospitalized for Alcohol Addiction." *Diseases of the Nervous System* 4 (1943): 246–51.

Vice, Sue, et al., eds. *Beyond the Pleasure Dome: Writing and Addiction from the Romantics.* Sheffield, England: Sheffield Academy Press, 1994.

Vice, Sue. "Intemperate Climate: Drinking, Sobriety, and the American Literary Myth." *American Literary History* 11, no. 4 (Winter 1999): 699–709.

Vidal, Gore. "This Critic This Gin and These Shoes." *New York Review of Books* 27, no. 14 (1980): 4, 6, 8, 10.

Voigt, Ellen Bryant. "Poetry and Gender." *Kenyon Review* 9, no. 3 (Summer 1987): 138–55.

Waggoner, Hyatt. *American Poets.* Baton Rouge: Louisiana University Press, 1984.

Waldron, Ann. "Writers and Alcohol." *Washington Post Health,* March 14, 1989, 13–14.

Walker, Cheryl. *Masks Outrageous and Austere: Culture, Psyche and Persona in Modern Women Poets.* Bloomington: Indiana University Press, 1991.

———. *The Nightingale's Burden: Women Poets and American Culture before 1900.* Bloomington: Indiana University Press, 1982.

Wall, James H. "A Study of Alcoholism in Women." *American Journal of Psychiatry* 93 (1937): 943–52.

Wetzsteon, Ross. *Republic of Dreams: Greenwich Village, the American Bohemia, 1910– 1960.* New York: Simon and Schuster, 2002.

Wilsnack, Richard, and Sharon C. Wilsnack, eds. *Gender and Alcohol: Individual and Social Perspectives.* New Brunswick, N.J.: Rutgers Center of Alcohol Studies, 1997.

Wilsnack, Sharon C., and Linda J. Beckman, eds. *Alcohol Problems in Women: Antecedents, Consequences, and Interventions.* New York: Guilford Press, 1984.

Wilson, Edmund. *The American Earthquake: A Documentary of the Twenties and Thirties.* Garden City, N.Y.: Doubleday, 1958.

———. *Shores of Light: A Literary Chronicle of the Twenties and Thirties.* New York: Farrar, Straus, and Young, 1952.

Woollcott, Alexander. *While Rome Burns.* New York: Viking, 1934.

Wright, Celeste Turner. "Elinor Wylie: The Glass Chimera and the Minotaur." *Twentieth Century Literature* 12, no. 1 (April 1966): 15–26.

Wylie, Elinor. *Collected Poems of Elinor Wylie.* New York: Knopf, 1932. (CPW)

Zabel, Morton Dauwen. "The Pattern of the Atmosphere." *Poetry: A Magazine of Verse* 11, no. 5 (August 1932): 273–82.

Index

Index

Index

Index

Index

Wanning, Tom, 146

Ward, Aileen, 151

Washington, University of, 155

Weaver, John V. A., 23

Wheelock, John Hall, 43, 49, 101

White, Katharine, 100

Whitman, Walt, 161

Wilder, Thornton, 2

Williams, Oscar, 115

Williams, Tennessee, 2

Williams, William Carlos, 38, 116

Wilson, Edmund, 2, 35, 38, 46, 47, 64, 69, 97, 99, *173*, *174*; "The Lexicon of Prohibition," 9

Wolf, Robert, 42

Wolfe, Thomas, 2

women and alcohol. *See* Alcohol

Wood, Peggy, 23

Woolf, Virginia, 4

Woollcott, Alexander, 22, 23

World War I, 22

Wright, James, 122–23

Wylie, Elinor, 18, 70, 78–92, 107; biographies of, 80; celebrity status, 15, 78; childhood, 79; death, 78, 84; drinking habits, 4, 19, 39, 46, 70, 80, 83, 102; marriages, 79, 84; pregnancies, 79, 82; works, xi, 20, 41, 52, 77, 93, 101, 102, 104, 156, *170*
—Books: *Angels and Earthly Creatures* (1929), 81; *Black Armour* (1923), 81, 86; *Nets to Catch the Wind* (1921), 81; *Trivial Breath* (1928), 81
—Essay: "Jewelled Bindings," 86

—Novels: *Jennifer Lorn* (1923), 81; *Mr. Hodge and Mr. Hazard* (1928), 81, 82; *The Orphan Angel* (1926), 81, 82; *The Venetian Glass Nephew* (1925), 81
—Poems: "Address to My Soul," 91; "A Proud Lady," 87; *A Red Carpet for Shelley*, 82; "Atavism," 90; "August," 90; "Bells in the Rain," 89; "Drowned Woman," 91; "Let No Charitable Hope," 86; "Nebuchandnezzar," 85, 89; *One Person*, 83, 86; "Portrait in Black Paint, With a Very Sparing Use of Whitewash," 80; "Priest. XXth Dynasty," 91; "Prophecy," 87–88; "Sanctuary," 89; "Sleeping Beauty," 87; "Spring Pastoral," 90; "The Eagle and the Mole," 87, 126; "The Loving Cup," 88–89; "The Tortoise in Eternity," 87; "This Corruptible," 85, 86; "Three Wishes," 89–90; "To a Blackbird Singing," 89; "Winter Sleep," 87
—Unpublished Poems: "I love you more than drink," 88

Wylie, Horace, 79, 81

Yaddo (N.Y.), 118, 133, 134, 154

Yeats, William Butler, 81

Young, Marguerite, 152, 155

Zabel, Morton Dauwen, 46, 82

Zaturenska, Maya, 81

B rett C. Millier is Reginald L. Cook Professor of American Literature at Middlebury College. She is the author of *Elizabeth Bishop: Life and the Memory of It,* associate editor, *Columbia History of American Poetry,* and author of articles in *New England Review,* the *Kenyon Review, Contemporary Literature,* and elsewhere.

The University of Illinois Press
is a founding member of the
Association of American University Presses.

Composed in 10.5/13 Bembo
with Glypha display
by Jim Proefrock
at the University of Illinois Press
Designed by Copenhaver Cumpston
Manufactured by Thomson-Shore, Inc.
University of Illinois Press
1325 South Oak Street
Champaign, IL 61820-6903
www.press.uillinois.edu